NEW SAT® MATH

ADVANCED
PRACTICE
SERIES

◇ Analysis of the New SAT Math

◇ Time-Saving Advice, Proven Strategies

◇ Essential SAT Tips and Tactics

ies
TEST
PREP

Authors
Khalid Khashoggi, CEO IES
Arianna Astuni, President IES

Editorial
Patrick Kennedy, Executive Editor
Christopher Carbonell, Editorial Director
Marc Wallace, Senior Editor

Contributors
Arianna Astuni
Christopher Carbonell
Lynn Harris
Patrick Kennedy
Khalid Khashoggi
Kevin Maldonado
Joseph Miller
Rajvi Patel
Bing Shen

··

Published by IES Publications

www.IESpublications.com

© IES Publications, 2017

ON BEHALF OF

Integrated Educational Services, Inc.

355 Main Street

Metuchen, NJ 08840

www.iestestprep.com

We would like to thank the IES Publications team as well as the teachers and students at IES Test Prep who have contributed to the creation of this book. We would also like to thank our Chief Marketing Officer, Sonia Choi, for her invaluable input.

The SAT* is a registered trademark of the College Board, which was not involved in the production of, and does not endorse, this product.

ISBN-10: 1545238243

ISBN-13: 978-1545238240

QUESTIONS OR COMMENTS? Visit us at iestestprep.com

TABLE OF CONTENTS

Unit 4: Passport to Advanced Math

Unit 5: Additional Topics in Math

Dear Student:

As a test prep educator for the past 20 years, I am both pleased and honored to bring you this *New SAT Math Practice Book*. Here, you will find a wealth of advice through the 58 skills we developed to address the required content for the SAT. In every class, my students absorb the techniques contained in this book, apply those techniques with care and precision, and radically improve their mathematics score. Now, I am bringing my SAT mathematics experience and knowledge directly to you, in the hope that you will enjoy similarly great successes.

In its current form, SAT mathematics is more a matter of problem solving than of anything else. The principles that you learn in Algebra I and II are crucial to succeeding on the SAT. With this book, you will not only review essential content, but you will gain a mastery of accuracy and timing through repeated practice. You will learn to pace your test-taking for maximum efficiency, and will systematically eliminate errors, as you adapt.

I encourage you to explore the full range of resources that IES has made available to help you achieve your target score. This book is ideal for students who wish to give the math section special attention, but is also designed to work in tandem with the other volumes in our Advanced Practice Series®. With these books—each one designed by expert editors and educators, each one proven to help students raise their scores—we will give you an approach to the SAT that is straightforward, rigorous, and designed to build confidence and precision.

So get ready to take control of the SAT Mathematics test, and achieve your target score!

Sincerely,

Khalid Khashoggi,
CEO IES

<u>58 Skills to Master the</u>

<u>New SAT Math</u>

Written by:

Marc Wallace
Head of Mathematics, IES Test Prep

UNIT 1

Unit 1: Test Taking Skills

The newly-revised SAT contains diversified questions that deal with the topics of Algebra, Geometry, Data Analysis, Probability, and Statistics, as well as a multitude of advanced-level mathematical concepts. All of these topics require unique skillsets, which will equip you to solve the problems efficiently and correctly. However, there are certain skills that blanket the entire test. Whether for a problem solving approach you are familiar with or for a situation that requires creativity, these skills are tools designed to organize your approach to answering questions and to keep you mathematically on task. This set of skills will be discussed in our first unit: Test Taking Skills.

CONTINUE

1 Translating Words into Math

"Writing an equation from a word problem is like translating a sentence. As you read a problem, you are translating from English to Math."

Let's take a look at some common English words and phrases and consider how they translate into Math:

English	Math
product, times	Multiplication
per, ratio, proportion	Division
difference, *less than*	Subtraction
sum, *more than*	Addition
square	x^2
square root	$\sqrt{x}$

Most Importantly:

* When you see "is", use an equal sign.

* "Of" means to multiply. (Half of x is $\frac{1}{2}x$.)

* For "What", "A certain number", etc...
  use a variable.

Example 1:

Three times what number is five less than two times the number?

$$3x = 2x - 5$$

Example 2:

What is three more than twice itself?

$$x = 2x + 3$$

Skill 1 Practice Exercises:

1

Eight less than the square root of a number is 8. What is the number?

A) 0
B) 4
C) 16
D) 256

Handwritten work:
$$\sqrt{x} - 8 = 8$$
$$\sqrt{x} = 16$$
$$x = \pm 4$$

2

Which of the following equations most clearly represents the equation defined by the following statement?

"Three less than two times a number is five less than two plus the number."

A) $3 - 2x = 5 - (2 + x)$
B) $2x - 3 = (2 + x) - 5$
C) $3 - 2x = 5 - 2 + x$
D) $2x - 3 = 2x - 5$

Handwritten work: $2x - 3 = (2 + x) - 5$

CONTINUE

3

When half of a number is added to the number the result is 9. What is the number?

A) 13.5
B) 9
C) 6
D) 3

$\frac{1}{2}x + x = 9$

$\frac{3}{2}x = 9$

$\frac{3x}{3} = \frac{18}{3}$

$x = 6$

4

Which would be best to use to find a number that is 10 more than half of itself?

A) $x = \frac{1}{2}x + 10$

B) $x + 10 = \frac{1}{2}x$

C) $x = \frac{1}{2}x - 10$

D) $x + 10 = 2x$

$y =$

$10 + x$

$x = (\frac{1}{2}x) + 10$

5

Twelve more than two times a number is five more than eleven. What is the value of three times the number?

A) 2
B) 4
C) 6
D) 12

$12 + 2x = 5 + 11$

$12 + 2x = 16$

$2x = 4$

$x = 2$

6

Each week, Roberson earns more than $210, but less than $390. If Roberson makes $15 per hour every hour that he works, which of the following is a possible number of hours that Roberson could have worked in a two-week period?

A) 12
B) 14
C) 28
D) 32

$210 < 15x < 390$

$420 < 15x < 786$

CONTINUE

7

Which of the following is equivalent to the average of the following: a number, the sum of the number and nine, and four times the number?

A) $x+1$

B) $2x+3$

C) $3x+\dfrac{9}{2}$

D) $6x+9$

$$\frac{x+(x+9)+4x}{3}$$

$$\frac{6x+9}{3}$$

$$2x+3$$

8

Which of the following is equivalent to the quotient when the sum of the square of a number, five times the number, and four is divided by the sum of the number and one, for $x \neq -1$?

A) $x+4$

B) $x+5$

C) $\dfrac{x^2+20x}{x+1}$

D) $\dfrac{x^2+5(x+4)}{x+1}$

$$\frac{x^2+5x+4}{x+1}$$

$$\frac{(x+4)(x+1)}{x+1}$$

Notes:

_____

_____

_____

_____

_____

_____

_____

_____

_____

_____

_____

CONTINUE

| **2** | *Using* Dashes |

"When building equations or sequences with multiple variables or ratios, use dashes as placeholders in order to stay organized."

Dashes are useful in problems where something in the problem is defined in terms of something else. We all know that variables are used as placeholders for unknown quantities. The question is, "what can be used to hold the place of unknown variables?"

When you are dealing with a word problem that has multiple instances of a variable or describes the relationship between multiple variables, dashes can be used as structured placeholders for your variables.

Example 1:

In a bag of jellybeans, there are red, green, and orange beans. There are three times as many red beans as green beans and twice as many green beans as orange beans. If there are 45 beans total in the bag, how many green jelly beans are there?

In Example 1, the number of red beans is defined in terms of the number of green beans, which in turn is defined in terms of the number of orange beans. Therefore, let the number of orange beans be represented by x, since they are fewest in number, and everything else can be defined in terms of that.

$$\frac{\_\_}{r}+\frac{\_\_}{g}+\frac{\_\_}{o}=45 \quad \rightarrow 6x+2x+1x=45$$

Therefore, $9x=45$ and $x=5$. Now, since we want green, which is $2x$, we just multiply by two to get 10.

Example 2:

There is an equal number of lions and tigers in a zoo. If a litter of 4 lion cubs is born and no tiger cubs are born, there will be twice as many lions as tigers. How many lions are there now?

$$\frac{\_\_}{lions}=\frac{\_\_}{tigers} \quad \rightarrow x+4=2x \quad \rightarrow x=4 \quad \rightarrow x+4=8$$

Skill 2 Practice Exercises:

1

The sum of two positive integers that differ by 12 is 68. What is the smaller integer?

A) 28
B) 40
C) 68
D) 80

x + (x+12) = 68
2x+12=68
*   -12 -12*
2x=56
x=28

2

On a weekend road trip Jessica drove x miles per hour for 4 hours, and her boyfriend Miles drove y miles per hour for 3 hours. Which of the following represents the total number of miles driven by Jessica and Miles on their weekend road trip?

A) $4x+3y$
B) $3x+4y$
C) $7xy$
D) $12xy$

x4+3y

CONTINUE

3

The sum of five more than x and x is 25. What is the value of four times x?

A) 6
B) 10
C) 24
D) 40

$x + 5 + x = 25$

$2x = 20$

$x = 10$

5

If Mike made twice as much as Steve, who made 3 times as much as Ike, and they made a total of $200, how much money did Steve make, in dollars?

A) 10
B) 20
C) 60
D) 120

$M = 2S$

$S = 3I$

$M + S + I = 200$

$S = 60$

$2S + S = \frac{S}{3} = 200$

$3S + \frac{S}{3} = 200$

$\frac{10S}{3} = 200$

$10S = 600$

4

The sum of four different positive integers is 46. What is the greatest possible value for one of these integers?

A) 15
B) 40
C) 47
D) 48

− − − −

40 1 2 3

6

What is the least possible average of three positive integers if two of the integers are ten?

A) 1
B) 5
C) 7
D) 10

$10 + 10 + 1$

$\frac{21}{3}$

CONTINUE

7

The number of students that graduated with honors from Eggerstown High School in the 1990s was three times the number of students who graduated with honors in the 1980s. If the total number of students who graduated with honors in the 1980s and 1990s combined is forty less than 780 and the number of students that graduated with honors in the 1980s was x, which of the following equations is true?

$780-40=x$

A) $3x - 40 = 780$

B) $3x + 40 = 780$

C) $4x - 40 = 780$

D) $4x = 740$

$x + y = 740$

$y = \frac{3x}{4}$

8

If 345 million votes were cast in the election between Richardson and Jefferson, and Jefferson won by 3,500,000 votes, what percent of the votes cast did Jefferson win?

A) 51.1

B) 50.5

C) 49.5

D) 48.9

Notes:

12

CONTINUE

3 *Splitting* the Difference

"When a question arises in which you are given a combined total of two quantities and you know the difference between these two quantities, remember to split the total, split the difference, and add/subtract the "split" difference to/from the "split" total in order to attain the desired quantity."

Let's take a look at an example:

Example:

There are 18 more boys than girls in the Spanish Honors Society which has a total of 42 members. How many of the members are boys?

First, split the total which yields the middle of all members:

$$\frac{42}{2} = 21$$

Second, split the difference between the boys and the girls:

$$\frac{18}{2} = 9$$

Finally, adding and subtracting the "split" difference, 9, to and from the "split" total, 21, yields the number of boys and girls. Since we know that there are more boys than girls:

$$Girls = 21 - 9$$
$$Boys = 21 + 9$$

Therefore, there are $\underline{21 + 9 = 30}$ **boys in the Spanish Honors Society.**

Skill 3 Practice Exercises:

1

There are 420 more cats than dogs in an animal shelter. If the total number of cats and dogs is 1200, how many cats are there?

A) 390
B) 810
C) 1020
D) 1240

2

There are 32 more boys than girls in a school of 540 students. How many girls go to the school?

A) 236
B) 238
C) 254
D) 286

13

CONTINUE

3

In 1492, Christopher Columbus sailed from Spain with a total of three ships. The number of smaller vessels he left with was one more than the number of larger vessels. How many smaller vessels did Christopher Columbus sail with?

$$\frac{3}{2} \qquad \frac{1}{2}$$

A) 0

B) 1

$$\frac{4}{2}$$

C) 2

D) 3

$$\frac{2}{2}$$

4

In 2015, 98 members of the Senate were either a Democrat or a Republican. If there were 10 more Republicans than Democrats in the Senate in 2015, how many Democrats were in the Senate?

A) 44

$$49 \qquad 5$$

B) 48

C) 50

$$49+5$$

D) 54

$$54$$

$$\begin{array}{r} 98 \\ -54 \\ \hline 44 \end{array}$$

5

There are 80 more men than women in a group of 600 people. How many women are in the group?

A) 220

$$300 + 80$$

B) 260

C) 340

$$300 - 40$$

D) 380

6

At the end of 2014, 201 members of the House of Representatives were voting Democrats. If the number of voting Republicans was 33 greater than the number of voting Democrats, how many total Democrats and Republicans who could vote sat in the House of Representatives at the end of 2014?

A) 201

$$\frac{201}{2} + \frac{33}{2}$$

B) 234

C) 369

$$\frac{234}{2}$$

D) 435

$$201 + \frac{33}{2}$$

CONTINUE

7

If there are 8,502 more nurses than doctors in a group of 88,888 doctors and nurses, how many doctors are in the group?

44444   4251

A) 40,193
B) 42,400
C) 44,444
D) 48,695

8

Governor Smythe won an election by 2,640 votes when there were 18,714 votes cast. What perentage of the vote did he win?

9357

A) 42.9
B) 51.7
C) 57.0
D) 57.1

Notes:

15

CONTINUE

4   *Making* T-Charts

"When you cannot solve algebraically and you have to resort to guessing and checking, use a T-Chart to stay organized."

When you realize that you cannot solve an equation algebraically, you must resort to "plug and chug" style mathematics. Once you've made the decision that you are going to use the guess-and-check method, a T-Chart can make things much more visually accessible. Basically, it's a chart of the "types" of numbers you are looking for. Questions that involve the use of T-Charts often involve continuous functions, but ask for integer solutions. Look for the phrase "positive integer" or "integers" in the question.

Example 1:

If $x^2 - y^2 = 5$, what is the value of $x + y$ if x and y are both positive integers?

By generating a table of integer values, *n*, and their respective perfect squares, you can check visually to find two squares that are five apart.

n	n^2
1	1
2	4
3	9
4	16

You can see that 9 and 4 are five apart: $x + y = 5$

Example 2:

The positive difference of the cube and the square of two different positive integers is 60. What is the product of these two integers?

n	n^2	n^3
1	1	1
2	4	8
3	9	27
4	16	64

Here, you can see that 64 and 4 are 60 apart. So, their respective bases, 2 and 4, have a product of <u>8</u>.

Skill 4 Practice Exercises:

1

The sum of the squares of two positive integers is 52. What is the sum of the two integers?

A) 10
B) 12
C) 24
D) 52

2

The positive difference of the squares of two negative integers is 5. What is the sum of the two integers?

A) –5
B) 5
C) 6
D) 13

CONTINUE

3

The sum of the squares of three positive integers is 35. What is the difference between the largest and the smallest integer?

A) 1

B) 2

C) 3

D) 4

$$\begin{array}{c|c} 1 & 1 \\ 2 & 4 \\ 3 & 9 \\ 4 & 16 \\ 5 & 25 \end{array}$$

4

The sum of the cubes of three positive integers is 73. What is the average of the squares of the three numbers?

A) $\frac{7}{3}$

B) 7

C) 21

D) $\frac{73}{3}$

$$\begin{array}{c|c} n & n^3 \\ 1 & 1 \\ 2 & 8 \\ 3 & 27 \\ 4 & 64 \end{array}$$

5

The difference between the cube of a positive integer and the square of the same positive integer is 48. What is the integer?

A) 2

B) 4

C) 6

D) 8

6

The cube of a negative integer is 80 less than the square of that same integer. What is the positive square root of the integer?

A) 2

B) 4

C) 16

D) There is no real solution.

$$n^3 = n^2 - 80$$

$$\begin{array}{c|c|c} n & n^2 & n^3 \\ 1 & & \\ 2 & & \\ 3 & & \\ 4 & & \\ 5 & & \\ 6 & & \end{array}$$

$$n^3 - n^2 - 80$$

$$-1) \quad 1 \quad -1 \quad 0 \quad -80$$

 CONTINUE

7

$$y = x^2$$
$$y = w - x^2$$

In one of the solutions to the system of equations above, w and x are both positive integers. Which of the following could be the value of w in that solution?

A) 4
B) 20
C) 32
D) 64

$x^2 = w - x^2$

$2x^2 = w$

$x^2 : \frac{w}{2}$

8

$$y = 2x^3 + 1$$
$$y = h - x^3$$

In the solution to the system of equations above, h is a constant and x is a positive integer. Which of the following could *not* be the value of h?

A) 4
B) 25
C) 65
D) 82

Notes:

CONTINUE

Mid-Unit 1 Review - No Calculator

25 MINUTES, 20 QUESTIONS

DIRECTIONS

For each question from 1-15, choose the best answer choice provided in the multiple choice bank and fill in the appropriate circle in the provided answer key. Alternatively, for questions **16-20**, answer the problem and enter your answer in the grid-in section of the answer key. Refer to the directions given before question 16 as to how to enter your answers for the grid-in questions. You may complete scratch work in any empty space in your test booklet.

NOTES

A. Calculator usage **is not allowed** in this section.
B. Variables, constants, and coefficients used represent real numbers unless indicated otherwise.
C. All figures are created to appropriate scale unless the question states otherwise.
D. All figures are two-dimensional unless the question states otherwise.
E. The domain of any given function is all real numbers x for which the function, $f(x)$, is a real number unless the question states otherwise.

REFERENCE

$A = \pi r^2$
$C = 2\pi r$

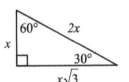
$A = lw$

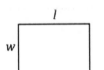
$A = \frac{1}{2}bh$

$c^2 = a^2 + b^2$

Special Right Triangle

Special Right Triangle

$V = lwh$

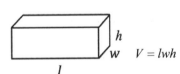
$V = \pi r^2 h$

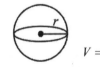
$V = \frac{4}{3}\pi r^3$

$V = \frac{1}{3}\pi r^2 h$

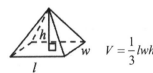
$V = \frac{1}{3}lwh$

There are $360°$ in a circle.
There are 2π radians in a circle.
There are $180°$ in a triangle.

CONTINUE ➡

1

Five more than the square root of a number is six less than twenty. What is the number?

A) 3
B) 9
C) 81
D) 361

$5 + \sqrt{x} = 14$

$\sqrt{x} = 9$

$x = ?$

2

The sum of three consecutive integers is 30. What is the smallest of the three integers?

A) 8
B) 9
C) 10
D) 11

3

There are 30 more red candies than green candies in a holiday candy jar. If the total number of candies in the jar is 118 and there are only red and green candies in the jar, how many of the candies are red?

A) 29
B) 44
C) 74
D) 89

4

The sum of the square and the cube of the same positive integer is 12. What is the integer?

A) 1
B) 2
C) 4
D) 6

CONTINUE

5

Which of the following equations could be solved to find a number that when added to twice itself returns a value that is half of the sum of itself and 10?

A) $2x = \dfrac{1}{2}x + 10$

B) $2x = \dfrac{1}{2}(x + 10)$

C) $x + 2x = \dfrac{1}{2}x + 10$

D) $x + 2x = \dfrac{1}{2}(x + 10)$

6

Meredith makes $12 per hour, Austin makes $15 per hour, and Kumar makes $18 per hour. Using x to represent the number of hours Kumar works, y to represent the number of hours that Meredith works, and z to represent the number of hours Austin works, which of the following expressions represents the total amount of money earned by Meredith, Austin, and Kumar?

A) $12x + 15y + 18z$

B) $12z + 15y + 18x$

C) $12y + 15x + 18z$

D) $12y + 15z + 18x$

7

There are 16 boys in a chemistry class. If the number of girls in the class is 12 less than the number of boys, how many total students are in the chemistry class?

A) 4

B) 20

C) 24

D) 28

8

The absolute difference of the cubes of two negative integers is 117. What is the sum of their squares?

A) −29

B) −7

C) 21

D) 29

CONTINUE

9

Every time that Gabriel reads from a novel, he reads at least 32 pages, but less than 40 pages. If Gabriel reads 2.5 pages per minute, which of the following is a possible number of minutes that Gabriel spent reading his book the last time he read?

A) 13
B) 16
C) 19
D) 21

10

If the sum of three positive even integers is 16, what is the greatest possible value for one of these integers?

A) 10
B) 12
C) 14
D) 16

11

At a golf driving range, a ball collecting cart drives across the range collecting golf balls. One afternoon, the cart collected 1,200 balls and there were 960 more white balls than any other color. What percentage of the golf balls collected by the cart were *not* white?

A) 10
B) 20
C) 80
D) 90

12

The difference of the squares of two different positive integers is 20. What is the average of the two integers?

A) 2
B) 5
C) 6
D) 10

CONTINUE

13

Which of the following expressions is equivalent to the sum of the square of a number, two times the number, and the number 1?

A) $x^2 + 2(x+1)$

B) $2x^2 + (x+1)$

C) $(x+1)^2$

D) $(2x+1)^2$

14

Resha bought one more ticket to the basketball game than David and David bought three more than twice as many tickets as Cindy. If x represents the number of tickets that Cindy bought to the basketball game and a combined total of 37 tickets were purchased by the Resha, David, and Cindy, which of the following equations is true?

A) $3x + 4 = 37$

B) $4x + 4 = 37$

C) $4x + 7 = 37$

D) $5x + 7 = 37$

15

A famous rock band has sold a total of 2.4 million records between their first two album releases. If they sold 800,000 more copies of their second album as opposed to their first, what fraction of their total album sales were accounted for by the first album?

A) $\dfrac{1}{4}$

B) $\dfrac{3}{10}$

C) $\dfrac{1}{3}$

D) $\dfrac{2}{3}$

23

CONTINUE

DIRECTIONS

For each question from 16-20, solve and enter your answer in the grid-in section of your answer sheet as described below.

A. Write out your answers in the boxes at the top of each column in order to help you fill in the circles accurately. Remember, you will only receive credit for the circles that are filled in correctly, not for the written answer at the top of the columns.

B. Mark only a single circle in each column.

C. There are no negative answers.

D. If the problem has more than one correct answer, grid only one of the correct answers.

E. When your answer is a **mixed number**, such as $1\frac{1}{2}$, it should be entered as 1.5 or $3/2$. You cannot enter a mixed number because there is no room to fill in a circle that represents a space.

F. If you enter a **decimal answer** with more digits then the grid can handle, the answer may be rounded or truncated, but it absolutely must fill the entire grid.

Answer: $\frac{8}{21}$

Answer: 6.4

Written answer →

Decimal point →

← Fraction line

Answer: 102 - both positions are correct

REMEMBER: You can begin writing your answers in any column as long as there is enough space. Leave unused columns blank.

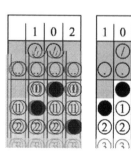

The ways to correctly grid $\frac{7}{9}$ are:

CONTINUE ➡

5 *Factoring* and *Foiling*

"Factoring and Foiling are skills that will be utilized throughout the test. It is very important to be efficient at both skills and to remember the three special binomial expansions."

Special Binomial Expansions

$$(X+Y)^2 = X^2 + Y^2 + 2XY$$
$$(X-Y)^2 = X^2 + Y^2 - 2XY$$
$$(X+Y)(X-Y) = X^2 - Y^2$$

You may wonder why the first two expansions above are out of order compared to how they were taught in school. It is important to memorize them in the order above because it matches the groupings that the SAT provides in a factoring question. Often on the SAT, the question will provide you with the value of two of the three expressions below and you will be asked to find the third:

Choose Any Two of Three

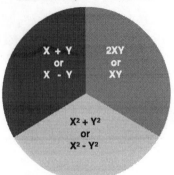

Example:

If $x^2 - y^2 = 42$ and $x - y = 3$, what is the value of $x + y$?

The three equations/expressions given are all part of the following equation. So, substitution allows us to solve for $x + y$ directly:

$$(x+y)(x-y) = x^2 - y^2$$
$$(x+y)(3) = (42) \rightarrow x+y = \frac{42}{3} = 14$$

Skill 5 Practice Exercises:

1

$$0 = x^2 - 14x + 33$$

What is the greatest value of x that satisfies the equation above? $(x-11)$

A) -3
B) 3
C) 11
D) 33

2

Which of the following values of x satisfies the equation $2x + 3 = x^2$?

$x^2 - 2x - 3$
$(x-3)(x+1)$

A) 0
B) 1
C) 2
D) 3

CONTINUE

3

If the expression $(mx+2)(nx+2)$ were written in the form $Ax^2 + Bx + C$, which of the following would be equivalent to B?

$mnx^2 + 2mx + 2nx + 4$

A) $m+n$

B) $2m+2n$

C) mn

D) $4mn$

4

$$(4x+1)(4x-1)=15$$

Which of the following values of x is a solution to the equation above?

$16x^2 - 1$

A) -4

B) -1

C) 2

D) 4

5

If $x^2 + y^2 = 16$ and $xy = 10$, what is the value of $x+y$?

A) 6

B) 12

C) 24

D) 36

1 2 5 10

$2xy = 20$

$x^2 + y^2 + 20 = 16 + 20$

$x^2 + y^2 + 20 = 36$

$x^2 + 2xy + y^2 = 36$

$(x+y)(x+y) = 36$

6

If $x-y=3$ and $x^2 + y^2 = 12$, what is the value of xy?

A) $\dfrac{3}{2}$

B) 2

C) $\dfrac{5}{2}$

D) 3

$(x-y)^2 = 9$

$x^2 - 2xy + y^2 = 9$

$12 - 2xy = 9$

$-2xy = -3$

$\dfrac{3}{2}$

28

CONTINUE

7

If $x^2 - y^2 = 27$ and $x - y = 3$, which of the following is equivalent to the value of x?

A) 2

B) 3

C) 6

D) 9

$(x-y)(x+y)$

$x^2 - y^2 = 3$

$3(x+y) = 27$

$3x + 3y = 27$

$x + y = 9$

$x - y = 3$

$2x = 12$

$x = 6$

8

If $x^2 - y^2 = 100$ and $x + y = 25$, which of the following is equivalent to the value of y?

A) $\dfrac{3}{2}$

B) $\dfrac{11}{2}$

C) $\dfrac{13}{2}$

D) $\dfrac{21}{2}$

$(x-y)25 = 100$

$x - y = 4$

$x + y = 25$

$\dfrac{2x}{2} = \dfrac{29}{2}$

$x = \dfrac{29}{2}$

$\dfrac{29}{2} - y = 4$

Notes:

29

CONTINUE

6   *Aiming* for Your Target!

"After you finish reading a question, the most important thing to make note of is 'what' the question is asking for. This is the target and you want to make sure that you get there quickly and efficiently."

Sometimes on the SAT, you are asked to solve for something other than a variable. Because you have been trained to "solve for x" and "simplify" in school, it may take you up to three times as long to solve for what the SAT asks you to find. Always "aim for your target" when you're answering a math question.

Example 1:

What is the value of $16x^2$ given that $4x^2 - 11 = 17$?

The target is "$16x^2$". You have to make sure that you are always mindful of getting to $16x^2$ as smoothly as possible.

$$4x^2 - 11 = 17$$
$$4x^2 = 28$$
$$(4)(4x^2) = (28)(4)$$

$$16x^2 = 112$$

Example 2:

If $x + y + z = 10$ and $x + y + 2z = 6$, what is the value of $x + y$?

What do you want? You want "*x* plus *y*." What do you not want? You don't want "*z*." So, eliminate *z* and let the rest unfold.

$$-2(x + y + z = 10)$$
$$x + y + 2z = 6$$

$$-2x - 2y - 2z = -20$$
$$\underline{x + y + 2z = 6}$$
$$-x - y = -14$$

$$x + y = 14$$

Skill 6 Practice Exercises:

1

If $5x = 22$, what is the value of $20x - 5$?

A) 83
B) 93
C) 435
D) 440

2

If $12x - 16 = 24$, what is the value of $3x$?

A) 2 $12x = 40$
B) 6
C) 10
D) 160

CONTINUE

3

If $(3x-6)(3x+6)=20$, what is $18x^2$?

A) 32
B) 56
C) 96
D) 112

(handwritten:) $9x^2 - 36 = 20$

$9x^2 = 56$

102

4

$$2x + y = 10$$
$$x + 2y = 20$$

Given the system of equations above, what is the value of $x+y$?

A) 3
B) 10
C) 15
D) 30

(handwritten:) $2(-2y + 10) + y = 10$

$-4y + 40 + y = 10$

$-3y + 40 = 10$

$-3y = -30$

$y = 10$

5

Suppose $2x+3y-z=14$ and $x+2y=15$. What is the value of $y+z$?

A) 16
B) 14
C) -14
D) -16

(handwritten:) $2x + 4y = 30$

$2x + 4y = 30$

$2x + 3y - z = 14$

$y + z = 16$

6

Gerald bought 2 apples and 5 oranges for $4.75. Mabel bought 4 apples and 1 orange from the same store for $2.75. What is the combined cost of 1 apple and 1 orange?

A) $0.50
B) $0.75
C) $1.00
D) $1.25

(handwritten:) $2x + 5y = 4.75$

$4x + y = 2.75$

$y = 2.75 - 4x$

$2x + 5(2.75 - 4x) = 4.75$

$2x + 13.75 - 20x = 4.75$

$-18x = -9$

$x = \frac{1}{2}$

31

CONTINUE

7

$$8a + 5b = 12$$
$$11a + 2b = 21$$

Given the system of equations above, what is the value of $a - b$?

$$-3a + 3b = -9$$

$$a - b = 3$$

A) −11

B) −3

C) 3

D) 11

8

If $xy = 5$, $yz = 3$, and $xz = 4$, what is the value of xyz?

A) $\sqrt{8}$

B) $\sqrt{60}$

C) 60

D) 120

$$xy \cdot yz \cdot xz =$$
$$\sqrt{x^2 y^2 z^2} = \sqrt{}$$

$$y = \frac{5}{x} \qquad z = \frac{4}{x}$$

$$\sqrt{\frac{20}{3}} \qquad \frac{5}{x}\left(\frac{4}{x}\right) = 3$$

$$\frac{20}{x^2} = 3$$

$$20 = 3x^2$$

Notes:

CONTINUE ➡

7   *Following* the Five Steps!

"Having all of the knowledge in the world can make you exceptional at mathematics. However, without control you will never give yourself the opportunity to become a great test taker."

If we were to identify one common area of the SAT that poses problems for all students at all levels, it would be careless mistakes. Careless mistakes are actually the most common type of error, as well as the most frustrating of them all. The question thus becomes…

"Is there a way to address careless mistakes?"

In order to address them, you need to understand the types of careless mistakes that exist:

The Misread Error:

In this case, a student does not fully absorb the important clue words or even the precise question that is being asked. Most of the time, this error occurs because a student simply moves too fast.

The Miscalculation Error:

The miscalculation error is also very common and predominantly involves moving through a problem at a pace that is too quick. Another reason a miscalculation can occur is distraction. Often, a student will be working out the simple steps of PEMDAS on a fairly routine simplification, but their mind will be focused on an earlier problem that led to confusion or uncertainty. This disconnect is what causes careless mistakes on routine problems.

So, we will address these errors by following a simple yet consistent answering structure.

"If you answer with structure, you turn your mathematics into an assembly line in which each response reaches the answer key with your seal of approval."

What Are the 5 Steps?

1. Read

This is about what you do while you are reading. Look for important words that will help to define the problem: *Positive, Negative, Even, Odd, Integer, Parallel, Perpendicular, Could, Must,* $a < 0$, $\ 0 < x < 1$, *etc.*

Underlining or mentally noting these key words will prepare you for the "what."

2. Emphasize the Target

This is the "what." You don't just want to find what the question is asking for. You want to emphasize the target and leave no chance of answering the wrong question.

So, if the question asks for the value of $4x^2$, you note that you want to get to $4x^2$ in the most efficient way possible.

3. Aim for Your Target (Plan)

Now that you know where you are going, you must take a moment to align your thinking with the problem. Quickly take note of how you will approach the problem prior to working it out. This will ensure that your work is all headed towards the goal and will prevent you from working for two minutes and then having to start over.

4. Do Your Work

The math has to take place somewhere. The main point in how you do your work differently than before is that you must have a set path and focus solely on the mathematical skill at hand. Make sure to eliminate any lingering thoughts from former problems.

5. Double Check

Well, your teachers always told you to check your work; now, doing so is more important than ever. Remember, the goal is to give each problem a seal of approval. As often as possible, you should leave the problem knowing that you will never need to return. There is no doubt. You are certain your answer is correct.

****

So, what assures you of success?

You must complete these steps for every question, no matter the difficulty level. Remember, you want to create a mathematical assembly line, devoid of error. Consistency and confidence are the root of control.

CONTINUE

These steps may seem daunting on paper, but in fact, they are much smoother in practice. At first, the process will slow you down, but with repetition, your efficiency will increase, along with your control.

Example:

In a set of 7 integers, the median is 5, the smallest number is 2, and the largest number is 8. If 3 is one of two modes in the set, which of the following could be true?

A) There is only one 8.
B) There are exactly two 8s.
C) There could be one or two 8s.
D) None of the above could be true.

1. Read: There are 7 integers in the list. The median of the list is 5. The smallest number is 2 and the largest is 8. 3 is one of two modes in the set.

2. Emphasize the Target: The problem asks what statement "could" be true. This means that you need to be creative and look for all cases that *do* work.

3. Plan: You will draw 7 dashes to hold places for the numbers, place in the given data, and look for any and all cases involving 8 that meet the given criteria.

4. Do Your Work:

<u>2</u> _ _ <u>5</u> _ _ <u>8</u>

Since 3 is one of two modes and only two spots remain…

<u>2</u> <u>3</u> <u>3</u> <u>5</u> _ _ <u>8</u>

What "could" happen? Well, 8 could be the other mode or it could not…

<u>2</u> <u>3</u> <u>3</u> <u>5</u> _ <u>8</u> <u>8</u>
<u>2</u> <u>3</u> <u>3</u> <u>5</u> _ _ <u>8</u>

So, the answer is <u>C</u>, one or two.

5. Double Check: You already know that there is one 8, the highest. So, it is possible that 5, 6, or 7 is the other mode. Or there could be two 8s, making 8 the other mode. This is clearly shown above. <u>C</u> **is correct!**

<u>**Skill 7 Practice Exercises:**</u>

1

If $\dfrac{x}{y} = 8$, what is the value of $\dfrac{2y}{x}$?

A) $\dfrac{1}{4}$

B) $\dfrac{1}{2}$

C) 4

D) 16

2

Daniel and James are boy scouts; every year, they become very competitive during the club's annual holiday wreath sale. This year, Daniel sold 25 less than two times the number of wreaths that James sold. How many wreaths did Daniel and James sell in total, if Daniel sold 25 wreaths?

A) 20
B) 25
C) 50
D) 75

CONTINUE

3

What is the square root of the lowest value of x that satisfies the equation $2x^2 = 32$?

A) $\sqrt{8}$

B) 4

C) 8

D) There is no real solution.

4

Given the equation $f(x) = x(x+2) - 15$, which of the following inequalities gives all possible true values of x, given that $f(x) < 0$?

A) $x > 3$

B) $0 < x < 3$

C) $-5 \le x \le 3$

D) $-5 < x < 3$

5

Line f is parallel to the line $y = \dfrac{1}{2}x + 6$ and goes through the point $(6,0)$. Line f also contains which of the following points?

A) $(-2,5)$

B) $(2,-2)$

C) $(4,4)$

D) $(6,-6)$

6

The difference between the cube and the square of a certain number is 180. The difference between the cube and the square of a different number is 18. What is the value of the quotient of the larger number divided by the smaller number?

A) 10

B) 3

C) 2

D) $\dfrac{1}{3}$

35

CONTINUE

7

A is equivalent to $36(x+1)$ for some value *x* and *B* is equivalent to $9x^2$ for the same value of *x*. What is the average of *A* and *B* in terms *x*?

A) $x+2$

B) $\dfrac{(3x+6)^2}{2}$

C) $(3x+6)^2$

D) $3x^2+18x+18$

8

Set *A* contains 6 integers and the median is equal to the range. Set *B* is created by multiplying every number in Set *A* by 3. If *m* is the median of Set *B* and *r* is the range of Set *B*, which of the following is true?

A) $m=r$

B) $m=3r$

C) $3m=r$

D) $m<r$

Notes:

_____

_____

_____

_____

_____

_____

_____

_____

_____

_____

CONTINUE

Test Taking Skills Unit Review:

1. *Translating* Words into Math

You must know the mathematical meanings of English words and use those meanings to create appropriate equations.

2. *Using* Dashes

Use dashes in order to organize multiple variables, multiple instances of a single variable, or even just a set of numbers.

3. *Splitting* the Difference

If you are given a combined total of two quantities and the difference between the two quantities, remember to "split" the total and to "split" the difference.

4. *Making* T-Charts

When you know that an equation cannot be solved algebraically, make a T-Chart to organize your guessing-and-checking.

5. *Factoring* and *Foiling*

Factoring and Foiling are skills that will be utilized throughout the test. It is very important to be efficient with them and to remember the special binomial expansions.

CONTINUE →

Test Taking Skills
Unit Review:

6. *Aiming* for Your Target!

When answering any question, you must always identify what the question wants and find the quickest, most direct route to that end.

7. *Following* the Five Steps!

In order to safely avoid careless mistakes, you must use a structured answering approach in order to maintain control over your answers.

CONTINUE ➡

Unit 1 Review - Calculator

55 MINUTES, 38 QUESTIONS

DIRECTIONS

For each question from 1-30, choose the best answer choice provided in the multiple choice bank and fill in the appropriate circle in the provided answer key. Alternatively, for questions **31-38**, answer the problem and enter your answer in the grid-in section of the answer key. Refer to the directions given before question 31 as to how to enter your answers for the grid-in questions. You may complete scratch work in any empty space in your test booklet.

NOTES

A. Calculator usage **is allowed**.
B. Variables, constants, and coefficients used represent real numbers unless indicated otherwise.
C. All figures are created to appropriate scale unless the question states otherwise.
D. All figures are two-dimensional unless the question states otherwise.
E. The domain of any given function is all real numbers x for which the function, $f(x)$, is a real number unless the question states otherwise.

REFERENCE

 $A = \pi r^2$
$C = 2\pi r$

 $A = lw$

 $A = \dfrac{1}{2}bh$

 $c^2 = a^2 + b^2$

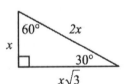 Special Right Triangle

 Special Right Triangle

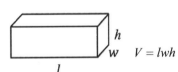 $V = lwh$

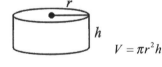 $V = \pi r^2 h$

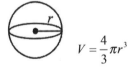 $V = \dfrac{4}{3}\pi r^3$

 $V = \dfrac{1}{3}\pi r^2 h$

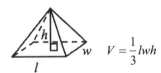 $V = \dfrac{1}{3}lwh$

There are $360°$ in a circle.
There are 2π radians in a circle.
There are $180°$ in a triangle.

CONTINUE ➤

1

18 less than 34 is equivalent to the square root of a number. What is the number?

$$34 - 18 = \sqrt{x}$$

A) 4
B) 16
C) 64
D) 256

2

The sum of a number and half of three times the number is 15. What is the value of half of three times the number?

A) 9
B) 12
C) $\frac{27}{2}$
D) 18

$$x + \frac{1}{2}(3x) = 15$$

$$x + 1.5x = 15$$

$$2.5x = 15$$

3

If there are 24 cars in a parking lot and there are 10 more 4-door cars than 2-door cars, how many 2-door cars are in the lot?

A) 2
B) 7
C) 17
D) 22

$$x + y = 24$$

$$x$$

$$-10 = y$$

4

If x is positive, y is negative, and $x^2 - y^2 = -5$, what is the value of $-\dfrac{x}{y}$?

A) $-\dfrac{9}{4}$
B) $-\dfrac{2}{3}$
C) $\dfrac{2}{3}$
D) $\dfrac{9}{4}$

CONTINUE ➡

5

$$0 = x^2 - 7x - 60$$

What is the greatest value of x that satisfies the equation above?

A) 5
B) 6
C) 10
D) 12 (circled)

6 10

20 3

12 5

$(x-12)(x+5)$

7

If $8x = 12$, what is the value of $4x - 4$?

A) -1
B) 2 (circled)
C) 8
D) 20

6

Nathaniel was on a quiz bowl team with Leonard. If Nathaniel and Leonard scored a combined total of 98 points and Nathaniel scored 12 more points than Leonard, how many points did Leonard score?

A) 37
B) 43 (circled)
C) 55
D) 61

$N + L = 98$

$L + 12 = N$

$2L + 12 = 98$

$2L = 86$

8

If $\dfrac{2a}{3b} = \dfrac{1}{2}$, what is the value of $\dfrac{9b}{2a}$?

A) $\dfrac{1}{6}$

B) $\dfrac{3}{2}$

C) 3

D) 6 (circled)

$\dfrac{4a}{2} = \dfrac{3b}{2}$

$2a = \dfrac{3b}{2}$

$9b$ $\dfrac{2}{3b}$ $\dfrac{9b}{\frac{3b}{2}}$

3

CONTINUE

9

Two times a number is equivalent to five more than three and a half times the number. Which of the following equations could be solved to find the number?

A) $2x - 5 = \frac{7}{2}x$

$2x = 5 + 3.5x$

B) $\frac{3}{2}x = 5$

C) $2x = 5 - (3 + \frac{1}{2}x)$

D) $2x = 5 - \frac{7}{2}x$

10

The average of x and eight more than x is 7. What is the value of $6x$?

A) −3

B) 6

C) 11

D) 18

$\dfrac{x + (8 + x)}{2} = 2$

$2x + 8 = 14$

$2x = 6$

$x = 3$

11

In a 278-page book, there are 78 less pages with pictures than pages without pictures. How many pages in the book have pictures?

A) 100

B) 134

C) 139

D) 178

$x + y = 278$

$x - 78 = y$

$2x - 78 = 271$

12

The difference between the cube and the square of a positive integer is 100. What is the greatest positive integer that is less than the number?

A) 3

B) 4

C) 5

D) 6

$x^3 + x^2 = 100$

42

CONTINUE

13

If $x + y = 9$ and $x - y = \dfrac{4}{3}$, what is the value of $x^2 - y^2$?

A) 3

B) $\dfrac{27}{4}$

C) 12

D) 13

(handwritten: $2x = \dfrac{18}{3} \dfrac{10\frac{1}{3}}{2}$; $x = \dfrac{31}{6}$)

14

The sum of the cubes of two different positive integers is 224. What is the average of the two integers?

A) 4

B) 5

C) 20

D) 112

(handwritten: $x^3 + y^3 = 224$)

15

$$x + y = 8$$
$$2x - y = 7$$

Given the system of linear equations above, what is the value of x?

A) 2

B) 3

C) 5

D) 8

(handwritten: $3x =$)

16

$$4(x + 10) = (x + 2)^2$$

What is the sum of the squares of the two values of x that satisfy the equation above?

A) 6

B) 12

C) 36

D) 72

(handwritten: $4x + 10 = x^2 + 4x + 4$; $0 = x^2 - 6$; 0; $4x + 40 = x^2 + 4x + 4$)

43

CONTINUE

17

Natalie can read as little as 3 pages per minute and as much as 5 pages per minute when she exercises her speed reading techniques. If Natalie practiced her speed reading techniques for three quarters of an hour, which of the following is a possible number of pages she could have read?

A) 120
B) 180
C) 720
D) 1200

18

Gary, Jill, and Armand held a fundraiser for their junior class prom. If Jill raised twice as much as Gary, Gary raised twice as much as Armand, and all together they raised $420, how much money, in dollars, did Gary raise?

A) 60
B) 120
C) 180
D) 240

19

If the number of people who graduated *without* honors was 48 more than the number of people who graduated *with* honors and a total of 200 people graduated, what percent of the graduating students graduated *without* honors?

A) 24
B) 36
C) 62
D) 64

20

The sum of the squares of two positive integers is 97. What is the average of the two numbers?

A) $\frac{11}{2}$

B) $\frac{13}{2}$

C) 7

D) 13

44

CONTINUE

21

$$x^2 - y^2 = 24$$
$$x + y = 6$$

The system of equations above is true for what value of x?

A) 2
B) 4
C) 5
D) 6

(handwritten work:)
$y = 6 - x$
$x^2 - (6-x)^2 = 24$
$x^2 - (36 - 12x + x^2) = 24$
$x^2 - x^2 + 12x - 36 = 24$
$12x - 36 = 24$

22

$$3x + 2y = 12$$
$$2x + 3y = 11$$

Given the system of equations above, what is the value of $x - y$?

A) 1
B) 9
C) 14
D) 23

(handwritten:) $x - y = 1$

23

Harold purchased 100 acres of land and 2 shacks for $240,000. Paul purchased 10 acres of land and 9 shacks for $90,000. What would it cost, in thousands of dollars, to purchase 10 acres of land and one shack?

A) 30
B) 330
C) 30,000
D) 330,000

(handwritten work:)
$100x + 2y = 240000$
$10x + 9y = 90000$
$2y = \dfrac{240000 - 100x}{2}$
$10x + 9(120000 - 50x) = 90000$
$y = 120000 - 50x$
$10x + 1080000 - 450x$
$-440x =$
$x = 2250$

24

Set A contains 10 integers and the median is equal to the range. Set B is created by multiplying every number in Set A by 2 and adding 20 to every number in the set. If m is the median of Set B and r is the range of Set B, which of the following is true?

A) $m = r$
B) $m + 20 = r$
C) $m = r + 20$
D) $m < r$

CONTINUE

25

Which of the following is equivalent to the sum of the square of the difference of a number x and 1 and two times the number?

A) $x^2 - 4x + 1$

B) $x^2 + 4x + 1$

C) $(x+1)(x-1)$

D) $x^2 + 1$

(handwritten work)
$(x^2 - x) + 1 - 2x$
$x^2 + x + 1$
$(x-1)^2 + 2x$
$x^2 - 2x + 1 + 2x$

26

If 824 votes were cast in a school's student council election between Jezebel and Lianna and Lianna lost by 62 votes, what percent of the votes cast did Jezebel win?

A) 42.5
B) 46.2
C) 53.8
D) 57.5

(handwritten work)
$L + J = 824$
$L + 62 = J$
$L =$
$L + L + 62 = 824$
$2L = 762$
381

27

If $x^2 - y^2 = \dfrac{1}{2}$ and $x - y = \dfrac{1}{8}$, what is the value of y?

A) $\dfrac{1}{8}$

B) $\dfrac{1}{4}$

C) $\dfrac{29}{16}$

D) $\dfrac{31}{16}$

(handwritten work)
$\dfrac{2}{8} - \dfrac{1}{8}$
$\dfrac{4}{64} - \dfrac{1}{64}$
$\dfrac{31}{16}$
$\dfrac{3}{8} - \dfrac{2}{8}$
$\dfrac{9}{64} - \dfrac{4}{64}$

28

The functions $y = 4x^2$ and $y = g - x^2$ intersect in Quadrant I of the xy-plane at the point (a,b). If a is a positive integer, which of the following could be the value of g?

A) 5
B) 9
C) 12
D) 27

CONTINUE

$x\left(\dfrac{32}{x}\right)=2$

$32=2$

29

If $xz^2 = 2$ and $xy^2 = 32$, which of the following could be the value of xyz?

A) 2
B) 4
C) 8
D) 16

$x = \dfrac{2}{z^2}$　　$x = \dfrac{32}{y^2}$

$\dfrac{32}{y^2} = \dfrac{2}{z^2}$

$\sqrt{z^2} = \sqrt{\dfrac{2}{x}}$

$z = \sqrt{\dfrac{2}{x}}$　$\dfrac{32z^2}{32} = \dfrac{2y^2}{32}$

$\sqrt{y^2} = \sqrt{\dfrac{32}{x}}$　$z^2 = \dfrac{y^2}{16}$

$\dfrac{\sqrt{32}}{\sqrt{x}}$　$\sqrt{\dfrac{2}{x}}$　$x\left(\dfrac{y^2}{16}\right) = 2$

$xy^2 = 32$

$y = 4a^2$

$y = 9 - a^2$

$5^{-a^2} = 4a^2$

$5 = 5a^2$

30

$$(x+a)(x+b) = x^2 + 12x + 27$$

Given that a and b are both positive integers, which of the following could be the value of b?

A) 1
B) 3
C) 6
D) 27

47

CONTINUE

DIRECTIONS

For each question from 31-38, solve and enter your answer in the grid-in section of your answer sheet as described below.

A. Write out your answers in the boxes at the top of each column in order to help you fill in the circles accurately. Remember, you will only receive credit for the circles that are filled in correctly, not for the written answer at the top of the columns.

B. Mark only a single circle in each column.

C. There are no negative answers.

D. If the problem has more than one correct answer, grid only one of the correct answers.

E. When your answer is a **mixed number**, such as $1\frac{1}{2}$, it should be entered as 1.5 or 3/2. You cannot enter a mixed number because there is no room to fill in a circle that represents a space.

F. If you enter a **decimal answer** with more digits then the grid can handle, the answer may be rounded or truncated, but it absolutely must fill the entire grid.

Answer: $\frac{8}{21}$ Answer: 6.4

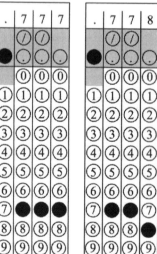

Answer: 102 - both positions are correct

REMEMBER:
You can begin writing your answers in any column as long as there is enough space. Leave unused columns blank.

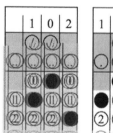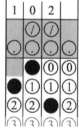

The ways to correctly grid $\frac{7}{9}$ are:

CONTINUE ➡

$(8-x)(8-x)$
$64-8x-8x+x$
$64+16x+x$

31

If the sum of two numbers that differ by 14 is 8, what is the value of the larger number?

$x(x+14)=8$

$x^2+14x-8=0$

$x^2-14x-8=0$

$x+(x+14)=8$ $2x=-22$
                $x=-11$
$2x+14=8$
        $2x=4$
          $x=2$

32

If x and y are both positive integers, what is the value of xy given that $x^2+y^2=25$?

4   3

12

$c=20$
$e=40-4c$
$2x=40-20-2c$
$x=80-40-4c$
$x=40-4c$

33

If $x+y=8$ and $x^2+y^2=63$, what is the value of xy?

$y=8-x$

$x^2+(8-x)^2=63$

$x^2+64-16x+x^2=63$

$2x^2-16+64=63$

$2x^2-16-1=0$

34

A foreign exchange student earned 10 more credits in core courses than she did in elective courses. Half of the number of credits she earned in core courses is 40 less than twice the number of credits she earned in elective courses. How many credits did the foreign exchange student earn all together?

$c=10+e$

$\frac{1}{2}c=40-2(10+c)$

$\frac{1}{2}c=40-20-c$

$\frac{3}{2}c=20\left(\frac{2}{3}\right)$

49

CONTINUE ➡

35

A local pizza parlor sold twice as many pizzas as it did the previous day for every day in a 7-day week. If the parlor sold a total of 254 pizzas that week, how many pizzas were sold on the last day?

$x + 2x + 4x + 8x + 16x + 32x + 64x = 254$

$127x = 254$

36

$$-2 \leq -\frac{1}{b} < 8$$

Given that the equation above is true, what is the greatest possible value for $12b$?

Questions 37-38 refer to the following information.

The five members of a school's student council raised a total of $1400 in order to afford the post-prom party they had planned. Three of the members raised the same amount of money, one of the members raised half the amount of money earned by each of the three members that raised the same amount, and the final member raised the average amount of money raised by the other 4 members.

37

How much money was raised by the student council member/members that raised the least amount of money in the group?

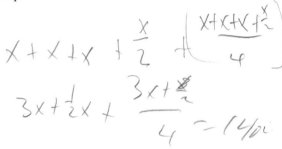

$$x + x + x + \frac{x}{2} + \left(\frac{x + x + x + \frac{x}{2}}{4} \right)$$

$$3x + \frac{1}{2}x + \frac{3x + \frac{x}{2}}{4} = 1400$$

38

One of the members that raised the most money and the member that raised the least amount of money both lost the money they had raised and were excused from the student council. The remaining three members raised the amount of money that was lost. If the remaining member who had earned the least amount of money raised twice as much of the lost money as the other two members combined, how much money in total was raised by the remaining member who had earned the least amount initially?

50

CONTINUE

UNIT 2

$= 1400$

$3.5x + \dfrac{3.5x}{4} = 1400$

$3.5x\left(1 + \dfrac{1}{4}\right) = 1400$

$x = 370$

$4x + 2x$

$480 = 2x + x + x$

$6x$

Unit 2: Heart of Algebra

Algebra is the most prominent mathematical language in high school. As one of the most vital skills required for success in advanced mathematics, it is utilized in many collegiate subject areas. Algebra is also the core of the newly-revised SAT. The skills covered in the Heart of Algebra unit will require students to analyze, solve, and create linear equations and inequalities. Further, it will be necessary for students to approach these equations, as well as systems of equations, in multiple fashions using multiple techniques. These topics and methods will be covered in this Heart of Algebra unit. An incredibly strong foundation in the core of algebra is the key to success in SAT mathematics.

CONTINUE ➡

8 Simplifying and Solving in One Variable

"When simplifying and solving, remember two things: follow the order of operations and keep your eyes open for the 'usual suspects'."

Simplifying linear expressions or solving linear equations and inequalities in one variable is as simple as you first learned. Combine like terms and use order of operations (PEMDAS) to simplify and/or solve. Of course, be extremely careful to pay attention to your "usual suspects":

1. **Negative Numbers** (Two negatives make a positive.)
2. **Distribution** (Distribute to all terms.)
3. **Inequalities** (When you divide or multiply by a negative number, flip the sign.)

Example 1:

What is the sum of $8-3x$ and $-7x-4$?

$$(8-3x)+(-7x-4)$$
$$8-3x-7x-4$$
$$8-10x-4$$
$$-10x+4$$

Example 2:

If $2(5x-19)+x=-8x$, what is the value of x?

$$2(5x-19)+x=-8x$$
$$10x-38+x=-8x$$
$$11x-38=-8x$$
$$-38=-19x$$
$$2=x$$

Example 3:

What is the greatest value of x that satisfies the inequality $4-2x \geq 10$?

$$4-2x \geq 10$$
$$-2x \geq 6$$
$$x \leq -3$$

The greatest value of x is -3.

Skill 8 Practice Exercises:

1

If $\dfrac{2x+3}{m}=7$ and $m=5$, what is the value of x?

A) 2
B) 10
C) 16
D) 19

(handwritten): $2x+3=3\cancel{5}$
$2x=32$
$x=16$

2

If $6x-3$ is 15 less than 27, what is the value of $2x$?

A) $\dfrac{5}{2}$
B) 5
C) $\dfrac{15}{2}$
D) 15

(handwritten): $6x-3=27-15$
$6x-3=12$
$\dfrac{6x}{3}=\dfrac{15}{3}$
$x=5$

CONTINUE

Heart of Algebra

3

The expression $3(x+1)+x(7-2)$ is equivalent to which of the following?

A) $12x+1$

B) $8x+3$

C) $8x+1$

D) $-2x+3$

$3x+3+7x-2x$

$8x+3$

5

If $5=h^2-11$ and $h>0$, what is the value of h?

A) 4

B) 2 16

C) -2

D) -4

4

Given that x is a positive integer, what is the greatest value of x that satisfies the inequality $-2x+3>3x-22$?

A) 2

B) 3

C) 4

D) 5

$-7>-7$

$-5>-10$

$-3>$

6

In the equation $2x+17=-4x+3$, what is the value of x?

A) -10

B) $-\dfrac{14}{3}$

C) $-\dfrac{10}{3}$

D) $-\dfrac{7}{3}$

$6x=-14$

$x=\dfrac{-7}{3}$

CONTINUE

7

$$11 + |2x + 4| = 3$$

For what value of x is the equation above equivalent to 3?

A) -2

B) 2

C) 4

D) There is no such value of x.

(handwritten work:)
$|2x + 4| = -8$
$2x + 4 = 8$ $2x + 4 = -8$
$-4 -4$
$2x = 4$ $2x = -12$
$x = 2$ $x = -6$
Absolute value
CAN NO EQUAL
A NEG #

8

Arnold will be depositing a check for $250 into his bank account five days from now. He plans to spend $20 per day for each of those five days. If Arnold wants to have at least $1,000 in his account after he deposits the check, what is the minimum amount of money, in dollars, that he must currently have in his account?

A) 850

B) 1,150

C) 1,250

D) 1,350

(handwritten: 100, 150, 5)

Notes:

CONTINUE

9   *Creating* in One Variable

"When creating expressions, equations, and inequalities, the most important step is to identify the variable and give it meaning."

The first step in creating is to identify the unknown quantity that the variable will represent. Once the variable has been given meaning, you can simply use the context of the problem and your word problem skills to develop the structure around the variable.

Example 1:

If Gina's grade average in her chemistry class is currently 85 and her average consistently increases by 2.2 points per month, which of the following expressions could be used to calculate Gina's current average given the number of months that have passed?

A) $85 + 2.2x$
B) $85 - 2.2x$
C) $2.2 + 85x$
D) $2.2 - 85x$

Identify the variable: *x, the number of months*
Identify the change per month: *2.2, so 2.2x*
Identify the direction: *The average is growing, so +.*

The expression must have $+2.2x$. The answer is <u>A</u>.

Example 2:

A scientist has filled a test tube with 500 cell samples. The scientist will be sampling 40 cells from the tube at a given time. The scientist must retain at least half of the original cells for outside testing sources; write an inequality, using s to represent the number of samples taken, that when solved will give the scientist a guideline as to how many samples he can take while retaining the required number of cells for outside testing sources.

Identify the variable: s, *the number of samples.*
Identify the change per sample: -40, *so* $-40s$.

Using the context of the problem: $500 - 40s \geq 250$

Skill 9 Practice Exercises:

1

Jeffrey can gut and clean 24 fish in an hour. A local fishery requires that their warehouse employees be able to gut and clean 45 fish per hour at a minimum. If Jeffrey continues to practice and increase the number of fish he guts and cleans by 3 per hour every week, *w*, that passes, which of the following represents the number of fish that Jeffrey can gut and clean in one hour, *w* weeks from today's date?

A) $3 + 24w$
B) $24 + 3w$
C) $21 - 3w$
D) $45 - 3w$

2

In the 1700s, *x* people joined a group of pioneers called the Exploring Riders of America. In the 1800s, three times as many people joined the group. If a total of 288 men and women joined the Exploring Riders of America in the 1700s and the 1800s combined, which of the following equations is true?

A) $288 - x = 2x$
B) $288 + x = 3x$
C) $288 = 4x$
D) $288 = 3x$

CONTINUE

3

Angela is traveling to visit a college that is 416 miles away. She has been traveling at a constant rate of 50 mph. If she is currently 206 miles from her destination, which of the following equations could be solved to determine the number of hours, h, that she has been on the road?

A) $416 - 50h = 206$

B) $50h + 206 = -416$

C) $50h - 416 = 206$

D) $206 - 50h = 416$

4

A computer science class currently has an enrollment of 60 students. If the classroom can handle a maximum of 120 students and the enrollment increases by 5 students per semester, which of the following inequalities can be solved to find the number of semesters, s, in which the classroom is at or exceeds capacity?

A) $s < 120 - 5$

B) $5s - 60 > 120$

C) $-5s + 120 \geq 60$

D) $5s + 60 \geq 120$

$60 + 5x \leq 120$

5

Dylan is planning a camping trip for himself and a group of d of his friends. Dylan has accumulated a total of $350 between his own money and the money he collected from his friends. If the gas for the entire trip will cost $58, how much money can Dylan budget for food and supplies per person in terms of d?

A) $\dfrac{292}{d}$

B) $\dfrac{292}{d+1}$

C) $\dfrac{350}{d}$

D) $350 - d$

6

Caitlin earns $18 per hour assembling mail advertisements for an advertising company. She also receives a daily stipend of $84. Jillian gets paid $24 per hour for performing market research for the same company, but receives no stipend for her work. Given that Caitlin and Jillian work the same number of hours, which of the following inequalities could be solved in order to find x, the number of hours that they must work in order for Jillian to earn more money than Caitlin?

A) $84x + 18 > 24x$

B) $18x + 84 < 24$

C) $84 < 6x$

D) $84 > 18x$

CONTINUE

7

Annika and Juanita go to a restaurant to have lunch. Annika's meal is x dollars and Juanita's meal is $8 more than twice as expensive as Annika's meal. If the two women split the bill after they leave a 15% tip and 7% sales tax is added, which of the following expressions represents the amount, in dollars, that each of them pay?

 $x = 2x+8$

A) $(1.2305)(\frac{3}{2}x+4)$

B) $(1.2305)(3x+8)$

C) $(1.15)(1.07)(x+4)$

D) $(1.15)(1.07)(2x+8)$

8

The population of a city with a current population of 10,200 increases by 20% every 40 years. Which of the following expressions can be used to estimate the population of the city t years from now?

A) $10,200(.2)^{40t}$

B) $10,200(1.2)^{40t}$

C) $10,200(.2)^{\frac{t}{40}}$

D) $10,200(1.2)^{\frac{t}{40}}$

Notes:

CONTINUE

10 — Interpreting in One Variable

"When interpreting you must make sure to read carefully and submerge yourself in the context of the problem."

Interpreting linear expressions, equations, and inequalities in one variable is one of the most useful skills you can attain, but also among the most difficult. When interpreting, you need to establish a clear understanding of what the variable represents and how it relates to the given numbers in the context of the problem. Imagining yourself in the context of the problem or recalling your understanding of the topics being discussed is highly useful. In this type of question, reading carefully is crucial to fully understanding the given information.

Example 1:

Eduardo is attempting to raise money for his school newspaper by selling ad spaces for graduation ads and announcements in next month's school newspaper. Each ad space costs $25, and Eduardo uses the equation $G(x) = 800 - 25x$ to determine the amount of money left before he reaches his goal, where x represents the number of ad spaces sold. What does the number 800 represent in Eduardo's equation?

From the context of the problem you can see that if x represents the number of ad sales, then $25x$ represents the amount of money that has already been earned. If you subtract this amount from 800, the number 800 must represent the amount of money that Eduardo wants to collect. So, <u>800</u> represents Eduardo's goal amount of money, in dollars.

Example 2:

If Martha's shoe size increases every year, y, that has passed since 2010 based upon the linear model $f(y) = 3 + .5y$, what does the value .5 represent?

Since you know that the model is linear, the coefficient of the variable, .5, is the slope or rate of change. So, in the context of this problem, <u>.5</u> represents Martha's increase in shoe size per year.

Skill 10 Practice Exercises:

In an experiment, the height of water in a glass was measured each time a marble was added to the glass. These height measurements were used to create the equation $h(m) = 0.6m + 12$, where m represents the number of marbles in the glass and $h(m)$ represents the height of the water, in centimeters. Which of the following best describes what the value 12 represents in the equation?

A) The number of marbles at the start of the experiment

B) The number of marbles added to the glass of water

C) The overall height of the glass

D) The height of the water in the glass when no marbles have been added

A tree removal service estimates the price in dollars of removing a tree using the expression $90h + 220$, where h represents the height, in feet, of the tree to be removed. Which of the following is the best interpretation of the number 90 in the expression?

A) The service charges $90 for each additional foot of tree height.

B) The service charges $90 for each additional tree to be removed.

C) The tree service charges $90 per hour to remove a tree.

D) The tree service charges $90 for each additional foot of height over 220 feet.

CONTINUE

3

Meredith works for a telemarketing service. Every day she is required to make a certain number of phone calls before the end of her shift. The number of calls she has left to complete on any given day can be calculated from the expression $72 - 6h$, where h is the number of hours that have passed since the start of her shift. What is the meaning of the value 72 in the expression?

A) Meredith makes 72 phone calls per hour.

B) Meredith starts each day with 72 phone calls to make.

C) Meredith will complete all of her calls in 72 hours.

D) Meredith makes 72 calls every six hours.

4

When Janelle runs on the treadmill at the gym her heart rate steadily rises for every minute that she continues to run. Janelle carefully monitors her heart rate using the formula $90 + 12x \leq 180$, where x represents the number of 5-minute intervals that have passed. Which of the following can be most reasonably concluded from the formula?

A) Janelle's at-rest heart rate is 180 beats per minute.

B) Janelle's heart rate rises 12 beats per minute every minute that she runs.

C) 35 minutes is the maximum amount of time that Janelle can run on the treadmill.

D) Janelle prefers to keep her heart rate at or below 180 beats per minute.

5

The average size of an SAT class at a private SAT school can be modeled by the expression $0.6x + 14.4$, where x is the number of summers that have passed since the school had opened. Which of the following best describes the meaning of the number 0.6 in the expression?

A) The total number students at the school when it first opened

B) The average number of students per class when the school first opened

C) The estimated increase in the average number of students per classroom each summer

D) The estimated increase in the total number of students at the school each summer

6

$$12h + 100 \geq 15h + 80$$

Stephen works for a office supply store at which he gets paid $12 per hour with a stipend of $100 on every paycheck. Alejandro has been working for the same company for a longer period of time. He gets paid $15 per hour, but only receives a stipend of $80 on each paycheck. Which of the following best describes the solution when the inequality above is solved for h?

A) The number of hours worked by both employees in which Stephen's paycheck is greater than or equal to Alejandro's paycheck

B) The number of hours worked by both employess in which Alejandro's paycheck is greater than or equal to Stephen's paycheck

C) The number of hours work by both employees in which they both have the same paycheck

D) The minimum number of hours worked in total by both employees

CONTINUE

7

At a local electrical supply store, the number of custom, automated, lighting quotes yet to be completed can be calculated from the expression $20 + 32w - 28w$, where w represents the number of weeks that have passed since the start of the year. Which of the following could explain the meaning of the constant 20 in the expression?

A) The total number of quotes yet to be completed

B) The total number of non-completed quotes carried over from the previous week

C) The total number of non-completed quotes carried over from the previous year

D) The number of new inquiries for quotes each week

8

Kimberly's weekly pay is represented by the following expression: $224.50 + 0.02(Sales)$. Which of the following statements is *not* true?

A) If Kimberly makes no sales, she will earn $224.50.

B) Kimberly earns a commission of 0.02% of her sales.

C) Kimberly will earn more than $500 in a week when she has $15,000 in sales.

D) Kimberly earns base pay as well as commission.

Notes:

$\frac{26}{3} > h$

61

CONTINUE

11   *Simplifying* and *Solving* Systems in Two Variables

"When working with systems of linear equations and inequalities, always remember to aim for your target!"

As you learned in Skill 7, when you are solving a system, the most important step is to identify what the question wants and to make sure that you always move toward that goal.

Example 1:

$$2x + y = 12$$
$$x - y = 3$$

Given the system of equations above, what is the value of y?

Although the system of equations can be solved easily for *x*, you want to aim for your target and solve for *y* by manipulating the equations:

$$2x + y = 12$$
$$\underline{-2(x - y = 3)}$$
$$3y = 6$$

$$y = 2$$

Example 2:

$$3x + 2y = 10$$
$$3x + 4y = 14$$

Given the system of equations above, what is the value of x + y ?

In this case, you want *x* and *y*, so you will not eliminate anything and will instead add:

$$3x + 2y = 10$$
$$\underline{3x + 4y = 14}$$
$$6x + 6y = 24$$

$$x + y = 4$$

Example 3:

If you know that $y < x + 2$ and $y > -x + 2$, which of the following coordinate points (x, y) satisfies this system of linear inequalities?

A) $(-1, -1)$
B) $(1, 5)$
C) $(2, -4)$
D) $(6, 0)$

One effective way to solve systems of linear inequalities is to "plug and chug." You can plug each point into both inequalities and see which point satisfies both. In this case:

$$(0) < (6) + 2 \text{ and } (0) > (-6) + 2$$
So, $\underline{D}$ is the correct answer.

Alternatively, when working with linear inequalities, you want to focus on the "target zone". This zone is the region of the *xy*-plane that satisfies both inequalities. You can graph both inequalities as linear equations, then shade the target region. After that, check to see which coordinate pair falls in that region. In this case:

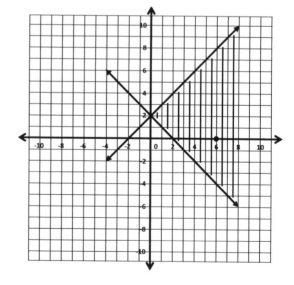

As you can see, the coordinate pair given in answer choice $\underline{D}$ falls in the "target region."

CONTINUE ➡

Skill 11 Practice Exercises:

1

$$y = 2x + 2$$
$$14 - x = y$$

Given the system of linear equations above, what is the value of x in the solution to the system?

A) 2
B) 4
C) 10
D) 14

Handwritten work:
$14 - x = 2x + 2$
$14 = 3x + 12$
$12 = 3x$
$x = 4$

2

$$3x + y = -4$$
$$-x - y = 2$$

According to the system of equations above, what is the value of x?

A) −2
B) −1
C) 1
D) 2

Handwritten work:
$2x = -2$
$x = -1$

3

$$y \leq 3$$
$$y \geq -3$$

Which of the following coordinate pair (x, y) satisfies the system of linear inequalities shown above?

A) $(-3, 10)$
B) $(0, -4)$
C) $(0, 3)$
D) $(3, 5)$

4

If $2x + 5y = 12$ and $2x - y = 0$, what is the value of $12x + 12y$?

A) 12
B) 24
C) 36
D) 60

Handwritten work:
$4x + 4y = 12$

CONTINUE

5

$$5x + 2y = -2$$
$$3y - 2x = 16$$

What is the solution (x, y) to the system of equations above?

A) $(4, -11)$

B) $(4, -2)$

C) $(2, -5)$

D) $(-2, 4)$

(handwritten work:)
$$15x + 6y = -6$$
$$-4x + 6y = 32$$
$$19x = -38$$
$$x = -2$$

6

$$d = 2.50 + .20m$$
$$h = 3.00 + .10m$$

In the set of equations above, d represents the price in dollars of a hot dog and h represents the price in dollars of a hamburger at a professional baseball stadium, m months into the season. What is the price of a hot dog when it is the same as the price of a hamburger?

A) $3.50

B) $4.50

C) $5.00

D) $7.00

(handwritten work:)
$$2.50 + .20m = 3 + .1m$$
$$.1m = .5$$
$$m = 5$$

7

A carpenter sells napkin holders for $5.50 each and cutting boards for $8.75 each. If the carpenter made a total of $48.25 selling a total of 7 napkin holders and cutting boards combined, how many cutting boards were sold?

A) 3

B) 4

C) 5

D) 6

(handwritten work:)
$$x + y = 7 \qquad y = 7 - x$$
$$5.50x + 8.75y = 48.25$$
$$5.50(7 - y) + 8.75y = 48.25$$
$$38.5 - 5.5y + 8.75y = 48.25$$
$$3.25y = 9.75$$
$$y = 3$$

8

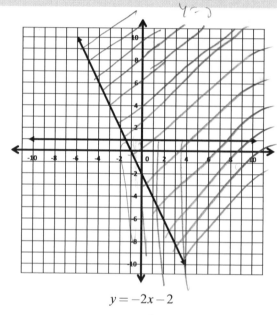

$$y = -2x - 2$$
$$y = 1$$

The system of equations given above is graphed on the xy-plane. If one were to graph the system of linear inequalities where $y > -2x - 2$ and $y < 1$, all of the solutions to the system would be located in which of the following quadrants?

A) I and II

B) II only

C) II, III, and IV

D) I, II, III, and IV

CONTINUE

Mid-Unit 2 Review - No Calculator

25 MINUTES, 20 QUESTIONS

$x = 7\eta$

$A = \pi r^2$
$C = 2\pi r$

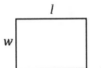

$A = lw$

$A = \dfrac{1}{2}bh$

$c^2 = a^2 + b^2$

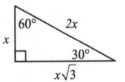

Special Right Triangle

Special Right Triangle

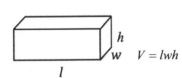

$V = lwh$

$V = \pi r^2 h$

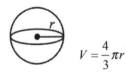

$V = \dfrac{4}{3}\pi r^3$

$V = \dfrac{1}{3}\pi r^2 h$

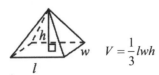

$V = \dfrac{1}{3}lwh$

There are $360°$ in a circle.
There are 2π radians in a circle.
There are $180°$ in a triangle.

CONTINUE ➤

1

If $t = 8$ and $\dfrac{2d+t}{4} = 16$, what is the value of d?

A) 6
B) 14
C) 28
D) 36

$\dfrac{2d+8}{4} = 16$

$2d + 8 = 64$

$2d = 56$

$d = 28$

2

Reagan wants to join the mathletes at his school, but he is nervous because they said that he must be able to answer 48 two-step math problems in under 30 minutes. Reagan can currently solve 28 two-step math problems in 30 minutes and knows that with practice, he will be able to increase that number by 5 problems per week. Which of the following expressions, using w for weeks, is equivalent to the number of two-step problems per half hour by which Raegan must improve in order to compete with the mathletes after w weeks have passed?

A) $48 + 5w$
B) $28 + 5w$
C) $48 - 5w$
D) $20 - 5w$

$28 + 5x = 48$

$5x =$

3

$$s(x) = 2 + 0.5x$$

The shoe size of a child can be estimated using the equation above where x represents the age of the child and $s(x)$ represents the comparable men's shoe size worn by the child. Which of the following best describes what the value 2 represents in the equation?

A) The shoe size of the child at birth
B) The shoe size of the child at the age of 1
C) The increase in the child's shoe size each year
D) The age of the child

4

$$y = 2x + 5$$
$$y = -x + 14$$

Given the system of linear equations above, what is the value of y in the solution to the system?

A) 3
B) 9
C) 11
D) 12

$2x + 5 = -x + 14$

$3x = 9$

$x = 3$

CONTINUE

5

$$\frac{250+10s}{s}$$

At a small coffee shop, each day the cash register starts with a total of $250 in the till. At the end of each day, the manager of the coffee shop uses the equation above to estimate the average amount of cash in the register per customer that visits the coffee shop. Which of the following is the most likely meaning of the constant 10 in the expression?

A) Each customer visits the coffee shop ten times a day.

B) Each customer spends an average of $10 at the coffee shop.

C) Ten customers visit the coffee shop each day.

D) The customers spent a combined total of $10 each day.

6

On Tuesday, Nigel and his brother asked x of their friends if they would like to go to Pennsylvania to play paintball. On Wednesday, Nigel and his brother asked twice as many friends the same question. If everyone responded yes and a total of 32 people went on the trip, which of the following equations could be solved to find x, the number of friends Nigel and his brother asked to go paintballing on Tuesday?

A) $2x+2=32$

B) $3x+2=32$

C) $2x=32$

D) $3x=32$

7

$$7x+2y=45$$
$$3y-5x=-41$$

What is the solution (x,y) to the system of equations above?

A) $(7,-2)$

B) $(5,5)$

C) $(3,10)$

D) $(1,19)$

(handwritten work:)
$21x+6y=135$
$-10x+6y=-82$
$31x=217$
$x=7$

8

A salesman at a home theater electronics store gets paid biweekly based on the expression $400+0.03s$, where s represents the dollar amount of sales that the salesman has made in that two-week period. Which of the following best describes the meaning of the number 0.03 in the expression?

A) The salesman receives 3 cents for every sale that he makes in a week.

B) The salesman receives 3 cents for every sale that he makes in two weeks.

C) The salesman receives a 3% commission on his sales every week.

D) The salesman receives a 3% commission on his sales every two weeks.

67

CONTINUE

9

Mani recently purchased 12 books at a garage sale for a total of $29. If each paperback book cost $2, each hardcover book cost $3, how many paperback books did Mani purchase at the garage sale?

$2x + 3y = 29$

$x + y = 12$

A) 4

B) 5

$2x + 2y = 24$

C) 7

D) 8

$y = 5$

$x = $

10

Mitchell has been driving his car for h hours at 60 miles per hour. He is currently 112 miles from his grandmother's house. In terms of h, which of the following expressions represents Mitchell's total round-trip distance for his trip to his grandmother's house?

$60h + 112$

A) $224 + 120h$ $120h + 224$

B) $112 + 60h$

C) $224 - 120h$

D) $112 - 60h$

11

$$25h \geq 2{,}200$$

Carrie works as a marketing consultant for a political campaign foundation. Carrie gets paid hourly and is exempt from paying taxes. If Carrie is attempting to raise $2,200 for a trip to Europe, which of the following best describes the solution when the inequality above is solved for h?

A) The number of hours Carrie must work to reach her vacation fund goal

B) The number of hours Carrie must work to exceed her vacation fund goal

C) The number of hours Carrie must work to assure that she has reached her vacation fund goal

D) The number of hours Carrie has left until she reaches her vacation fund goal

12

Thomas, his two younger brothers, and f of his closest friends are going on a field trip for school. Each person is required to give a deposit of $15 prior to the trip. In terms of f, if the total amount of money collected for all of the people going on the field trip was $200, which of the following expressions represents the average amount of money paid by each person in addition to the deposit?

A) $\dfrac{200 + 15f}{f + 3}$ $(3 + f) 15$

B) $\dfrac{200 + 15(f + 3)}{f + 3}$

C) $\dfrac{200 - 15f}{f + 3}$

D) $\dfrac{200 - 15(f + 3)}{f + 3}$

CONTINUE

13

$$|2x+3|+5=6$$

For which of the following values of x is the equation above true?

(handwritten: $2x+3=1$ $2x+3=-1$ $2x=-2$ $2x=-4$ $x=-1$ $x=-2$)

A) -2 and -1

B) -1 and 1

C) 1

D) There is no such value of x.

14

Daniella went to a store to buy a new hairdryer. The hairdryer was on sale at a 30% discount. If Daniella paid 5% sales tax and her final bill was $22.75, which of the following equations could be solved to find x, the original list price of the hairdryer?

(handwritten: $(x)(.7)(1.05)=22.75$ $x=\dfrac{22.75}{(.7)(1.05)}$)

A) $22.75(0.7)(1.05)=x$

B) $x(0.7)(1.05)=22.75$

C) $22.75(1.3)(1.05)=x$

D) $x(0.7)(0.05)=22.75$

15

Sohil gets paid hourly during the week and receives time-and-a-half on the weekends. If Sohil worked half as many hours on the weekend as he did during the week and his total pay for the week can be calculated using the expression $12h+18(\frac{1}{2}h)$, which of the following statements is true?

A) h is the number of hours Sohil worked on the weekend.

B) Sohil worked a total of h hours this week.

C) Sohil made $18 for every half hour he worked on the weekend.

D) Sohil made $18 per hour during the weekend.

CONTINUE

DIRECTIONS

For each question from 16-20, solve and enter your answer in the grid-in section of your answer sheet as described below.

A. Write out your answers in the boxes at the top of each column in order to help you fill in the circles accurately. Remember, you will only receive credit for the circles that are filled in correctly, not for the written answer at the top of the columns.

B. Mark only a single circle in each column.

C. There are no negative answers.

D. If the problem has more than one correct answer, grid only one of the correct answers.

E. When your answer is a **mixed number**, such as $1\frac{1}{2}$, it should be entered as 1.5 or 3/2. You cannot enter a mixed number because there is no room to fill in a circle that represents a space.

F. If you enter a **decimal answer** with more digits then the grid can handle, the answer may be rounded or truncated, but it absolutely must fill the entire grid.

Answer: $\frac{8}{21}$

Answer: 6.4

Written answer →
Decimal point →
← Fraction line

The ways to correctly grid $\frac{7}{9}$ are:

Answer: 102 - both positions are correct

REMEMBER: You can begin writing your answers in any column as long as there is enough space. Leave unused columns blank.

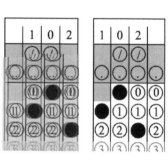

CONTINUE →

16

$$4 - x^2 = -32$$

The equation above is true for what value of x, where $x > 0$?

$36 = x^2$

$\boxed{4}$

18

If four more than $8x$ is equivalent to five less than twenty five, what is the value of $24x$?

$4 + 8x = 25 - 5$

$8x = 16$

$\boxed{48}$

17

$$x + 3y = 18$$
$$4x + 2y = 2$$

Given the system of equations above, what is the value of $x + y$?

$5x + 5y = 20$

$x + y = \boxed{4}$

19

If $x + 19y = 21$ and $19x + y = 23$, what is the value of $10x + 10y$?

$19x + y = 23$

$x + 19y = 21$

$18x - 18y = 2$

$x - y = \dfrac{2}{18}$

$10x - 16y = \dfrac{20}{18}$

$\boxed{22}$

CONTINUE

20

Ernesto is going on vacation. He has to purchase some new luggage that will cost him $240 and a new Hawaiian shirt that will cost $40. Ernesto's parents are giving him $200 toward his trip. If Ernesto plans to spend $55 per day and he plans to return home with no money, how much money is in Ernesto's vacation fund before the trip, if his trip is 8 days long?

$$((?240 + 40) + 55(8)) - 200 =$$

$$280 =$$

$$\boxed{520}$$

CONTINUE

12   *Creating* in Two Variables

"When creating expressions, equations, inequalities, or systems from scratch, you must identify the variables, understand how they relate to each other, and use the context of the problem to translate the words into math."

After you have identified the variables, take note of which coefficients pair with which variables. Once you have created the expressions, you can use them to build the individual equations or inequalities.

Example 1:

Tian recently went to a convenience store and purchased two cookies and a bottle of soda for $2.10. On another day, he purchased one cookie and two sodas for $2.70. If Tian plans to go to the convenience store in the future to buy one cookie and one soda, how much money, in dollars, should he expect to spend?

Identify the variables:
c, the price of a cookie in dollars
s, the price of a bottle of soda in dollars

Identify the expressions:
$2c+s$, *two cookies and one soda*
$c+2s$, *one cookie and two sodas*

Create the system, aim for your target, and solve:

$$2c+s=2.10$$
$$\frac{c+2s=2.70}{3c+3s=4.80}$$
$$c+s=1.60$$

Example 2:

Giana makes $20 per hour and $5 per quilt that she sells while representing her craft company at a trade show. Angeline, Giana's partner, only makes $10 per hour, but receives a higher rate of $10 per quilt since she is one of the main seamstresses for the quilt project. The two women have agreed that they would like to make at least $300 each before they shut down their table at the trade show. If the coordinate pair (h,q) represents the number of hours of work, h, and the number of quilt sales, q, and Giana and Angeline have made the same number of sales, which of the following coordinate pairs will satisfy their goal?

A) $(5,30)$
B) $(10,20)$
C) $(15,10)$
D) $(20,0)$

Identify the variables:
h, hours worked
q, number of quilts sold

Identify the expressions:
$20h+5q$, *Giana's earnings*
$10h+10q$, *Angeline's earnings*

Create the system and solve:

$$20h+5q\geq300$$
$$10h+10q\geq300$$

Since graphing is fairly challenging with the given variables, just use your answer choices, plug in, and find the solution that satisfies both inequalities.

$$20(10)+5(20)=300\geq300$$
$$10(10)+10(20)=300\geq300$$

The correct answer is <u>B</u>.

CONTINUE

Skill 12 Practice Exercises:

1

A music downloading service charges $9 for every full album that gets downloaded and $0.90 for every individiual song that gets downloaded. If a person downloads a albums and s individual songs, which of the following expressions is equivalent to the total cost for all of this individual's purchases from the music downloading service?

A) $9a+.9s$ $9a + 5.9$

B) $9s+.9a$

C) $9+.9as$

D) $9a+90s$

2

Ernesto purchased a new mp3 player and downloaded 20 songs for a total of $190. Marta purchased three mp3 players for her daughters and paid in advance for 30 total music downloads, which cost her a total of $510. If m represents the cost of each mp3 player purchased and d represents the cost of a single music download, which of the following systems of equations could be solved to find out the cost of an mp3 player and a single song download combined?

$m + 20d = 190$

$3x + 3a = 510$

A) $20m+d=190$
   $30m+3d=510$

B) $m+20d=190$
   $3m+30d=510$

C) $20m+d=510$
   $30m+3d=190$

D) $m+20d=510$
   $3m+30d=190$

3

A door-to-door salesman has a total of 120 households to visit on a given day. If the salesman can visit 45 households in 3 hours, which of the following equations can be solved to find R, the number of remaining households he must visit given h, the number of hours he has been working for on that day?

A) $R=120-45h$

B) $R=120-15h$

C) $R=45+120h$

D) $R=15+120h$

4

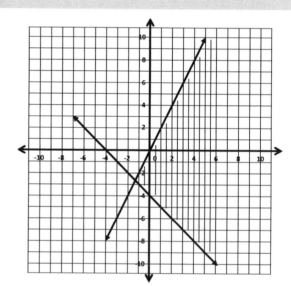

The xy-plane above displays the solution region for which of the following systems of linear inequalities?

A) $y\le -x-4$
   $y\le 2x$

B) $y\le -x-4$
   $y\ge 2x-4$

C) $y\ge -x+4$
   $y\le x$

D) $y\ge -x-4$
   $y\le 2x$

CONTINUE

5

A construction worker is transporting 35-pound bags of mortar and 50-pound bags of concrete in an oversized wheelbarrow. If m represents the number of bags of mortar, c represents the number of bags of concrete, and the wheelbarrow can handle a maximum of 16 bags or a total of 600 pounds, which of the following systems of inequalities represents this relationship?

A) $m+c \le 600$
   $35m+50c \le 16$

B) $m+c \le 16$
   $50m+35c \le 600$

C) $m+c \le 600$
   $50m+35c \le 16$

D) $m+c \le 16$
   $35m+50c \le 600$

Handwritten: $35m+50c \le 600$
Handwritten: $m+c \le 16$

6

A traveling salesman rents a car for $20 per hour and sells magazine subscriptions for $10 per subscription. The salesman plans to earn $200 on a normal workday. Another salesman rents retail space for $50 per hour and sells secondhand USB based scanners for $30 per device. The second salesman plans to earn $650 on a normal workday. If both salesmen work the same number of hours, make the same number of sales, and achieve their respective earning goals, how many hours did the salesmen work?

A) 5
B) 6
C) 8
D) 10

Handwritten:
$200 = 10y - 20x$
$650 = 30y - 50x$
$600 = 30y - 60$
$50 = x \cdot 10$
$x = 5$

7

If 5 more than a value a is equivalent to the sum of twice the value of a and five times another value b, what is a in terms of b?

A) $a = 2.5b - 2.5$
B) $a = 5b - 5$
C) $a = 5 - 5b$
D) $a = 5b + 5$

Handwritten:
$a + 5 = 2a + 5b$
$5 - 5b = a$

8

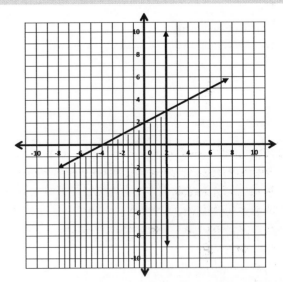

The xy-plane above displays the solution region for which of the following systems of linear inequalities?

A) $y \le 2$
   $y \le \frac{1}{2}x + 2$

B) $y \ge 2$
   $y \ge \frac{1}{2}x + 2$

C) $x \le 2$
   $y \le \frac{1}{2}x + 2$

D) $x \le 2$
   $y \le -\frac{1}{2}x + 2$

75

CONTINUE

13 — *Interpreting* in Two Variables

"When interpreting in two variables, pay close attention to the meaning of each variable and of each coefficient attached to a variable."

As before, when interpreting you have to have a clear understanding of what each variable represents and how it relates to the given numbers in the context of the problem. Reading carefully, being involved in the problem, and making the words as real as possible will make it easier to interpret the meanings of the expressions that make up a mathematical equation.

Example 1:

In the equation $25h + 30y = 500$, h represents the number of hours that Haley works and y represents the number of hours that Yolanda works. If the total amount of money earned by Haley and Yolanda is $500, what is the meaning of the coefficient 25 in the equation?

A) The total amount of money that Haley earns
B) The amount of money that Haley earns per hour
C) The total amount of money that Yolanda earns
D) The amount of money that Yolanda earns per hour

Generally, you know that the total amount of money earned from working is the total number of hours worked times the hourly rate. In this case you have two workers, and since 25 is the coefficient attached to *h* and *h* is the number of hours that Haley worked, 25 must be Haley's hourly rate.

The correct answer is _B_.

Example 2:

$$25,000x + 30,000y = 1,400$$
$$50,000x + 10,000y = 1,300$$

At a certain wholesale company, one employee made $25,000 worth of sales in the United States and $30,000 worth of international sales, and earned a commission of $1,400. Another employee, who conducts more business within the United States, had $50,000 worth of sales in the Unites States and $10,000 worth of sales internationally, and earned a commission of $1,300. The two commission payments are calculated in the system of equations given above. If the coordinate (a,b) is the solution to the system of equations given above, what does the value of a represent?

A) The commission rate for sales in the United States common to both employees
B) The commission rate for international sales common to both employees
C) The number of sales in the United States common to both employees
D) The number of international sales common to both employees

Since (a,b) is a solution to the system of equations, you know that it is a coordinate pair that makes both equations correct. You can also see that *a* is in the *x*-coordinate position, which makes it attached to United States sales. Finally, since you can see that the employees' pay is lower than their sales, you can conclude that *a* and *b* are both decimals. More importantly, you can see that these are percentages in decimal form. Given this data, *a* is the commission rate for sales in the United States common to both employees.

The correct answer is _A_.

CONTINUE

Skill 13 Practice Exercises:

1

Geraldine begins each week with a number of processing chip repairs that must be completed. The number of processing chips that she has left to fix, C, given the number of days that have passed, d, can be estimated with the equation $C = -48d + 240$. What is the meaning of the number 240 in the equation?

A) Geraldine can repair all of the processing chips in 240 days.

B) Geraldine can repair 240 processing chips every day.

C) Geraldine has 240 processing chips to repair at the beginning of the week.

D) Geraldine will finish all of the repairs in 240 work days.

2

The average grade point average of a senior graduating from Glennstown Memorial High School during the years 1990 through 2000 can be modeled with the equation $y = 0.05x + 2.8$, where x represents the number of years since 1990, and y represents the average grade point average for graduating seniors. Which of the following best describes the meaning of the coefficient 0.05 in the equation?

A) The average grade point average of all students at Glennstown Memorial High School in the year 1990.

B) The average grade point average of all graduating seniors at Glennstown Memorial High School in the year 1990.

C) The estimated increase in the average grade point average for all students at Glennstown Memorial High School each year.

D) The estimated increase in the average grade point average for all graduating seniors at Glennstown Memorial High School each year.

3

$$y = \frac{3}{5}x + 2$$

In the equation above, what is the meaning of the number $\frac{3}{5}$?

A) For every increase of 3 units in the value of x, y will increase by 5 units.

B) For every increase of 3 units in the value of y, x will increase by 5 units.

C) For every increase of $\frac{3}{5}$ units in the value of x, y will increase by 2.

D) For every increase of $\frac{3}{5}$ units in the value of y, x will increase by 2.

4

$$3x - y = 5$$
$$2x + y = 10$$

If (q, r) is the solution to the system of equations above, which of the following best describes this coordinate pair?

A) (q, r) is the y-intercept of $3x - y = 5$.

B) (q, r) is the y-intercept of $2x + y = 10$.

C) (q, r) is the point where $2x + y = 10$ intersects $3x - y = 5$.

D) (q, r) is the point where $2x + y = 10$ and $3x - y = 5$ intersect the origin.

CONTINUE

5

$$P = 37.5(1.01)^t$$

The population of a small town can be calculated using the equation above where P represents the population of the town in hundreds of residents given t, the number of years that have passed since the town's inception. Which of the following gives the best meaning for the number 1.01 in the equation?

A) The population, P, increases by .01% each year.

B) The population, P, increases by 1% each year.

C) The population, P, increases by 1.01% each year.

D) The population, P, increases by 101% each year.

6

A mobile blood bank collects 50 pints of blood every day that the bank is on the road. A local school blood drive collects 15 pints of blood every hour that the drive lasts. If m represents the number of days that the mobile blood bank is on the road and d represents the number of hours that the school blood drive lasts, then given the inequality $50m + 15d \geq 350$, which of the following could describe what the value 350 represents?

A) The total amount of time that both the blood bank and the school blood drive will be operating

B) The total number of pints that the blood bank and the school blood drive will produce in one hour

C) The maximum number of pints of blood that the blood bank and the school blood drive would like to collect together

D) The minimum number of pints that the blood bank and the school blood drive would like to collect together

7

$$2g + 6b = 9.00$$
$$5g + 2b = 9.50$$

On her way to a big family picnic, Janis purchased 2 gallon jugs of water and 6 smaller bottles of water for $9.00. Because it was a particularly hot afternoon, Janis had to return to the store later to purchase 5 more gallon jugs of water and 2 more bottles of water. This second trip cost her $9.50. Given the system of equations above, which of the following best describes the expression $g + b$?

A) The combined cost of purchasing one gallon jug of water and one bottle of water

B) The combined number of gallon jugs of water and bottles of water that Janis purchased

C) The value of $g + b$ is more than $3.00.

D) The value of $g + b$ is exactly $3.00.

8

An escalator is moving downward at a rate of 20 vertical feet per minute and a man is running up the escalator at a rate of 50 vertical feet per minute. Part of the way through the man's ascent, the escalator stops. If the top of the escalator is 40 vertical feet higher than the bottom of the escalator and $50x - 20y = 40$, what could the variable y represent?

A) The amount of time that the escalator spends moving before it stops

B) The amount of time that it takes the man to reach the top of the escalator

C) The total vertical distance that the escalator travels before it stops running

D) The total vertical distance that the man travels before the escalator stops running

78

CONTINUE

14 Determining Coefficients for No Solutions or Infinite Solutions

"Keep it simple. When using the elimination method, if 0 equals a non-zero constant, there are no solutions; when 0 equals 0, there are infinitely many solutions."

Often, you will be asked to determine a coefficient in an equation or a system of equations that will yield no solutions or infinitely many solutions. The goal is to force one of the following situations:

$$0 = b$$, where b is a non-zero constant

(This implies that there is <u>no solution</u>.)
(These are <u>parallel</u> lines.)

$$0 = 0$$

(This implies that there are <u>infinitely many solutions</u>.)
(These are <u>coincident</u>, or the same line.)

Example 1:

$$-4x + 5y = 200$$
$$bx - 5y = 300$$

Given the system of equations above, for what value of b does the system have no solutions?

In order to obtain no solutions, you should eliminate both variables and create a statement that makes no sense. In this case, a non-sensical statement is exactly what you are looking for.

If you substitute 4 for *b*:

$$-4x + 5y = 200$$
$$(4)x - 5y = 300$$
$$\overline{\hspace{4cm}}$$
$$0 = 500$$

the variables are eliminated and the statement makes no sense. Hence, there are <u>no solutions</u>.

The correct value for *b* is <u>4</u>.

Example 2:

$$9x - 6y = 3$$
$$ax - 2y = 1$$

If the system of equations above is true for all values of x and y, what is the value of a?

A) 3
B) 2
C) 1
D) 0

In the case of infinite solutions, you are looking for two equations that are exactly the same. This way, when the variables are canceled, so are all of the constants. You want to end up with $0 = 0$.

$$9x - 6y = 3$$
$$-3(ax - 2y = 1)$$
$$\overline{\hspace{4cm}}$$

$$9x - 6y = 3$$
$$-3ax + 6y = -3$$
$$\overline{\hspace{4cm}}$$

If you substitute 3 for *a*:

$$9x - 6y = 3$$
$$-3(3)x + 6y = -3$$
$$\overline{\hspace{4cm}}$$
$$0 = 0$$

The variables are eliminated, as are all of the constants. You end up with $0 = 0$ **and <u>infinitely many solutions</u>.**

The correct answer is <u>A</u>.

CONTINUE

Skill 14 Practice Exercises:

1

$$y = -2x + 6$$
$$4x + 2y = 3$$

How many coordinate pairs satisfy the system of equations above?

$2y = -4x + 3$

A) 0
B) 1
C) 2
D) Infinitely many

2

$$mx + 5y = 10$$
$$2x + 5y = 20$$

In the system of equations above, m is a constant. For what value of m will the system of equations have no solution?

A) −2
B) −1
C) 0
D) 2

3

$$ax + 4y = 10$$
$$bx + 8y = 20$$

If the system of equations above has infinitely many solutions and a and b are constants, what is the value of $2a - b$?

A) $2a + b$
B) $2ab$
C) 0
D) 1

$2ax = 0$

bx

$2ax - bx$

$2a = b$

4

$$100x + 200y = 300$$
$$250x + my = 750$$

For what value of m will the system of equations above have infinitely many solutions?

A) 1
B) 200
C) 400
D) 500

80

CONTINUE

5

Given that the equations $y = 8x + 2$ and $y = 8x + b$ do not intersect, which of the following values *cannot* be a value of b?

A) 0
B) 2
C) 4
D) 8

6

$$rx + 7y = 70$$
$$2x + 4y = 40$$

In the system of equations above, r is a constant. For what value of r will the system of equations have infinitely many solutions?

A) $\dfrac{8}{7}$

B) $\dfrac{7}{2}$

C) 7

D) 14

7

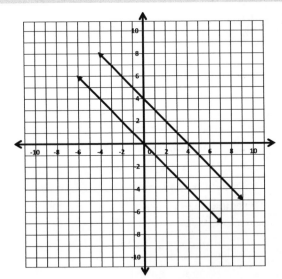

The system of equations graphed on the xy-plane above has how many solutions?

A) 0
B) 1
C) 2
D) Infinitely many

8

$$2x + 2y < 8$$
$$4x + hy > 16$$

Which of the following defines all values of h where there is no coordinate pair (x, y) that satisfies the system of linear inequalities above?

A) $h \le 4$
B) $h \ge 4$
C) $h = 4$
D) $h = 0$

$x + y < 4$

$4x + 4y > 4$

$x +$

81

CONTINUE

15   *Recognizing* Connections Between Linear Equations and Their Graphs

"When working with linear graphs, always think
$$y = mx + b \text{."}$$

Important things to remember:

1. **Parallel lines have the same slope.**
2. **Perpendicular lines have negative reciprocal slopes.**
3. **The equation of a horizontal line is** $y = $ constant.
4. **The equation of a vertical line is** $x = $ constant.

Example 1:

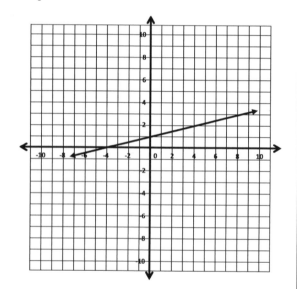

Which of the following linear equations is the best approximation of the line graphed in the xy-plane above?

A) $y = \frac{1}{2}x + 1$
B) $y = \frac{1}{4}x + 1$
C) $y = \frac{1}{4}x - 1$
D) $y = -\frac{1}{2}x - 1$

Start with a *y*-intercept of +1. This eliminates answers *C* and *D*. Then inspect the slope. From the point $(0,1)$**, we *rise* 1 and *run* 4. This makes *B* the correct answer.**

Example 2:

The graph of a linear function crosses the x-axis at 2 and passes through the point $(1,3)$*. With x and y as variables, what is the equation of the line?*

Here you are given two points: $(2,0)$ **and** $(1,3)$**.**

All you have to do is use the slope formula with which you are familiar, $m = \dfrac{y_2 - y_1}{x_2 - x_1}$**, to find the slope and then plug in either point to find the *y*-intercept:**

$$m = \frac{y_2 - y_1}{x_2 - x_1} = \frac{(3) - (0)}{(1) - (2)} = -3$$

$$y = -3x + b$$
$$(0) = -3(2) + b$$
$$6 = b$$

Therefore, the equation is $y = -3x + 6$**.**

Example 3:

Assuming that the axes are drawn to scale, which of the following graphs displays a linear equation with a positive y-intercept and a fractional negative slope?

A)

B)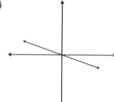

C)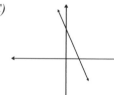

D)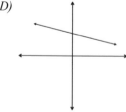

As before, starting with the positive *y*-intercept, you can eliminate answer *B*. Now, focusing on the negative fractional slope, look for a line that falls from left to right and a slope that is shallow, not steep. *D* is the obvious choice.

CONTINUE ➡

Skill 15 Practice Exercises:

1

A graph on the *xy*-plane displays a horizontal line that passes through the point $(0,8)$. What is the equation of the line?

A) $y = x + 8$
B) $y = x - 8$
C) $y = 8$
D) $x = 8$

2

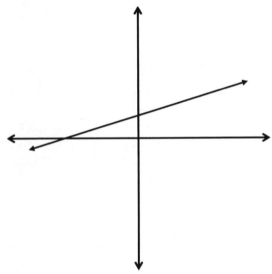

Assuming that the axes are drawn to scale, which of the following linear equations could be graphed in the *xy*-plane above?

A) $y = 5x + 2$

B) $y = x + 2$

C) $y = \frac{4}{9}x + 2$

D) $y = -\frac{1}{10}x + 2$

3

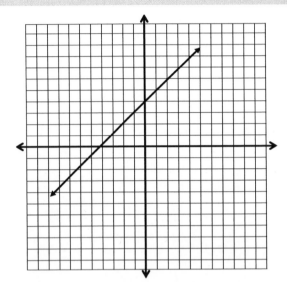

Assuming that the axes are drawn to scale, which of the following linear equations could be perpendicular to the equation graphed above?

A) $y = -12x - 1$
B) $y = -x - 12$
C) $y = x$
D) $y = 0$

4

The graph of which of the following linear functions has no solutions in Quadrant III?

A) $y = \frac{1}{2}x + 10$

B) $y = 5x - 110$

C) $y = -\frac{1}{3}x - 1$

D) $y = -3x + 1$

CONTINUE

5

Assuming that the graphs below are drawn to scale, if the line $3x - 9y = 18$ were to be translated down 4 units and to the right 4 units, which of the following graphs would best represent the graph of the new linear equation?

A)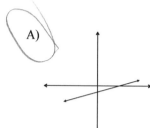

$3(x-4) - 9(y-4) = 18$

$3x - 12 - 9y + 36 = 18$

$3x - 9y + 24 = 18$

$3x - 9y = -6$

$3x = 9y +$

$\dfrac{-9y = -3x - 6}{-9} \quad \dfrac{}{-9}$

$y = \dfrac{x}{3} - \dfrac{2}{3}$

B)

C)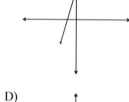

D)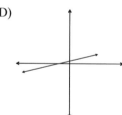

6

Which of the following is the slope of a line that only has solutions in Quadrant II and Quandarant III of the xy-plane??

A) -1

B) 0

C) 1

D) Undefined

7

Which of the following is the equation of a line where the absolute value of the line's x-intercept is lower than the absolute value of the line's y-intercept?

A) $y = -3x + 5$ $y = 5 \quad 3x$

B) $y = -x - 2$

C) $y = -\dfrac{2}{3}x + 4$

D) $y = \dfrac{2}{3}x - 2$

8

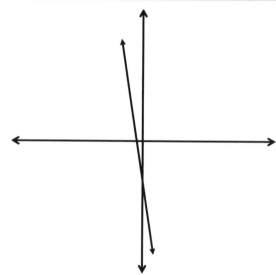

Assuming that the axes are drawn to scale, which of the following linear equations could be the equation of a line that is perpendicular to the line pictured above and has the same x-intercept?

A) $y = \dfrac{1}{15}x - \dfrac{5}{2}$

B) $y = \dfrac{1}{15}x + \dfrac{1}{5}$

C) $y = 15x - \dfrac{8}{5}$

D) $y = 15x + \dfrac{1}{3}$

84

CONTINUE

Heart of Algebra
Unit Review:

8. *Simplifying* and *Solving* in One Variable

Make sure to follow the order of operations carefully. Be mindful of common traps: double negatives, distributing errors, flipping inequality symbols, etc.

9. *Creating* in One Variable

Quickly identify the variable and give it meaning. From there, you can build an expression, a series of expressions, or an equation/inequality.

10. *Interpreting* in One Variable

In a question that requires interpreting, be sure to read very carefully and do your best to submerge yourself into the context of the problem.

11. *Simplifying* and *Solving* Systems in Two Variables

When it comes to solving systems, the golden rule is to aim for your target. Always do your best to move toward your answer as efficiently as possible.

12. *Creating* Systems in Two Variables

In addition to identifying the variables and giving them meaning, you must take careful note of how the variables interact with each other when creating mathematical systems.

CONTINUE ➡

Heart of Algebra
Unit Review:

13. *Interpreting* in Two Variables

Pay close attention to what each variable represents, which coefficients they are connected to, and the effect of each variable's coefficient in the context of the problem.

14. *Determining* Coefficients for No Solutions or Infinite Solutions

Under the elimination method, a system with no solutions will simplify to 0 equals a non-zero constant. A system with infinitely many solutions will simplify to 0 equals 0.

15. *Recognizing* Connections Between Linear Equations and Their Graphs

Think $y = mx + b$. Parallel lines have the same slope. Perpendicular lines have negative reciprocal slopes. Horizontal lines have y and no x. Vertical lines have x and no y.

CONTINUE

Unit 2 Review - Calculator

55 MINUTES, 38 QUESTIONS

DIRECTIONS

For each question from 1-30, choose the best answer choice provided in the multiple choice bank and fill in the appropriate circle in the provided answer key. Alternatively, for questions **31-38**, answer the problem and enter your answer in the grid-in section of the answer key. Refer to the directions given before question 31 as to how to enter your answers for the grid-in questions. You may complete scratch work in any empty space in your test booklet.

NOTES

A. Calculator usage **is allowed**.
B. Variables, constants, and coefficients used represent real numbers unless indicated otherwise.
C. All figures are created to appropriate scale unless the question states otherwise.
D. All figures are two-dimensional unless the question states otherwise.
E. The domain of any given function is all real numbers x for which the function, $f(x)$, is a real number unless the question states otherwise.

REFERENCE

$A = \pi r^2$
$C = 2\pi r$

$A = lw$

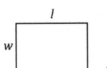

$A = \frac{1}{2}bh$

$c^2 = a^2 + b^2$

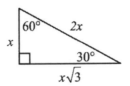

Special Right Triangle

Special Right Triangle

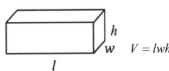

$V = lwh$

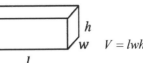

$V = \pi r^2 h$

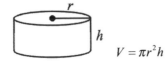

$V = \frac{4}{3}\pi r^3$

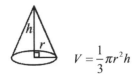

$V = \frac{1}{3}\pi r^2 h$

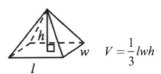

$V = \frac{1}{3}lwh$

There are $360°$ in a circle.
There are 2π radians in a circle.
There are $180°$ in a triangle.

CONTINUE ➡

1

If $3x+8=12$, what is the value of $6x-1$?

$6x+16=24$

$6x+1=-1$

A) 1

B) 3

C) 7

D) 39

2

If Sneha is traveling by car at a constant rate of k miles per hour and travels for a total of 45 minutes, which of the following expressions represents the total distance, in miles, that Sneha has traveled?

A) $45k$

$k\frac{3}{4}$

B) $\dfrac{k}{45}$

C) $\dfrac{3k}{4}$

D) $\dfrac{4}{3}k$

3

A chemistry teacher uses the expression $220-12s$ to calculate the number of remaining pH strips in the supply cabinet of her science classroom. If s represents the number of strips she gives each student in her class, what does the number 12 most likely represent?

A) The number of students in her class

B) The number of days that she distributes the pH strips

C) The total number of strips used per class

D) The maximum number of students who can receive a single pH strip

4

$$4a+b=11$$
$$a-b=-1$$

Given the system of linear equations above, what is the value of a?

$5a=10$

A) 1

B) 2

C) 3

D) 4

CONTINUE

5

At a streetside farmer's market, apples cost $0.50, pears cost $0.75, and kiwis cost $1.00. If a customer bought z apples, y pears, and x kiwis, which of the following expressions is equivalent to the total value of the customer's purchase in dollars?

$.5z + .75y + 1x$

A) $.5z + .75y + x$

B) $.5x + .75y + z$

C) $x + .5y + .75z$

D) $z + .5y + .75x$

6

Reginald was given a shoebox filled with 852 baseball cards on his 10th birthday. Since then, Reginald's baseball card collection has been growing at a steady pace. On any birthday after Reginald's 10th birthday, the size of his baseball card collection can be calculated using the equation $T = 52b + 852$, where T is the number of cards in his collection b birthdays after his 10th birthday. What is the best interpretation of the value 52 in the equation?

A) Reginald collects 52 more baseball cards each year between his birthday and the end of the calendar year.

B) Reginald receives 52 baseball cards each year on his birthday.

C) Reginald's baseball card collection has grown by 52 cards since his 10th birthday.

D) Reginald's baseball card collection will reach 894 cards on his 52nd birthday.

7

$$2x + 5y = 18$$
$$15y + 6x = 54$$

How many coordinate pairs satisfy the system of equations above?

A) 0

B) 1

C) 2

D) Infinitely many

$5y = -2x + 18$

$y = -\frac{2}{5}x + \frac{18}{5}$

$\frac{15y}{15} = \frac{-6x + 54}{15}$

$y = \frac{-6x}{15} + \frac{54}{15}$

8

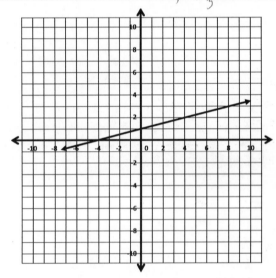

Which of the following linear equations could be the equation of a line that is parallel to the line pictured above?

A) $y = -1x + 2$

B) $y = -4x - 4$

C) $y = \frac{1}{4}x + 2$

D) $y = 7$

CONTINUE

9

If $5 + x = \dfrac{x + 23}{j}$ and $j = 3$, what is the value of x?

A) 3

B) 4

C) 15

D) 19

$5 + x = \dfrac{x + 23}{3}$

$15 + 3x = x + 23$

$2x = 8$

10

If gas costs \$2.45 per gallon and a customer fills her tank for d dollars, which of the following expressions represents the number of gallons of gas that the customer has purchased?

A) $2.45d$

B) $\dfrac{d}{2.45}$

C) $\dfrac{2.45}{d}$

D) $\dfrac{2.45d}{100}$

$2.45x = d$

$\dfrac{2.45}{d} = \dfrac{1}{x}$

$2.45x = d$

$2.45 = \dfrac{d}{x}$

11

Lydia can estimate her monthly savings account balance using the expression $3{,}284(1.01)^m$, where m represents the number of months that have passed since Lydia's account balance was \$3,284. Which of the following statements is *not* true?

A) Lydia's savings account balance is growing.

B) Lydia's savings account balance changes by 1% of its current value each month.

C) Lydia's savings account balance will be larger than \$3,700 in one year.

D) Lydia's savings account balance increases by 12% each year.

12

$$x + y = 10$$
$$2x + y = 19$$

Given the system of linear equations above, what is the value of $3x + 2y$?

A) 1

B) 9

C) 29

D) 48

$x = 9$

$y = 1$

$27 + 2$

CONTINUE

13

A boy scout troop has a goal of raising G dollars from their annual wreath sales event. If 5 days into the wreath sales event, the boy scout troop has raised a total of \$995 and the amount of money raised by the troop has increased linearly over the 5 days, which of the following equations could be solved to find G, the goal amount of dollars, given d, the number of days that have passed since the start of the event?

A) $G - 199d = 0$
B) $G - 995d = 0$
C) $G - 199 = d$
D) $G - 995 = d$

14

$$y = -2x + 7$$

In the equation above, what is the meaning of the number -2?

A) For every decrease of 2 units in the value of x, y will increase by 7 units.
B) For every decrease of 2 units in the value of y, x will increase by 7 units.
C) For every decrease of 2 units in the value of x, y will increase by 1 unit.
D) For every decrease of 2 units in the value of y, x will increase by 1 unit.

15

$$4x + 5y = 14$$
$$ax + \frac{5}{2}y = 7$$

In the system of equations above, a is a constant. For what value of a will the system of equations have infinitely many solutions?

A) 1
B) 2
C) 4
D) 8

$5y = -4x + 14$

$y = \frac{-4x}{5} + \frac{14}{5}$

$\frac{5}{2}y = -ax = 7$

$-\frac{2}{5}ax$

16

Which of the following is the equation of a line that only has solutions in two non-adjacent quadrants of the xy-plane?

A) $y = -x$
B) $y = x + 1$
C) $x = -4$
D) $y = 13$

91

CONTINUE

17

$$15x + (2x - 8) - (8x - 11)$$

The expression above can be simplified to the form $Ax + B$, where A and B are constants. What is the value of $A + B$?

$4x + 3$

A) 3

B) 7

C) 9

D) 12

18

For three months each summer, James raises $800 each month. Then, starting on the 1st of September, each month he spends $250 from his summer savings. If James' remaining summer savings balance can be calculated m months from September 1st using the expression $Q - 250m$, what is the value of Q?

A) 750

B) 800

C) 2,400

D) 9,600

19

A flooring company estimates the price in dollars to fabricate a custom square carpet using the expression $200 + 25x^2$, where x is the measure in feet of one side of the carpet. What is the most likely meaning of the number 25 in the expression?

A) The cost in dollars of fabricating the entire carpet

B) The cost in dollars per linear foot to fabricate the carpet

C) The cost in dollars per additional square foot to fabricate the carpet

D) The cost in dollars per additional square yard to fabricate the carpet

20

$$4x + y = 12$$
$$x + 4y = 13$$

Given the system of equations above, what is the value of $x + y$?

A) $\frac{1}{5}$

B) 1

C) 4

D) 5

$5x + 5y = 25$

$x + y = 5$

CONTINUE

21

Renaldo recently went to the supermarket and spent $5.50 on 3 avocados and 4 horseradish nuggets. Mary Beth went to the same supermarket and spent $6.00 on 2 avocados and 12 horseradish nuggets. Using a for the number of avocados and h for the number of horseradish nuggets, which of the following systems of equations can be solved to find the price of each avacado and each horseradish nugget?

$3a + 4h = 5.5$

$2a + 12h = 6$

A) $5.5 = 4h + 3a$
   $6 = 12h + 2a$

B) $5.5 = 4a + 3h$
   $6 = 12a + 2h$

C) $5.5 = 4h + 3a$
   $6 = 2h + 12a$

D) $5.5 = 3h + 4a$
   $6 = 12h + 2a$

22

Meredith is selling candles for $3.50 each to raise money for her school's student council luncheon. Nona is selling bath salts for $7.25 each to raise money for the school's student council luncheon as well. If Meredith sells c candles, Nona sells b bath salts, and the inequality $3.5c + 7.25b \geq 470$ must be true in order for the luncheon to take place, what is the meaning of the number 470 in the inequality?

A) The total number of candle and bath salt sales combined for Meredith and Nona

B) The minimum number of candle and bath salt sales combined that Meredith and Nona must make

C) The maximum amount of money that Meredith and Nona can make selling candles and bath salts

D) The minimum amount of money that Meredith and Nona must make

23

$$jx - 16y = 24$$
$$-kx + 2y = -3$$

If the system of equations above has infinitely many solutions and j and k are constants, what is the value of $j - 8k$?

$jx - 16y = 24$

$-8kx + 16y = -24$

A) 0

B) 1

C) $-8jk$

D) $j + 8k$

24

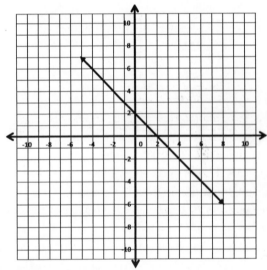

Which of the following equations could be perpendicular to the equation graphed in the xy-plane above?

A) $y = 2x + 2$

B) $y = x + 2$

C) $y = -x - 2$

D) $y = -2x - 2$

CONTINUE

25

An alliance of protestors has gained 6 new protestors each five-day week that the protest has lasted, but lost 1 member every other day due to people returning to work. Given the expression $6(\frac{d}{5}) - \frac{1}{2}d$, where d represents the number of days that have passed since the beginning of the protest, what is the most likely meaning of the number $-\frac{1}{2}$ in the equation?

A) The alliance loses half of its protestors every week that the protest lasts.

B) The alliance loses half of a member every day that the protest lasts.

C) On average, the alliance loses half of a member each day that the protest lasts.

D) The alliance loses half of its protestors every day that the protest lasts.

26

Suppose that Dale makes $80 for every comic book that he sells and $75 for every autographed novella that he sells. If c represents the number of comic books that Dale sells, n represents the number of autographed novellas that Dale sells, and Dale would like to make a total of $775, which of the following equations could be used to determine the number of comic books and autographed novellas that Dale must sell to meet his goal?

A) $80c + 75n = 775$
B) $75c + 80n = 775$
C) $80c + 775 = 75n$
D) $775 - 80n = 75c$

27

$$15.00h + 22.50w = 540.00$$

At her job, Roberta receives an hourly pay rate during the week; whenever she works on weekends, she gets paid time-and-a-half for overtime. If the equation above represents Roberta's pay for her most recent week of work, which of the following statements *cannot* be validated?

A) Roberta earned a total of $540.00 during the week.

B) Roberta worked h weekday hours during the week.

C) Roberta earns $22.50 per hour on the weekends.

D) Roberta worked both weekday and weekend hours during the week.

28

$$40x + 576y = 216$$
$$20x + 384y = 124$$

A group of people in charge of a 5K running event purchased 40 1-gallon jugs of orange juice and 24 cases of water each containing 24 individual water bottles for a total of $216. Some additional employees purchased 20 more 1-gallon jugs of orange juice and 16 more cases of water for $124. In the system of equations above, what does the expression $384y$ most likely represent?

A) The dollar cost for a single bottle of water

B) The dollar cost for a single case of water

C) The total amount of money spent on water by the additional employees

D) The total number of water bottles purchased by the additional employees

CONTINUE

29

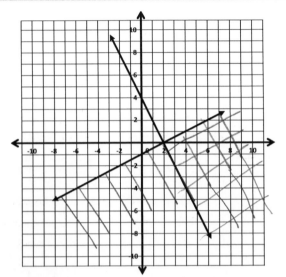

The equations $y = -2x + 4$ and $y = \frac{1}{2}x - 1$ are graphed in the xy-plane above. If the system of inequalities $y \leq \frac{1}{2}x - 1$ and $y \geq -2x + 4$ were graphed, all solutions to the system would lie in which of the following quadrants?

A) I and II

B) I and IV

C) III and IV

D) I, II, III, and IV

30

$$q^2 x + 2y = 12$$
$$4x + 18y = 14$$

In the system of equations above, q is a positive constant. For what value of q will the system of equations have no solutions?

A) $\frac{4}{9}$

B) $\frac{2}{3}$

C) 2

D) 3

$2x + 9y = 7$

$\dfrac{-2}{9}$

$\dfrac{-4}{9(2)}$

$\dfrac{2}{-9}$

CONTINUE

DIRECTIONS

For each question from 31-38, solve and enter your answer in the grid-in section of your answer sheet as described below.

A. Write out your answers in the boxes at the top of each column in order to help you fill in the circles accurately. Remember, you will only receive credit for the circles that are filled in correctly, not for the written answer at the top of the columns.

B. Mark only a single circle in each column.

C. There are no negative answers.

D. If the problem has more than one correct answer, grid only one of the correct answers.

E. When your answer is a **mixed number**, such as $1\frac{1}{2}$, it should be entered as 1.5 or 3/2. You cannot enter a mixed number because there is no room to fill in a circle that represents a space.

F. If you enter a **decimal answer** with more digits then the grid can handle, the answer may be rounded or truncated, but it absolutely must fill the entire grid.

Answer: $\frac{8}{21}$

Answer: 6.4

Written answer →
Decimal point →
← Fraction line

The ways to correctly grid $\frac{7}{9}$ are:

Answer: 102 - both positions are correct

REMEMBER:
You can begin writing your answers in any column as long as there is enough space. Leave unused columns blank.

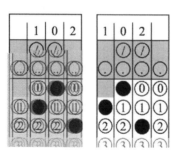

CONTINUE →

31

$$3(d-1) = d + 15$$

What value of d satisfies the equation above?

$3d - 3 = d + 15$

$2d = 18$

$d = 9$

$3d - 3 = 9 + 15$

32

$$y = 9x - 11$$
$$y = bx + 40$$

If there is no solution to the system of equations above, what is the value of $2b$?

33

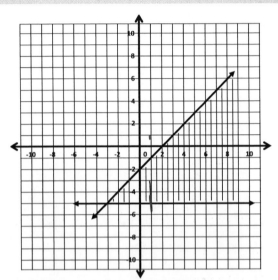

Given the system of linear inequalities graphed in the xy-plane above, if both inequalities are translated 4 units to the right and 6 units up, all coordinate points (x, y) that satisfy the new system of linear inequalities lie in how many quadrants?

34

Nathaniel surveyed 50 people from each of f cities and 32 people from each of g suburban communities for a total of 1,070 people. Erika surveyed 25 people from each of f cities and 43 people from each of g suburban communities for a total of 805 people. What is the total number of cities and suburban communities that Nathaniel and Erika each visited?

$50f + 32g = 1070$

$25f + 43g = 805$

$50f + 86g = 1610$

$55g = 540$

$g = $

CONTINUE

35

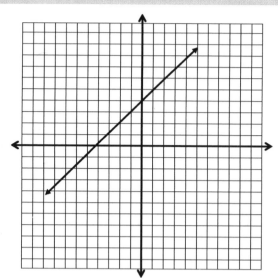

Assuming the axes above are drawn to scale, if a line with

the equation $y = mx + b$ is perpendicular to the line above

and they share a common y-intercept, what is the value of

$\left| \dfrac{m}{b} \right|$?

$6-4$

$\dfrac{1}{4}$

36

A female clothing sales associate makes $12 per hour and a commission of 3% on the clothing that she sells. Her paycheck from last week totaled $111. A male clothing sales associate makes $15 per hour, but only gets a commission of 2% on the clothing that he sells. His paycheck from last week totaled $130. If both of the sales associates worked the same number of hours and sold the same value of clothing last week, how many hours did either sales associate work last week?

$12x + 0.03y = 111$

$15x + 0.02y = 130$

$180x + .45y = 1665$

$180x + .24y = 1560$

$.21y = 105$

$y = 500$

Questions 37-38 refer to the following information.

An Eagle Scout has been running a program to raise money to protect local wildlife in his town. In his second year he raised twice as much money as he did in his first year. The third year he raised $300 more than three times what he raised in the second year.

37

The average amount of money the Eagle Scout raised over the first three years expressed in terms of d, the amount of money that he raised in the first year, is $3d + V$, where V is a positive integer constant. What is the value of V?

100

38

If the Eagle Scout raised a total of $2,100 over the first three years, how much more money did he raise in the third year as compared to the first two years combined?

900

CONTINUE

$x + 2x + 3(2x) + 300$

$3x + 6x + 300$

$\dfrac{9x + 300}{3}$

$3x + 100 = d$

UNIT 3

$200 =$

$3x + 100 = 2100$

$3x = 2000$

$x + 2x + 6x + 300 = 2100$

$9x + \cancel{300} = 1800$

$9x = 1800$

$x = 200$

1800

Unit 3: Problem Solving and Data Analysis

In the College Board's progressive strategy of preparing students for college, a great emphasis has been placed on problem solving and data analysis skills. The goal is to get students to use more brain power. Students need to nurture their problem solving skills in order to create, analyze, and interpret in a variety of contexts. Students will also use their quantitative reasoning skills to a much higher degree than on earlier versions of the SAT. Questions involving ratios, rates, proportions, and statistical analysis will require in-depth knowledge and mathematical understanding at a much more comprehensive level. These problem-solving skills, which cover a vast array of topics, both collegiate and career oriented, will be covered thoroughly in this unit, "Problem Solving and Data Analysis."

CONTINUE

16 | *Understanding* Proportional Relationships, Ratios, and Rates

"It is vital to know your different proportional relationships and to know when to apply them."

Whether you are given a proportional relationship, a ratio, a rate, or even a set of scale drawings, you must be able to isolate the relationship between the variables. Once you understand this relationship, you can use the relationship to solve single and multi-step problems. Let's look at some basic relationships:

1. **Direct Proportionality:** $y = kx$ or $\dfrac{y}{x} = k$

   When two variables are directly proportional, you can simply utilize a proportion to solve for the unknown quantity. So, if you see the words "directly proportional," you should think, "use a proportion."

2. **Inverse Proportionality:** $y = \dfrac{k}{x}$ or $yx = k$

   When two variables are inversely proportional, they multiply to the same constant. You can simply multiply to find the constant and use that constant to solve for the unknown quantity. So, when you see the words, "inversely proportional," you should think, "multiply."

3. **Parts to the Whole:** A ratio of 4:5 implies that there are 9 total parts. So, even though a ratio compares two parts to each other, if you add the numbers in the ratio, you can find out what portion of the whole each part is. In the case of 4:5, if you add the parts of the ratio, you have $\frac{4}{9}$ of the whole and $\frac{5}{9}$ of the whole.

4. **Rates:** Suppose you are told that a car is traveling at 45 miles per hour. This means that the car will travel 45 miles in one hour. So, if you want to know how far the car will travel in 3 hours, just multiply: $3(45) = 135$. Also remember that Distance = Rate x Time. This can be very useful in other contexts that require the use of rate in solving problems.

5. **Scale Drawings:** When dealing with scale drawings, remember to build proportions. Just be sure to build any given proportion using appropriate measurements in corresponding locations.

Example 1:

The length of an exam is directly proportional to the number of hours of study required to receive a passing grade on the exam. If a 45-minute exam requires 8 hours of study time, how many hours should a student study for an exam that lasts 1.5 hours?

You have seen the words "directly proportional," so you know to use a proportion. You just have to make sure that we maintain the appropriate balance of units in the proportion.

In this case, the question is asking for how many hours a student must study for an exam whose length is in hours. Convert the original ratio, which provides the exam length in minutes, to hours and proceed by solving the proportion. 45 minutes is 0.75 hours.

$$\frac{0.75 hours}{8 hours} = \frac{1.5 hours}{x}$$

$$0.75x = 12$$
$$x = 16 \ hours$$

Example 2:

In a certain recipe, the ratio of cups of flour to cups of water is 4:1. If Sherlynn has a bag with 8 cups of flour and plans to use the entire bag, how many cups of flour and water total will she need to complete the recipe?

By adding up the parts to the whole, you can see that 4+1 = 5 total parts. So, the 8 cups of flour will be $\frac{4}{5}$ of the entire recipe. Take the words and translate them into math:

$$8 \ cups \ are \ \tfrac{4}{5} \ of \ the \ total$$

$$8 = \tfrac{4}{5}(T)$$
$$10 = T$$

There are <u>10</u> cups total in the recipe.

CONTINUE →

Skill 16 Practice Exercises:

1

If $y = kx$, where k is a constant, and $x = 12$ when $y = 84$, what is the value of x when $y = 14$?

A) 2
B) 7
C) 14
D) 98

$$84 = 12k$$
$$\frac{84}{12} = \frac{12k}{12}$$

$$7 = k$$

$$14 =$$

2

If $y = \dfrac{k}{x}$, where k is a constant, and $y = 16$ when $x = 3$, what is the value of y when $x = 8$?

A) $\dfrac{16}{3}$
B) 6
C) $\dfrac{128}{3}$
D) 48

$$16 = \frac{k}{3}$$

$$48 = k$$
$$\times 8$$
$$384$$

$$16 \times 3 = 48$$

$$y = \frac{48}{x}$$

3

On a map, every 2 inches represent 30 miles. If two cities are 5 inches apart on the map, how many miles apart are the two cities?

A) 15
B) 60
C) 75
D) 150

4

Rachel rides her mountain bike at a rate of x miles per hour. Her brother, Travis, can travel twice as far in half the amount of time. Which of the following gives the ratio of Rachel's speed in miles per hour to Travis's speed in miles per hour?

A) 1:4
B) 1:2
C) 2:1
D) 4:1

CONTINUE

5

Maybel is making a pie. The recipe calls for 3 cups of frozen blueberries for every 1/2 cup of sugar in order to make a 20 ounce pie. If Maybel has exactly 8 cups of blueberries and 1 cup of sugar, what is the largest pie, in ounces, that she can bake?

A) 2

B) 16

C) 20

D) 40

6

1 in.

2 in.

4 in

Michelle is designing a fountain for a park near her house as part of a public works program. The fountain will be cross-shaped, as shown in the diagram above. Michelle has started by creating a scale drawing at one hundredth of the size of the actual fountain. If in Michelle's drawing the longer edges of the fountain measure 2 inches long and the shorter edges measure one inch long, the actual fountain will measure how far across from left to right?

A) 16 feet 8 inches

B) 33 feet 4 inches

C) 50 feet

D) 400 feet

Questions 7-8 refer to the following table.

Year	2011	2012	2013	2014
Educational Programs	80	100	20	10
Extra-Curricular Programs	0	0	70	80

The table above shows the budget increase in thousands of dollars for educational programs and extra-curricular programs from the year 2011 through 2014 for a school district in California.

7

What is the average dollar increase in the budget for educational programs for the years 2011 through 2014?

A) 50

B) 52.5

C) 50,000

D) 52,500

8

The average increase in dollars budgeted for educational programs for the years 2011 through 2014 is how much higher than the average increase in dollars budgeted for extra-curricular programs for the years 2011 through 2014?

A) 15

B) 60

C) 15,000

D) 60,000

103

CONTINUE

17   *Maintaining* or *Changing* Ratios

"When attempting to maintain a ratio or change a ratio, use parts-to-the-whole to create a proportion that sets the modified totals equal to the desired ratio."

It is easiest to understand the concept of maintaining or changing ratios through examples. Let's look at one of each:

Example 1: (Maintaining a ratio)

On a pearl necklace, there is a 1:6 ratio of white pearls to black pearls. There are 42 pearls currently on the necklace. If 6 black pearls are added, how many white pearls must be added to maintain the ratio?

If you use Parts-to-the-whole, you will find that there are currently 6 white pearls and 36 black pearls on the necklace. 6 black pearls are added to make a total of 42 black pearls. We need to add "x" white pearls to maintain the 1:6 ratio.

$$\frac{White}{Black} = \frac{6}{36} = \frac{6+x}{36+6} = \frac{6+x}{42}$$

Once the modified ratio of the totals has been created, set it equal to the ratio you wish to maintain, cross-multiply, and solve:

$$\frac{6+x}{42} = \frac{1}{6} \rightarrow 6(6+x) = 42(1)$$

$$36 + 6x = 42 \rightarrow 6x = 6 \rightarrow \underline{x = 1}$$

Example 2: (Changing a ratio)

Using the same original necklace from above, how many white pearls must be added to the 42 original pearls in order to "create" a ratio 1:4?

$$\frac{White}{Black} = \frac{6+x}{36} \rightarrow \frac{6+x}{36} = \frac{1}{4}$$

$$4(6+x) = 36(1) \rightarrow 24 + 4x = 36 \rightarrow 4x = 12 \rightarrow \underline{x = 3}$$

1

The ratio of tulips to violets is 5:6 and the total number of flowers is 99. If 10 tulips are added, how many violets must be added to maintain a ratio of 5:6?

A) 12

B) 11

C) 10

D) 8

2

In a battalion, there are 5 cavalry to every 12 infantry. When 25 cavalry are added, how many infantry must be added to the battalion to maintain the original ratio?

A) 24

B) 36

C) 60

D) 72

CONTINUE

3

A nuclear scientist is creating a new element. He starts with an element that has a proton-to-neutron ratio that is 13 to 71. He then sets off a nuclear reaction in which some neutrons are converted to energy and lost. The new proton-to-neutron ratio is 1 to 5. How many neutrons were lost?

A) 65

B) 13

C) 8

D) 6

$$\frac{13}{84} \qquad \frac{71}{84}$$

$$\frac{1}{6} \qquad \frac{5}{6}$$

4

A fruit punch is made by mixing passionfruit juice with cranberry juice. For every 2 parts passionfruit juice, there are 3 parts cranberry juice. How many ounces of passionfruit juice should be added to 25 ounces of the mixed fruit punch in order to create a mixture that has a ratio of passionfruit juice to cranberry juice that is 2:1?

A) 10

B) 15

C) 20

D) 25

$$\frac{2}{5} \qquad \frac{3}{5}$$

$$\frac{10}{4} \qquad \frac{15}{25}$$

5

In a recent study, 32 largemouth bass and 24 smallmouth bass have had their fins tagged. If 12 more smallmouth bass have their fins tagged, how many more largemouth bass must have their fins tagged so that the number of tagged largemouth bass remains $\frac{4}{7}$ of the total?

A) 9

B) 16

C) 18

D) 24

$$\frac{36}{32+x} = \frac{4}{7}$$

$$252 = 128 = 4x$$

6

A class of new recruits in basic training consists of a total of 54 males and females. There are 36 more males than females in the class. If 35 additional males join the class, how many additional females must join the class in order to maintain the initial ratio of males to females?

A) 5

B) 7

C) 9

D) 175

$$F+36 + F = 54$$

$$2F = 18$$

$$F = 9$$

$$45$$

$$\frac{9}{45} \qquad \frac{9+x}{80+x} = \frac{1}{5}$$

$$45+5x = 80$$

CONTINUE

7

A ratio of $a{:}b$ must be maintained at all times. If k is added to b, what must be added to a in order to maintain the ratio?

A) k

B) ak

C) $\dfrac{ab}{k}$

D) $\dfrac{ak}{b}$

$$\frac{a+x}{b+k} = \frac{a}{b}$$

$$ab + bx = ab + ka$$

$$bx = ka$$

$$\frac{ka}{b}$$

8

Two numbers are in a ratio of $c{:}d$. Which of the following must be added to c in order to create a ratio of $\dfrac{c}{d^2}$?

A) $\dfrac{c}{d} - c$

B) $\dfrac{d}{c} - c$

C) $\dfrac{c}{d^3} - c$

D) $\dfrac{c}{d^3} + c$

$$\frac{c+x}{d} = \frac{c}{d^2}$$

$$cd^2 + xd^2 = cd$$

$$\frac{xd^2}{d^2} = \frac{cd - cd^2}{d^2}$$

$$x = \frac{c}{d} - c$$

Notes:

CONTINUE

18   *Solving* with Percentages

"**Converting percentages to decimal form is the most effective way to solve percentage questions efficiently.**"

For percentage-based questions, converting to decimal form by dividing the percentage by 100 and then multiplying allows you to solve with minimal steps and to address multiple percentage changes in a single expression or equation. Remember your important forms:

1. Percents in Decimal Form: x percent $=> \frac{x}{100}$

2. Growth Factor: x percent increase $=> (1+\frac{x}{100})$

3. Decay Factor: x percent decrease $=> (1-\frac{x}{100})$

Example 1:

88 is what percent of 352?

Translate the words into math. Remember to convert your decimal back to a percentage.

$$88 = (x)(352)$$
$$\frac{88}{352} = x$$
$$.25 = x$$

88 is <u>25%</u> of 352.

Example 2:

A 20% increase followed by a 30% increase followed by a 40% decrease is the same as a one-time decrease of what percent?

In order to increase, use a growth factor. In order to decrease, use a decay factor. Make one equation and solve.

$$(1+.20)(1+.30)(1-.40) = (1-x)$$
$$(1.20)(1.30)(0.60) = (1-x)$$
$$0.936 = 1-x$$
$$x = 1-.936 = 0.064$$

The one time decrease would be <u>6.4%</u>.

Skill 18 Practice Exercises:

1

The number of female students in a math class is 20% greater than the number of male students in the class. If there are 24 female students in the class, how many male students are in the class?

A) 20
B) 25
C) 30
D) 35

$x \cdot (1.2) = 24$

2

A discounted dress shirt costs 36% less than a shirt that cost \$50. What is the cost of the discounted dress shirt?

A) 20
B) 28
C) 32
D) 38

CONTINUE

3

The length of a rectangle is increased by 40% and its width is increased by 20%. The new area of the rectangle is equivalent to what percent of its old area?

A) 32

B) 68

C) 108

D) 168

1.4

1.2

4

If x is 80% of y and y is 150% of z, then x is what percent larger than z?

A) 12

B) 20

C) 120

D) 230

$x = .8y$

$y = 1.5z$

$x = .8(1.5z)$

$x = 1.2z$

5

A magician earns $300 when he puts on a show for 50 people. The magician earns $450 if he puts on a performance for 75 people. If the magician puts 52% of his earnings into his savings account after each performance and charges a constant rate for each customer, how many dollars does the magician deposit into his savings account on a night that he performs for 10 people?

A) 28.80

B) 31.20

C) 60

D) 100

$\dfrac{156}{25}$

6

1

60

6

A balloon filled with helium rises in oxygen because its atomic mass, which is approximately 4 amu (atomic mass units), is less than the atomic mass of oxygen. If the atomic mass of helium is 75% less than the atomic mass of oxygen, which of the following best approximates the atomic mass, in amu, of oxygen?

A) 1

B) 3

C) 12

D) 16

$4 = .25x$

108

CONTINUE

7

If the number of seniors that graduated with honors in 2016 is 40% higher than the number of seniors who graduated with honors in 2015 and a total of 192 seniors graduated with honors in both years combined, how many seniors graduated with honors in 2016?

A) 80
B) 96
C) 112
D) 120

$x + 1.4x = 192$

$2.4x = 179$

8

In a group of adults, 65% have a desire to try skydiving. Of those adults who have a desire to try skydiving, 40% actually skydive. If 39 adults in the group have a desire to try skydiving, but DO NOT actually skydive, how many adults are in the group?

A) 100
B) 120
C) 150
D) 156

$39 = .19x$

$97.5 = .65x$

Notes:

CONTINUE

19　*Combining* Percentages & Averages

"Combining percentages and averages can be accomplished by creating a number line and remembering that the combined percentage or average gets pulled toward the larger quantity."

Since combined percentages and combined averages work the same way, let's look at one example of a combined percentage:

Example:

A beverage that consists of 25% orange juice is mixed with another beverage that consists of 40% orange juice. How many ounces of the 25% juice must be mixed with the 40% juice to create 24 ounces of a beverage that consists of 30% orange juice?

Draw a number line with the two percentages on either end and place the combned percentage where it belongs on that number line:

$$25\% ----- 30\% ---------40\%$$

Note that 30% is closer to 25% which means that there is "more" of the 25% beverage in the mixture. Note the distance between 30% and either end of the number line. Then, switch those distances to create the ratio of 25% to 40%:

$$25\% ----- 30\% ---------40\%$$

$$30 - 25 = 5 \qquad\qquad 40 - 30 = 10$$

Therefore, after switching the two differences...

$$\underline{25\% : 40\%}$$
$$10 : 5$$
$$2 : 1$$

Then, using parts-to-the-whole, one can see that the 25% solution makes up $\frac{2}{3}$ of the mixture's total:

$$\frac{2}{3}(Total) = \frac{2}{3}(24oz.) = \underline{16oz.}$$

1

In a class, the boys averaged 50% on a test while the girls averaged 90% on the same test. If the combined average was 80%, then the boys make up what fraction of the class?

A) $\frac{1}{4}$

B) $\frac{1}{3}$

C) $\frac{2}{3}$

D) $\frac{3}{4}$

[handwritten work]
$0.5x + 0.9y = 0.8$
$\overline{x+y}$
$50\% ----- 80\% - 90\%$
$30 \qquad\qquad 10$
$10 : 30$
$1 : 3$
$\frac{1}{4}$

2

A solution that is 5% saline is mixed with a solution that is 17% saline to form a solution that is 14% saline. How many liters of a 4-liter mixed 14% saline solution are accounted for by the 17% saline solution?

A) 1

B) 2

C) 3

D) 4

[handwritten work]
$5\% ----- 14\% \quad 17\%$
$9\% \qquad\qquad 3\%$
$3 : 9$
$1 : 3$
$\frac{3}{4}$

CONTINUE

3

Out of 120,000 test takers, the boys averaged 1498 on the SAT and the girls averaged 1510. If the combined average was 1506, how many boys took the test?

A) 20,000
B) 40,000
C) 60,000
D) 80,000

1498   1506   1510

8   4

$x+y=120000$ 4:8

1:L

$\frac{1}{3}$

4

Class *A* averaged 75 on a test and class *B* averaged 90 on the same test. The combined average for both classes was an 80. If there are 12 students in class *B*, how many total students took the test?

A) 6
B) 18
C) 24
D) 36

75   80   90

5   10

10:5   2:1

$0.05x + 0.17y = .14(x+y)$

$0.05 + 0.17y(.14(4)$

$x+y=4$

$0.05x + .17y = .56$

$0.05(4-y) + .17y = .56$

$.2 - 0.05y + .17y = .56$

$.2 + .12y = .56$

5

TWA sold 400 tickets for a total of $32,000. The price of a first-class ticket was $90 and the price of an economy-class ticket was $40. How many first-class tickets were sold?

A) 80
B) 160
C) 240
D) 320

50   31 9 10

$x+y = 400$

$90x + 40y = 32000$

$9x + 4y = 3200$

$4x + 4y = 1600$

$5x = 1600$

$x = 320$

$y = 60$

6

Hana purchased a combined total of 60 tulips and roses for $600. The roses cost $12 each and the tulips cost $7 each. How many tulips did Hana buy?

A) 12
B) 18
C) 24
D) 36

$x+y = 60$

$7x + 12y = 600$

$12x + 12y = 720$

$-5x = -120$

CONTINUE

7

How many liters of a 12% peroxide solution must be mixed with 15 liters of a 27% peroxide solution to obtain a 24% peroxide solution?

A) 3.75

B) 5

C) 45

D) 60

(handwritten: 12 24 27 ; 12 3 ; 3:12 ; 1:4)

8

Tickets to a concert are sold in advance for $5 or on the day of the concert for $8. If the combined average for all ticket sales was $6 per ticket and 100 tickets were sold on the day of the concert, how many tickets were sold in advance?

A) 50

B) 200

C) 300

D) 400

(handwritten: 2:1 ; 1/3)

Notes:

_____

_____

_____

_____

_____

_____

_____

_____

_____

_____

CONTINUE ➡

20 | *Solving* with Units and Unit Conversions

"Where units are concerned, pay attention to the *given* units and the *target* units for your answer. Always convert units in order to approach your target."

Simplifying expressions or solving equations involving units is as easy as doing the same without units. You just need to make sure that all of the units match before you proceed. Pay particular attention to density units, since they often require more than one unit conversion.

Even if the units are made up, if the conversion factor is given you can use it to proceed effectively.

In most cases, a conversion factor will be given in the question. However, it cannot hurt to know the major ones:

1 kilometer (*km*) = 1,000 meters (*m*)

1 meter (*m*) = 100 centimeters (*cm*)

1 centimeter (*cm*) = 10 millimeters (*mm*)

1 mile (*mi*) = 5280 feet (*ft*)

1 yard (*yd*) = 3 feet (*ft*)

1 foot (*ft*) = 12 inches (*in*)

1 mile (*mi*) = 1.609 kilometers (*km*)

1 inch (*in*) = 2.54 centimeters (*cm*)

1 m^3 = 1,000,000 cm^3

1 ft^3 = 1728 in^3

1 liter (*l*) = 1,000 cubic centimeters (cm^3)

1 kilogram (*kg*) = 2.204 pounds (*lbs*)

1 pound (*lb*) = 453.6 grams (*g*)

1 *km/h* = .6214 *mi/h*

1 *mi/h* = 1.467 *ft/s*

1 gm/cm^3 = 1,000 kg/m^3

1 gm/cm^3 = 62.43 lb/ft^3

Example 1:

A sample blank of a ceramic tile weighs 1.2 pounds. If the weight of the sample blank were to increase by 150 grams, what would be the weight of the new sample blank in grams? (1 pound = 453.6 grams)

Since the target unit is grams, you should convert pounds to grams and then proceed.

1.2 pounds = (1.2)(453.6) grams = 544.32 grams

So, 544.32 + 150 = 694.32 grams.

Example 2:

A machine parts manufacturer produces and sells solid steel bearings for use in industrial vehicles. The manufacturer will be converting its units of measurement for density from gm/cm^3 to kg/m^3. If the current density of the bearings is 8 gm/cm^3 and the manufacturer plans to build the bearings using a new alloy with exactly one quarter of the current density, what will the density of the bearings cast in the new alloy be in kg/m^3 ?

(1,000 grams = 1 kilogram)

(1,000,000 cubic centimeters = 1 cubic meter)

Since the target unit is kg/m^3, you must convert the original 8 gm/cm^3 to the new unit of density, and then proceed with the modification.

$$\frac{8gm}{1cm^3} \bullet \frac{1kg}{1,000gm} \bullet \frac{1,000,000cm^3}{1m^3}$$

$$\frac{8,000,000kg}{1,000m^3} = 8,000kg/m^3$$

$$(\tfrac{1}{4})8,000 = 2,000kg/m^3$$

The density will be 2000 kg/m^3 .

CONTINUE

Skill 20 Practice Exercises:

1

If a person measures 77 inches tall and says that they are f feet 5 inches tall, what is the value of f?

A) 4
B) 5
C) 6
D) 7

2

Diego's car weighs exactly 2.01 tons. If 1 ton is equivalent to 2,000 pounds, what is the weight of Diego's car in pounds?

$2.01 \text{ tons} \left(\dfrac{2000}{1 \text{ t}} \right.$

A) 2,020
B) 4,020
C) 4,100
D) 4,200

3

$$1 \text{ yard} = 3 \text{ feet}$$
$$1 \text{ mile} = 5280 \text{ feet}$$

Based on the information given above, if Nathaniel can jog 3,520 yards in 15 minutes, what is his average speed in miles per hour?

A) 2.67
B) 8
C) 16
D) 24

4

In Mrs. Jennings' political science class, students earn points on a point system that was made up by Mrs. Jennings' daughter. Students earn what are called *murpees,* and every 50 *murpees* are equivalent to one *girkee.* If a certain student has earned two and a half *girkees*, how many additional *girkees* must the student earn to reach a total of 250 *murpees*?

$2.5 \text{ girkees} \left(\dfrac{50 \text{ murpees}}{girkee} \right.$

A) 2.5
B) 5
C) 75
D) 125

CONTINUE

5

One centimeter is equivalent to ten millimeters and one meter is equivalent to one hundred centimeters. If a mountain climber has multiple ropes which measure 3 meters in length each, how many millimeters in length is each rope?

A) 100

B) 300

C) 1,000

D) 3,000

6

On NASA's New Horizons Pluto mission, the Atlas V rocket reached the moon in approximately one-third of a day. If the moon is approximately 240,000 miles from earth, which of the following is closest to the average speed of the Atlas V rocket in miles per hour?

A) 30,000

B) 72,000

C) 80,000

D) 720,000

7

Allen is carving a cube of wood from an old tree stump as a part of an art presentation for a 3-dimensional art seminar. The immense cube measures 3 feet in all directions. If the density of the wood that Allen is carving is a uniform $12 \, lb / ft^3$, what will his finalized project weigh in pounds?

A) 27

B) 108

C) 324

D) 648

8

Harlan runs a metal shop and has just received a pallet that contains 32 cubic feet of aluminum sheet metal. If the weight of the metal including the pallet is 5,940 pounds and the pallet alone weighs 500 pounds, what is the approximate density of the aluminum in kilograms per cubic meter?

(1 cubic meter = 35.3 cubic feet)

(1 kilogram = 2.204 pounds)

A) 170

B) 270

C) 1700

D) 2700

115

CONTINUE

21	*Identifying* and *Predicting with* Models That Relate to Scatterplots

"The fastest way to connect a model to a scatterplot is to have a strong knowledge of the characteristics of the graph of each model type."

The behavior of a scatterplot can be modeled by many different types of equations, including linear equations, quadratic equations, and exponential equations. It is very important to know the standard forms of each of these equation types, how the coefficients relate to the graphs, and how to utilize these equations to predict outcomes.

Common Models for Scatterplots:

Linear Models: $y = mx + b$, where m is the slope of the line and b is the y-intercept. Scatterplots that are best represented by linear models appear to increase or decrease at a constant rate. They simply look like lines.

Quadratic Models: $y = ax^2 + bx + c$, where a defines the vertical stretch of the equation, $-\frac{b}{2a}$ defines the x-coordinate of the vertex, and c is the y-intercept. Scatterplots that are best represented by quadratic models appear to have the symmetrical shapes of common parabolas, or u-shapes, whether inverted or not.

Exponential Models: $y = ab^x + c$, where a defines the vertical stretch of the equation, b defines the common growth factor or decay factor, and $a + c$ defines the y-intercept. Scatterplots that are best represented by exponential models are curved and tend to rise more rapidly as you move left to right (in the case of a growth model), or tend to drop steeply and then taper off from left to right (in the case of a decay model). Scatterplots best represented by exponential models do *not* turn back on themselves.

By using these characteristics and paying close attention to the scale on each axis, you can identify the appropriate model that matches a scatterplot. Then, you can simply plug in the requested input value to predict an outcome.

Example 1:

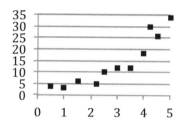

Given the data points plotted in the scatterplot above, which of the following models best fits the given data?

A) $y = 5x$

B) $y = x + 5$

C) $y = 2^x + 4$

D) $y = (2)2^x + 4$

The scatterplot appears to curve upward from left to right. Furthermore, the scale of the y-axis is five times the scale of the x-axis, so this curve would be even more extreme than if the scales were identical. It also does not curve back on itself. These are the characteristics of an exponential model, so you can eliminate choices A and B. To test the difference between choices C and D, simply substitute a value, such as 5, into the equation. In the equation given in choice D, if you substitute a 5, you end up with 68, which is much too high of a value given the graph. The correct answer is clearly choice _C_.

Example 2:

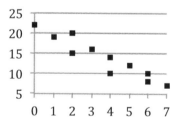

The data points displayed in the scatterplot above can best be modeled by the equation $y = 22 - 2.1x$. For what x-value can we most likely expect a y-value of 0?

Since you are given the equation, all you need to do is plug in 0 for y and solve. The answer is an x-value of approximately _10.5_.

CONTINUE

Skill 21 Practice Exercises:

1

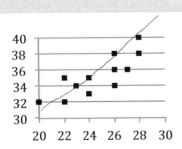

Which of the following equations best fits the data given in the scatterplot above?

A) $f(x) = \frac{3}{4}x + 32$

B) $f(x) = \frac{3}{4}x + 17$

C) $f(x) = \frac{1}{4}x + 32$

D) $f(x) = \frac{4}{3}x + 17$

2

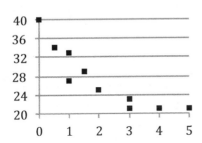

Which of the following equations best fits the data given in the scatterplot above?

A) $y = -5x + 40$

B) $y = 20(0.5)^x + 20$

C) $y = 2(x-3)^2 + 21$

D) $y = -x + 40$

3

A scatterplot is drawn comparing the height of a baby to the child's age in months. The scatterplot followed a linear trend that appeared to rise slightly from left to right. Which of the following could be used to predict the child's height, $f(x)$, in inches, in terms of x, the age of the child in months?

A) $f(x) = .6x + 18$

B) $f(x) = -.6x + 48$

C) $f(x) = .7x$

D) $f(x) = 12x + 18$

4

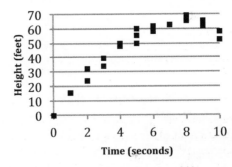

A group of physicists recorded the height measurements, in feet, of multiple objects that had been launched into the air by a compressed spring located at ground level. These height measurements were taken over a period of 10 seconds and were marked in relation to the time, in seconds, that had passed since the object left the spring. Which of the following models would best be suited to determine the height of an object, in feet, that has left the spring in relation to the time that has passed, in seconds?

A) $y = -x^2 + 16x$

B) $y = x^2 - 16x + 64$

C) $y = 64 - x^2$

D) $y = 8x + 1$

CONTINUE

Questions 5-6 refer to the following scatterplot.

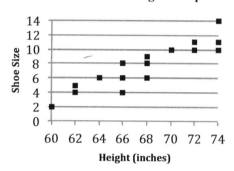

Shoe Size

Height (inches)

5

Which of the following types of models would best fit the data presented in the scatterplot above?

A) A linear model with a negative slope and a positive y-intercept.

B) A linear model with a positive slope and a y-intercept of zero.

C) A linear model with a positive slope and a negative y-intercept.

D) A linear model with a positive slope and a positive y-intercept.

6

Given the scatterplot above, shoe size can best be explained by height, in inches, using the equation $s(h) = 0.85h - 49$, where h represents height and $s(h)$ represents shoe size. The fact that $s(67)$ is approximately equal to 8 allows us to make which of the following assumptions?

A) One data point was collected from a 67 inch-tall person with a shoe size of 8.

B) Given that a person has a size 8 shoe, it can be estimated that the person's height is 67 inches.

C) Given the line of best fit, it can be estimated that a person who is 67 inches tall has a shoe size of 8.

D) All 67 inch-tall people have shoe sizes that are approximately size 8.

Questions 7-8 refer to the following scatterplot.

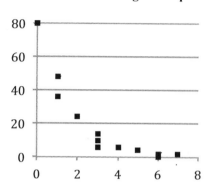

7

Which of the following models best fits the data in the scatterplot above?

A) $y = -10x + 80$

B) $y = -40x + 80$

C) $y = 80(\frac{4}{5})^x$

D) $y = 80(\frac{1}{2})^x$

8

If one were to estimate the output value, y, for an input of $x = 2.5$, which of the following would be the best estimate?

A) 2

B) 6

C) 10

D) 14

CONTINUE

22 — Recognizing Graphical Characteristics of Two-Variable Relationships

"As with scatterplots, pay close attention to what type of relationship the two variables share and recall the characteristics of that relationship's graphical representation."

The steps to follow:

1. Recognize the Relationship.
2. Recall the Characteristics of the Graph.
3. Match the Relationship with the Graph.

Example:

A battery powered desktop heater requires that four AAA batteries be changed every 2 hours that the heater operates. If the x-axis represents the number of hours that have passed and the y-axis represents the number of remaining AAA batteries, which of the following graphs best depicts the relationship between remaining batteries and time?

A)
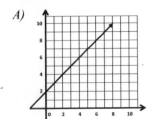

B)
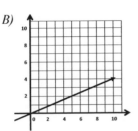

C)
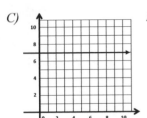

D)
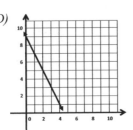

Since you are looking for a graph that depicts remaining batteries given time, and you know that the number of batteries is decreasing, you just need to spot the negative slope. The answer is *D*.

1

A radioactive isotope has been steadily decreasing in mass by 20% every 20 years. If a 400 gram sample of the isotope was collected in the year 1900, which of the following bar graphs best represents the remaining amount of the isotope over time?

A)
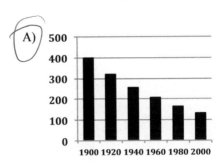

B)
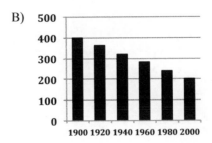

C)
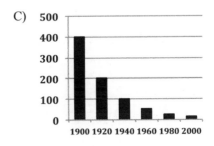

D)
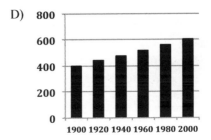

119

CONTINUE

Questions 2-3 refer to the following scatterplot.

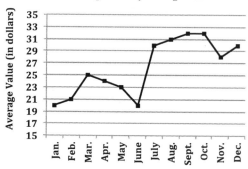

Average Monthly Closing Value

The line graph above shows the average monthly closing value for a particular stock that is listed on the New York Stock Exchange.

2

The stock had an increase in average closing price followed by a decrease in which of the following intervals?

A) January - March

B) February - April

C) April - June

D) July - September

3

The stock had its greatest decrease in average monthly closing value during which of the following time periods?

A) February - March

B) May - June

C) June - July

D) October - November

4

A ball bounces off of the ground, rises into the air, falls, and does not hit the ground again for 4 seconds. If the function $f(x)$ is used to estimate the height of the ball in feet, x seconds after it originally struck the ground, which of the following could be $f(x)$?

A) $f(x) = x^2 - 4x$

B) $f(x) = x^2 - 8x + 12$

C) $f(x) = -2x^2 + 8x$

D) $f(x) = -x^2 + 8x - 12$

5

A bison population has been decreasing along an exponential curve ever since the year 2000. In the year 2000, the population consisted of 320 bison. One year later the population decreased to 240 bison and by 2003, the population had reached 135 bison. If this population of bison were to be graphed on the xy-plane over time, in years, which of the following characteristics would best describe the graph?

A) The graph would decay by less than half of its y-value for every change of one unit on the x-axis.

B) The graph would decay by more than half of its y-value for every change of one unit on the x-axis.

C) The graph would linearly decrease steeply from left to right.

D) The graph would linearly decrease from left to right with a slope of approximately -1.

120

CONTINUE

Questions 6-7 refer to the following graph.

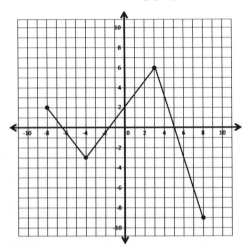

The complete graph of the function *f* is shown in the *xy*-plane above.

6

For what value of *x* is the value of $f(x)$ at its maximum?

A) −4

B) −3

C) 3

D) 6

7

If the function $f(x)$ reaches its maximum at an *x*-value of *u* and its minimum at an *x*-value of *v*, what is the value of $f(u) - f(v)$?

A) −3

B) 3

C) 9

D) 15

8

A condominium's property value increases in a fairly steady fashion. Its value growth stays fairly steady at around 5% of its value per year. If the property was initially valued at $60,000, which of the following bar graphs best depicts percentage growth over time?

A)
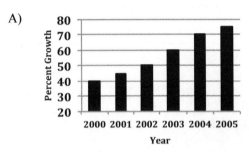

B)
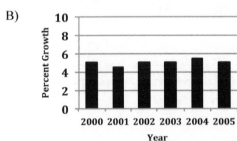

C)
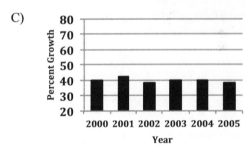

D)
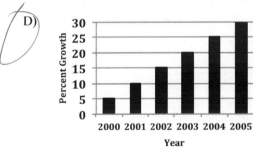

121

CONTINUE

23 *Identifying* the Strength of Association Between Two Variables

"Less scatter means a stronger association."

When investigating the strength of an association, it is important to notice how closely the data points approximate a line or a curve. The more tightly the points are packed together and the more visibly they represent a trend, the stronger the association.

In addition, pay attention to the direction of the association as well. If a question asks for a strong *positive* association, you can eliminate any sets of data in which one variable decreases as the other variable increases.

Example:

Which of the following scatterplots shows a strong linear association between the two variables?

A)   B)

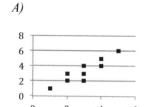

C)   D)

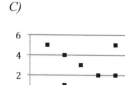

For this question, look for a strong linear association. If you focus on the strength of the association first, you can immediately eliminate C and D, which are much too scattered. Then, if you focus on the fact that you are looking for a linear relationship, _A_ becomes the obvious choice since B, although strong, presents a quadratic relationship.

1

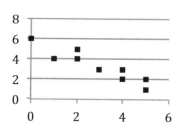

The scatterplot above displays which of the following kinds of linear association?

A) Weak positive linear association

B) Strong positive linear association

C) Weak negative linear association

D) Strong negative linear association

2

Which of the following pairs of variables would most likely have a strong negative association?

A) Hours of exercise and weight

B) Hours of exercise and weight lost

C) Hours watching TV and likelihood of getting a tumor

D) Hours of work and money earned

CONTINUE

3

Which of the following pairs of variables would most likely have a strong positive association?

A) Hours worked and salary

B) Physical height and points on driving record

C) Physical height and shoe size

D) Hours of exercise and weight

4

Which of the following graphs in the *xy*-plane best shows a strong positive association between *x* and *y*?

A)
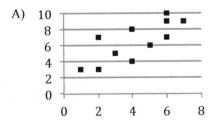

B)
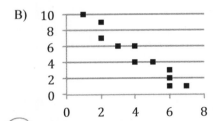

C)
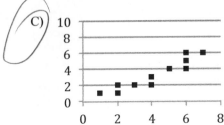

D)
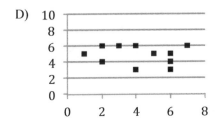

5

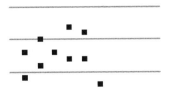

The scatterplot above displays which of the following kinds of linear association?

A) Strong positive linear association

B) Weak positive linear association

C) Weak negative linear association

D) Neither positive nor negative association

6

A student decided to conduct a study on the relationship between two variables, *a* and *b*. When he created a scatterplot of variables *a* and *b* on the *x* and *y* axes, respectively, he noticed that regardless of the value of *a*, the *b* values seemed to gather around the number twelve without deviating by more than one. Which of the following statements can the student make about the association between variables *a* and *b*?

A) The variables have a strong positive association.

B) The variables have a strong linear association.

C) The variables have a strong negative linear association.

D) The association between the variables cannot be determined.

123

CONTINUE

7

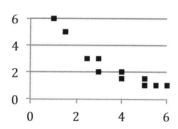

Which of the following associations best describes the scatterplot above?

A) Strong negative exponential association
B) Weak negative exponential association
C) Strong positive linear association
D) Strong negative linear association

8

If the value of a home increased by approximately 3% each year, the association between the percentage of growth in the home's value and time would best be described by which of the following?

A) Strong, positive, and linear
B) Strong and linear
C) Positive and linear
D) Strong and positive

Notes:

CONTINUE

Mid-Unit 3 Review - No Calculator

25 MINUTES, 20 QUESTIONS

> * Note: On the actual SAT, there are no problems from the Problem Solving and Data Analysis unit in the No Calculator section of the test. This review was created solely for consistency of structure and practice in this book.

DIRECTIONS

For each question from 1-15, choose the best answer choice provided in the multiple choice bank and fill in the appropriate circle in the provided answer key. Alternatively, for questions **16-20**, answer the problem and enter your answer in the grid-in section of the answer key. Refer to the directions given before question 16 as to how to enter your answers for the grid-in questions. You may complete scratch work in any empty space in your test booklet.

NOTES

A. Calculator usage **is not allowed** in this section.
B. Variables, constants, and coefficients used represent real numbers unless indicated otherwise.
C. All figures are created to appropriate scale unless the question states otherwise.
D. All figures are two-dimensional unless the question states otherwise.
E. The domain of any given function is all real numbers x for which the function, $f(x)$, is a real number unless the question states otherwise.

REFERENCE

$A = \pi r^2$
$C = 2\pi r$

$A = lw$

$A = \frac{1}{2}bh$

$c^2 = a^2 + b^2$

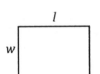

Special Right Triangle

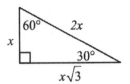

Special Right Triangle

$V = lwh$

$V = \pi r^2 h$

$V = \frac{4}{3}\pi r^3$

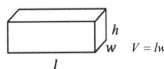

$V = \frac{1}{3}\pi r^2 h$

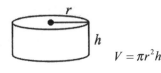

$V = \frac{1}{3}lwh$

There are $360°$ in a circle.
There are 2π radians in a circle.
There are $180°$ in a triangle.

CONTINUE

1

If $y = kx$, where k is a constant, and $y = 52$ when $x = 13$, what is the value of y when $x = 4$?

A) 4
B) 12
C) 16
D) 24

$$\frac{52}{13} = \frac{k13}{13}$$

$k = 4$

16

2

If the sides of a square are increased by 50%, by what percent is the area of the square increased?

A) 25
B) 100
C) 125
D) 225

$1 : 2.15$

$\times 1.5$
1.5
$7\ 5$
$1\ 5$
2.25

3

1 foot = 12 inches

1 meter = 3.28 feet

Based on the information given above, if a heptathlete throws a shot put 12.5 meters, approximately how many inches can the heptathlete throw the shot put?

A) 3.5
B) 41
C) 150
D) 490

4

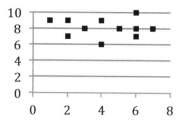

If $y = f(x)$, which of the following equations best fits the data points plotted in the xy-plane above?

A) $x = 8$
B) $f(x) = 8$
C) $f(x) = -x + 8$
D) $f(x) = x + 8$

CONTINUE

Questions 5-6 refer to the following graph.

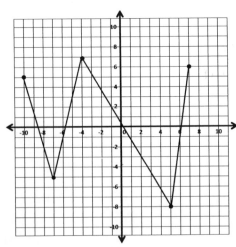

The complete graph of the function *f* is shown in the *xy*-plane above.

5

For what value of *x* is the value of $|f(x)|$ at its maximum?

A) −10

B) −4

C) 5

 D) 7

6

If the function $f(x)$ reaches its maximum at an *x*-value of *a* and its minimum at an *x*-value of *b*, what is the average of *a* and *b*?

A) $-\dfrac{9}{2}$

B) $\dfrac{1}{2}$

C) $\dfrac{9}{2}$

D) 6

$-8 +$

$\dfrac{-1}{2}$

7

Which of the following pairs of variables would most likely have a strong linear association?

A) Amount of change in a car's cup holder and time

B) Height above a trampoline and time

C) Checking account balance and time

D) Distance traveled on a freeway and time

8

In a flock of 200 seagulls, 120 are females. If 30 female seagulls leave the flock, how many male seagulls must leave the flock in order for the ratio of males to females to stay the same as the initial ratio?

A) 10

B) 20

C) 30

D) 45

120F : 80M

90F :

CONTINUE

9

If a is 120% of b and c is 150% of b, then a is what percent smaller than c?

A) 20

B) 30

C) 70

D) 80

(handwritten work):
$a = 1.2b$
$c = 1.5b$
$\dfrac{a}{1.2} = \dfrac{c}{1.5}$
$a = .8c$

10

If $f(x)$ represents the height in inches of an adult that is 80 years old or older and x represents the number of years since the adult's 80th birthday, which of the following linear models could define the relationship between x and $f(x)$?

A) $f(x) = 68.5 - 0.25x$

B) $f(x) = 67 + 0.1x$

C) $f(x) = 5.75 - 0.5x$

D) $f(x) = 5.75 - 0.05x$

11

A pancake recipe calls for 1 cup of pancake mix, 1/4 of a cup of milk, and 1 egg in order to make 4 pancakes. What is the maximum number of pancakes that can be made if there is one six-cup box of pancake mix, 1 cup of milk, and 1 dozen eggs?

A) 16

B) 20

C) 24

D) 48

12

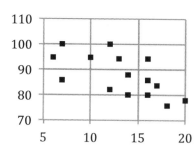

The scatterplot above displays which of the following kinds of linear association?

A) Weak positive linear association

B) Strong positive linear association

C) Weak negative linear association

D) Strong negative linear association

128

CONTINUE

13

$$1kg = 2.204 lbs.$$
$$1m^3 = 35.3 ft^3$$

Jeremy hired a contractor to help him put a patio in his backyard. The contractor asked him to find out the density of the loose gravel that is available at the local mason supply store in town. Jeremy discovered that the density of the loose gravel is 95 pounds per cubic foot. Given the conversions shown above, if Jeremy's contractor wanted the density in kilograms per cubic meter, what approximate density in kilograms per cubic meter would Jeremy tell the contractor?

A) 6
B) 1,500
C) 3,300
D) 7,400

$$\frac{95 lbs}{ft^3} \left(\frac{35.5 ft^3}{1} \right) \left(\frac{}{2.204} \right)$$

14

If 3 gallons of a 30% saline solution are mixed with x gallons of a 5% saline solution to make a 10% saline solution, what is the value of x?

A) 3
B) 6
C) 9
D) 12

$$3(.3) + x(.05) = .1(3+x)$$
$$.9 + x.05 = .3 + .x$$
$$.6 = .05x$$

15

The ratio of wooden beads to glass beads on a necklace is 2:7. There are a total of 63 beads currently on the necklace. If wooden beads were to be added to the necklace until the ratio of wooden beads to glass beads was increased to 5:7, how many total beads would be on the necklace?

A) 21
B) 35
C) 70
D) 84

$$2:7$$

$$\frac{2}{9}(63)$$

$$14:x$$

$$\frac{14}{x} = \frac{5}{7}$$

$$\frac{14+x}{} = \frac{5}{7}$$

$$63+x$$

$$98 + 7x = 315 + 5x$$

$$\frac{14+x}{49} = \frac{5}{7}$$

$$245$$

CONTINUE

DIRECTIONS

For each question from 16-20, solve and enter your answer in the grid-in section of your answer sheet as described below.

A. Write out your answers in the boxes at the top of each column in order to help you fill in the circles accurately. Remember, you will only receive credit for the circles that are filled in correctly, not for the written answer at the top of the columns.

B. Mark only a single circle in each column.

C. There are no negative answers.

D. If the problem has more than one correct answer, grid only one of the correct answers.

E. When your answer is a **mixed number**, such as $1\frac{1}{2}$, it should be entered as 1.5 or $3/2$. You cannot enter a mixed number because there is no room to fill in a circle that represents a space.

F. If you enter a **decimal answer** with more digits then the grid can handle, the answer may be rounded or truncated, but it absolutely must fill the entire grid.

Answer: $\frac{8}{21}$

Answer: 6.4

The ways to correctly grid $\frac{7}{9}$ are:

Answer: 102 - both positions are correct

REMEMBER:
You can begin writing your answers in any column as long as there is enough space. Leave unused columns blank.

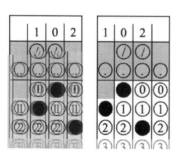

CONTINUE

16

In a nuclear fallout shelter, there is enough food to feed 16 people for 3 months. If 8 additional people enter the shelter safely, how many months will the food last?

$$\frac{16 \text{ peop}}{3 \text{ mont}}$$

8   1.5
16   3
24   4.5

(4.5)

17

If a person ran for two and one-eighteenth hours, but said that they ran for M minutes and S seconds, what is the value of $M + S$?

123 minuts
+20
(143)

18

The number of juniors in a high school who drive 2-door cars is 25% higher than the number of seniors who drive 2-door cars. If a total of 540 juniors and seniors drive 2-door cars, how many juniors drive 2-door cars?

$$x + y = 540$$
$$x = 1.25y$$
$$1.25y + y = 540$$

[300]

19

A residual for a data point in a scatterplot is calculated by subtracting the predicted y-value generated by using the best-fit line from the actual y-value of the data point. For a scatterplot that has a best-fit line with the equation $y = 1.5x + 13$, what is the residual for a data point with the coordinates $(5, 23)$?

23

2.5

CONTINUE

20

A class of 39 students earned an average of 85% on their most recent exam. Another class of n students earned an average of 92% on the same exam. If the combined average of both classes was an 89%, how many students were in the class with the higher average?

$$\frac{3315 + 92n}{34 + n} = 84$$

$$3315 + 92n = 3471 + 84n$$

$$n = 52$$

$$\boxed{52}$$

CONTINUE

24   *Comparing* Linear Growth with Exponential Growth

"Pay attention to the context of the problem. Understanding the relationship between the variables will allow you to determine the appropriate model given a clear understanding of the context."

Comparing linear and exponential models is like comparing arithmetical sequences to geometric sequences. If a quantity is changing by a constant amount over each period, you have linear growth or decay. If a quantity is being multiplied by a constant amount, you have exponential growth or decay. Once you have decided which type of model you are dealing with, you can recall that model's long run characteristics.

Example:

Geraldine makes $100 per day every day that she works. Melody makes $5 on the first day that she works and her pay doubles each day thereafter. On which day will Melody first make more money per day than Geraldine?

You know that Geraldine makes $100 per day every day. This is a constant rate. So, Geraldine's daily pay is modeled by a linear equation $y = 100$.

Melody's pay, on the other hand, doubles each day. Therefore, her daily pay follows an exponential model: $y = 5(2)^{x-1}$.

According to the characteristics of these two models, Geraldine's daily pay will follow a steady line with a slope of 0. Melody's daily pay will continually curve upward and will eventually surpass Geraldine's.

Since the question only concerns the women's daily pay rates, it is easiest to guess and check until you find the first day on which Melody's pay exceeds 100 dollars.

$$5(2)^{(6)-1} = 5(32) = 160 > 100$$

Melody's pay will be higher from the <u>6th</u> day on.

1

If the sale price for a $2.00 loaf of bread were to increase by 5% each year, the final sale price after 4 years would be approximately how many dollars greater than the final sale price of the bread if the price were to increase by exactly $0.10 each year?

A) 0.03 $2(1.05)^{4}$
B) 0.43
C) 2.03
D) 2.43 $y = 2 + .1x$

2

Patty's coin collection has been growing over the last few weeks. In the third week she had 50 coins, in the fifth week she had 80 coins, and in the tenth week her collection had grown to 155 coins. Which of the following models could be used to determine the number of coins that Patty has, $c(w)$, given the number of weeks she has been collecting, w?

A) $c(w) = 5w + 15$
B) $c(w) = 15w + 5$
C) $c(w) = 2(5)^{w-1}$
D) $c(w) = 5(2)^{w-1}$

133

CONTINUE

3

An old man offered his grandchildren an option. He said that he would give each of them $50 on each of their birthdays for 10 years or he would give each of them $1 on each of their birthdays and double the amount each year for ten years. How many more dollars would the grandchildren receive on their 10th birthday if they chose the option to take $1 and double each year rather than the other option?

A) 61

B) 206

C) 462

D) 523

1
2
4
8
16
32
64
128
256
512

4

$$y = 22.56 + 4x$$
$$y = 20(1.2)^x$$

If (x, y) is the only solution to the system of equations above and x is positive, what is the value of x?

A) 1

B) 2

C) 3

D) 4

$22.56 + 4x = 20 (1.2)^x$

$1.128 + \dfrac{x}{5} = 1.2^x$

$\log_{1.2} \left(1.128 + \dfrac{x}{5}\right) = x$

$\dfrac{\log 1.128 + \dfrac{x}{5}}{\log 1.2} = x$

$\log 1.128 + \dfrac{x}{5} = x \log 1.2$

$1.128 + \dfrac{x}{5} = 16^{x \log 1.2}$

5

If the sale price of a collectable baseball card that originally sold for $10 increased by 8% each year, the final selling price in dollars after 8 years would be approximately how much less than the final selling price if the baseball card were to have increased by $1.50 each year?

A) 3.00

B) 3.49

C) 3.50

D) 5.60

$10(1.08)^8$

6

$$f(x) = 960(0.5)^x$$
$$f(x) = 225 - 35x$$

If (a, b) and (c, d) are the two unique solutions of the form $(x, f(x))$ that satisfy the system of equations above, which of the following could be the value of $b - d$?

A) 3

B) 6

C) 35

D) 105

CONTINUE

7

There are two fallen trees decaying in the woods. On the day that they fell, both trees had an initial mass of 500 kilograms. The first tree loses 100 kilograms of mass each year that passes. The second tree loses 20% of its mass each year that passes. The first tree will have more mass than the second tree during which of the following time periods?

A) 0-1 years

B) 0-3 years

C) 0-5 years

D) The first tree will never have more mass than the second tree.

8

After an antibacterial solution was applied to an extremely tiny sample of a dirty wash cloth, the number of bacterial cells after one minute had passed was 8,000,000. After three minutes, the number of bacterial cells had diminished to 500,000 and after five minutes, the number of bacterial cells had diminished to 31,250. Which of the following models could be used to determine the number of bacterial cells, B, t minutes after the antibacterial solution was applied?

A) $B = 8,000,000 - 1,593,750t$

B) $B = 9,992,187.5 - 1,992,187.5t$

C) $B = 8,000,000(.25)^t$

D) $B = 32,000,000(.25)^t$

Notes:

CONTINUE

25   *Understanding* Relative Frequency and Conditional Probability in Tables

"When analyzing a two-way table, focus on the row headings, column headings, and margin totals that the question conditionally defines."

In learning about SAT mathematics, you have seen many two-way tables that categorize data into frequency cells. These tables, also known as contingency tables, define one categorical variable for the rows and another categorical variable for the columns. Collected data is added to the frequency in the appropriate cell.

In the case of <u>relative frequencies</u>, the total frequency in a single cell should be compared to a condition of one or both of the categorical variables. Take a closer look at an example to see how this works:

Example 1:

Grade Level		Favorite Color			Total
		Red	Blue	Green	
	Middle School	10	20	10	**40**
	High School	20	30	40	**90**
	College	10	20	30	**60**
Total		**40**	**70**	**80**	**190**

In a research study, students from middle school, high school, and college were asked to identify a favorite color from among red, blue, and green. What percentage of the college students prefer the color green?

In this question, the two-way table compares the categories of Grade Level and Favorite Color. The frequencies are easy to identify in the table. However, the question presents a condition when it asks, "What percentage of the college students...".

You must find the relative frequency of college students who prefer green compared to the total number of college students *only*. So, this would be 30 out of 60, *not* out of the total 190.

$$\frac{30}{60} = \frac{1}{2} = 50\%$$

Often, when probability questions arise, the language can appear challenging and can fill a student with anxiety. It is important to remember that a <u>conditional probability</u> is exactly the same as a relative frequency in a two-way table. The only difference is that the answer is given in decimal or fractional form, *not* as a percentage.

Example 2:

	A-Grade Stock	B-Grade Stock	After Market	Total
Acceptable	45	35	50	130
Defective	5	7	10	22
Total	50	42	60	152

An auto parts store has recently begun to keep track of acceptable and defective brake pads given the grade quality of the parts. If a set of non-aftermarket break pads were to be randomly selected from the store, what is the probability that the set will have a defect?

As soon as you see the word "probability," you should immediately think:

$$\frac{Favorable}{Total}$$

The phrase "If a set of non-aftermarket break pads..." tells you that the *Total Outcomes*, or the bottom of the fraction, has changed. For the remainder of this problem, the "After Market" column no longer exists.

So, you are really looking for the number of defective A-Grade and B-Grade break pads over the total number of A-Grade and B-Grade break pads:

$$\frac{5+7}{50+42} = \frac{12}{92} = \frac{3}{23}$$

CONTINUE

Skill 25 Practice Exercises:

▼

Questions 1-2 refer to the following table.

	Males	Females	TOTAL
Cereal	4	4	8
Pancakes	16	0	16
Eggs &Toast	8	12	20
TOTAL	28	16	44

A group of 44 adults were asked whether they eat cereal, pancakes, or eggs & toast for breakfast. Their responses were categorized by gender in the two-way table above.

1

If a single adult were to be randomly selected from the group of people surveyed, what is the probability that the adult is male?

A) $\frac{1}{5}$

B) $\frac{2}{11}$

C) $\frac{7}{10}$

D) $\frac{7}{11}$

2

Given that a female is selected at random, what is the probability that she *does not* eat eggs & toast for breakfast?

A) 0.04

B) 0.25

C) 0.67

D) 0.25

▼

Questions 3-4 refer to the following table.

	Math	Verbal	TOTAL
Freshman	10	0	10
Sophomore	14	10	24
Junior	18	12	30
Senior	16	20	36
TOTAL	58	42	100

100 high school students were interviewed and were asked, "On which section of the standardized aptitude test did you score higher, math or verbal?" Their responses were categorized by grade level in the table above.

3

Which of the following grade levels accounted for 60% of the students interviewed?

A) Juniors

B) Seniors

C) Freshmen and Juniors

D) Sophomores and Seniors

4

What percentage of the juniors performed better on the math section of the aptitude test?

A) 60

B) 40

C) 18

D) 12

▲

137

CONTINUE

Questions 5-6 refer to the following table.

	Black	Red	TOTAL
Heart	0	13	13
Diamond	0	13	13
Club	13	0	13
Spade	13	0	13
TOTAL	26	26	52

The four suits in a regulation deck of playing cards (Hearts, Diamonds, Clubs, and Spades) are categorized by color in the table above.

5

If a black card were to be randomly selected from a regulation deck of playing cards, what is the probability that the card is a Spade?

A) 0

B) $\frac{1}{4}$

C) $\frac{1}{2}$

D) 1

6

What is the probability of randomly selecting two diamonds in a row from a regulation deck of playing cards *without replacement*?

A) $\frac{1}{17}$

B) $\frac{1}{8}$

C) $\frac{4}{51}$

D) $\frac{33}{68}$

$$\frac{1}{4}\left(\frac{12}{51}\right)$$

$$\frac{12}{204}$$

7

	Shake	Bar	TOTAL
Pre-workout	24	6	30
Post-workout	8	18	26
TOTAL	32	24	56

Considering the chart above, what percentage of those who drink protein shakes have their shake after their workout?

A) $\frac{1}{4}$

B) 25

C) 50

D) 75

8

	Less than 10	10 or more	TOTAL
Before School	12	2	14
During School	23	22	45
After School	40	41	81
TOTAL	75	65	140

140 students in Arnet High School were asked when they send most of their daily text messages and how many they send each day. What percentage of the students who said during or after school send 10 or more text messages?

A) 45

B) 49

C) 50

D) 51

138

CONTINUE

26 *Making* Inferences About Population Parameters Based on Sample Data

"Pay close attention to the population from which the sample is taken. In many cases, this information will be all that you need to make an appropriate inference about the population."

Statistics, which are calculated from a sample of the population, can be used to make inferences about the entire population so long as the sample size is large enough and the inference is made about the same population from which the sample was taken. For example, you *cannot* make an inference about the entire population of the state of New Jersey if you have only sampled women. You *could,* however, make an inference about women in the state of New Jersey. What this means is that you don't need to take a census of an entire population, which is impossible in many cases, in order to get a good idea of what an exact average or probability is for the entire population.

Some important things to know:

1. *Statistics* **are calculated based on the sample:**

   "I have calculated my *sample statistic* from my sample to be a mean SAT score of 1000."

2. *Parameters* **are related to the actual population:**

   "I infer, given my appropriate sample size and appropriate sampling techniques, that the *population parameter* of the mean SAT score is 1000, given the results of my sample."

3. *Confidence Intervals* **are ranges calculated from your sample; you should have a certain level of confidence that the true population parameter lies within such an interval:**

   "After careful sampling and calculation, I am 95% confident that the true population mean national SAT score falls between 950 and 1050."

On the new SAT, your statistical knowledge and accuracy do not need to be too extensive. Just remember that you can calculate a statistic, *mean* or *probability*, from a sample and use it to estimate the population parameter.

Example 1:

In a random sample of 1,000 biomedical engineers from the United States, 250 have been continuously employed by their initial employers. Which of the following statements can be inferred from the sample?

A) *25% of biomedical engineers worldwide have been continually employeed by their first employers.*

B) *75% of biomedical engineers worldwide have had more than one employer.*

C) *75% of biomedical engineers in the United States have had more than one employer.*

D) *25% of male biomedical engineers in the United States have been continually employed by their first employer.*

First and foremost, you must take note of the population from which the sample was taken. In this case, the population is "biomedical engineers from the United States." By identifying the population, you can quickly eliminate the inferences that are made from populations that do not match the population of the sampling. *A* and *B* refer to biomedical engineers worldwide and *D* refers only to male biomedical engineers in the United States. All three of these do not represent the population from which you actually sampled.

So, without even calculating the percentage, you know that the correct answer is *C*.

Example 2:

In a random sample of 500 high-school-aged female volleyball players from China, the mean grade point average is 94%. What can be inferred about the population?

Remember, you must clearly identify your population. In this case, the population is high-school-aged female volleyball players from China.

"You can infer that the mean grade point percentage for all high-school-aged female volleyball players from China is 94%."

CONTINUE

Skill 26 Practice Exercises:

1

Ricardo asked 12 of his closest friends whether they planned to stay in-state for college or wanted to go out-of-state for college. Only 3 of his friends said out of state. Which of the following can Ricardo infer?

A) 25% of the students in Ricardo's school plan to attend out-of-state schools for college.

B) 33% of Ricardo's closest friends plan to attend out-of-state schools for college.

C) 25% of Ricardo's closest friends plan to attend out-of-state schools for college

D) 67% of the students in Ricardo's school plan to stay in-state for college.

2

In a clinical trial, 220 injured athletes at a physical therapy clinic were randomly selected. Half of the athletes were given a new pill that had an active ingredient said to reduce back pain and the rest of the athletes were given a pill of equal size and color that had no active pain relieving agent. The data showed that the athletes who took the pill that was stated to have an active pain relieving agent showed marked improvement in their back pain. Based on the experimental design and the stated results, which of the following is an appropriate conclusion?

A) The back pain pill will improve back pain in athletes better than any other pain pill on the market.

B) The back pain pill will improve back pain in athletes who participate in physical therapy better than any other pill on the market.

C) The back pain pill will improve back pain in athletes who currently have bad enough back pain that they must seek out a physical therapist.

D) The back pain pill will improve back pain in all people who have bad enough back pain that they must seek out a physical therapist.

Questions 3-4 refer to the following table.

	Running	Swimming	Hiking	Total
Daily	5	2	0	7
Weekly	15	8	0	23
Monthly	5	10	5	20
Total	25	20	5	50

In a recent survey, fifty 35-year-old males were asked what physical activity they prefer as a form of exercise and how often they perform that activity.

3

Which of the following best describes the population from which an inference could be made using the sample taken above?

A) 35-year-old males from the United States

B) 35-year-old males

C) 35-year-old males who exercise regularly

D) 35-year-olds

4

"40% of 35-year-old males prefer to _____."

Which of the following *could not* conclude the statement above and create a correct inference about the population?

A) exercise monthly

B) swim as a form of exercise

C) run daily or weekly

D) exercise daily or weekly

CONTINUE

5

$$1 \quad 2 \quad 2 \quad 3 \quad 3 \quad 4 \quad 5 \quad 5 \quad 6 \quad 6 \quad 7$$

The 11 scores above are the AP Chemistry exam scores of 11 randomly-selected sophomores taking AP Chemistry at Ward Ridge High School. Which of the following can we infer?

A) The mean AP Chemistry exam score for sophomores at Ward Ridge High School is approximately 4.

B) The mean AP Chemistry exam score for students at Ward Ridge High School is approximately 4.

C) The mean AP Chemistry exam score for all high school sophomores is approximately 4.

D) The mean score on the AP Chemistry exam is approximately 4.

6

At the Olympic Games in Rio De Janiero, Donovan asked 1,000 randomly selected attendees who were at a VIP luncheon, "Is Rio De Janiero a more beautiful city than your home town?" When surveying the people, Donovan handed each person a card that said yes or no and asked the people to mark their answer and drop it in the survey box on their way out of the Olympic village. If all 1,000 people responded and 51% of the respondents said "Yes," which of the following can Donovan infer?

A) 51% of adults worldwide believe that Rio De Janiero is more beautiful than their home city.

B) Approximately 50% of adults worldwide believe that Rio De Janiero is more beautiful than their home city.

C) 51% of middle to upper class people worldwide believe that Rio De Janiero is more beautiful than their home city.

D) Approximately 50% of middle to upper class people worldwide believe that Rio De Janiero is more beautiful than their home city.

7

A market researcher conducted a survey to see if people in a city prefer the taste of a beer from the tap or from the bottle. The market researcher handed out 242 surveys at a local bar and received 230 of the surveys back. Which of the following factors is the most obvious reason as to why a usable conclusion *cannot* be drawn about the beer preference of the population from this city?

A) The number of non-responses

B) The location of the survey

C) Size of the population

D) Size of the sample

8

If a statistics student were to survey 1,000 high school students who currently take advanced placement courses and attempt to calculate a statistic for the mean number of AP courses taken by these students, which of the following would best describe the difference between an inference based on a 95% confidence interval for the true population parameter and a 90% confidence interval for the true population parameter?

A) The 95% confidence interval for the true mean number of advanced placement courses would be wider than the comparable 90% confidence interval.

B) The 90% confidence interval for the true mean number of advanced placement courses would be wider than the comparable 95% confidence interval.

C) A 95% confidence interval and a 90% confidence interval would have the same width.

D) A comparison between a 95% confidence interval and a 90% confidence interval cannot be determined.

141

CONTINUE

27 — *Calculating* Measures of Center

"Calculating mean, median, or mode is always the same, regardless of the form in which you receive the data."

Mean, median, and mode are basic statistics that you should know how to calculate regardless of the form in which you receive the data. Remember the following:

Mean:

Sum of Data Points
# of Data Points

In order to calculate the mean, calculate the sum of all of your data points and divide by the number of data points that you have. In most cases, the mean is your best choice for a measure of center. However, means are strongly affected by outliers, points that fall far outside the normal trend. So, if your data set includes outliers, the median would be a better choice for measuring the center.

Median:

"The Middle Number"

In order to calculate the median, you must make sure that the numbers are in ascending order; once they are, the median is the center number. If there is no center number, the median will always be the average of the two numbers closest to the middle. As stated above, the median is less affected by outliers. So, when your data set has some outliers, use the median as a measure of center instead of the mean.

Mode:

"The Most Common Number"

The mode is always the easiest measure of tendency to spot. All you have to do is look for the most repeated data point in the set or the most popular one. Remember, a data set can have multiple modes.

Example 1:

$$72 \quad 74 \quad 78 \quad 78 \quad 80 \quad 80 \quad 80 \quad 82$$

Given the set of 8 test scores above, find the Mean, Median, and Mode of the set.

Mean:

$$\frac{72+74+78+78+80+80+80+82}{8} = \frac{624}{8} = 78$$

Median:

$$72 \quad 74 \quad 78 \quad \underline{78 \quad 80} \quad 80 \quad 80 \quad 82$$

$$\frac{78+80}{2} = \frac{158}{2} = 79$$

Mode:

<u>80</u> is the most common score.

Example 2:

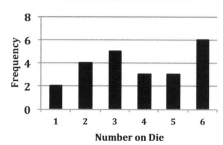

Numbers Rolled on a Die

A standard die was rolled 23 times and the number that showed on the die was recorded each time. Which of the following is the median number rolled on the die?

A) 3
B) 3.5
C) 4
D) 4.5

The numbers are already in order. Just use the frequencies to count and find the middle roll, the 12th roll. The correct answer is <u>C</u>.

CONTINUE

Skill 27 Practice Exercises:

▼

Questions 1-2 refer to the following table.

Group A	1:50	1:58	2:02	2:18	3:10
Group B	2:02	2:08	2:10	2:10	2:52
Group C	1:48	2:32	2:32	2:32	3:12

15 students were separated into 3 equal groups. The students in each group were given an academic puzzle to complete and the times it took in minutes and seconds for each student to complete the puzzle are listed in the table above.

1

What is the median time to complete the puzzle in minutes and seconds of the group with the lowest median?

A) 2:02
B) 2:10
C) 2:15
D) 2:32

2

What is the mode time to complete the puzzle in minutes and seconds of the group with the greatest mode?

A) 2:02
B) 2:08
C) 2:10
D) 2:32

▲

3

Class A: 88 80 94 92 92 90 96

Class B: 90 88 86 88 86 90 90

Samples of seven test scores were taken from two classes that took the same exam. What is the absolute value of the difference between the medians of the two classes?

A) 2
B) 4
C) 6
D) 8

4

114 ft. 186 ft. 186 ft. 186 ft. 188 ft. 190 ft.

190 ft. 193 ft. 195 ft. 195 ft. 198 ft. 199 ft.

The distances for the top 12 competitors in the javelin throw at a recent track and field event are recorded above. An unbiased newspaper reporter will be writing an article on the results of the event. Which of the following statements would the newspaper reporter most likely print?

A) The most common throw distance among the competitors was 186 feet.
B) The mean distance of a javelin throw in the competition was 185 feet.
C) The median distance of a javelin throw in the competition was 190 feet.
D) The top competitor threw the javelin 85 feet further than the 12th place competitor.

143

CONTINUE

5

Class A: 60 80 90 90 92 92 96 96 96

Class B: 84 84 84 88 88 90 90 92 92

Which of the following statements is true?

A) The median of class A is greater than the median of class B.

B) The mean of class A and the mean of class B are equal to each other.

C) The mode of class A is more than 10 greater than the mode of class B.

D) All of the above

6

$$A : \{55, 82, 82, 84, 85, 86, 86, 90, 92, 95\}$$
$$B : \{59, 67, 75, 82, 88, 94, 95, 97, 99, 99\}$$

Mrs. Allendale teaches AP chemistry and has two classes with ten students in each class. The scores of all ten students in each class are listed above. After the test was graded, Mrs. Allendale reported that the mean test score for Class B was 85.5 and the median test score for Class A was 85.5 as well. Which of the following is the best reason why Mrs. Allendale reported a different measure of central tendency for each class?

A) Mrs. Allendale only reported the mean for Class B because their standard deviation was higher.

B) Mrs. Allendale only reported the median for Class A because one student scored much lower than the rest of the students in that class.

C) Mrs. Allendale wanted each class to have the same score so that she could keep the spirit of competition alive between her two classes.

D) Mrs. Allendale did not want one class to feel inferior to the other class because one class had a higher score than the other.

7

If the average test score of a class of 10 students is 20% higher than another class of 6 students, then the sum of the test scores in the higher class must be what percent of the sum of the test scores in the lower class?

A) 200

B) 100

C) 50

D) 20

8

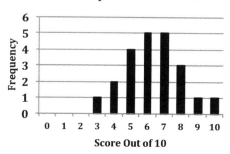

Girls Aptitude Test Scores

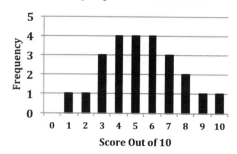

Boys Aptitude Test Scores

24 boys and 24 girls were given a monitored aptitude test, and a score from 0 to 10 was assigned to each student. The students' scores are shown on the histograms above. How many total modes does the group with highest number of modes have?

A) 1

B) 2

C) 3

D) 4

CONTINUE

28   *Comparing* Measures of Spread

"Spread measures the width of a distribution of data. Whether you are assessing the spread visually or calculating the spread, the more information that is farther away from the center, the larger the spread."

On the SAT, the spread of a distribution is measured using two factors: the range and the standard deviation. In most cases, the standard deviation is a better measure of spread since the standard deviation incorporates more data. The range, in contrast, is simply the distance between the highest data point and the lowest.

Range:

Highest - Lowest

The range is generally calculated in tandem with the median. It measures the width of a distribution by providing the absolute distance between the highest data point and the lowest data point.

Standard Deviation:

"The square root of the average of the squared distances from the mean."

The standard deviation is a measure of how far, on average, each point lies from the mean. The standard deviation is generally calculated in tandem with the mean. The easiest way to recognize a standard deviation is to note where the data lies. A lower standard deviation means that more data lies close to the center. This is easy to recognize in a data display, like a histogram; just look for a spike in the center or a standard bell curve shape. Quite simply, data that follows a standard bell curve shape has a lower standard deviation than data that stays uniform across a histogram or even rises at the outer edges. So, an inverted bell curve, one that is high on the sides and low in the center, has a very high standard deviation. When analyzing sets of numbers, you must take note of the mean and of how far away each of the individual numbers is from that mean. One easy way to address this is to make a quick histogram of the data points in a set and visually note its shape.

Example:

Which of the following histograms displays the distribution with the highest standard deviation?

A)

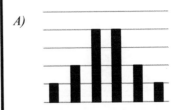

B)

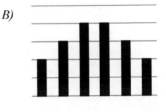

C)

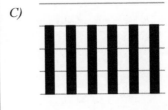

D)

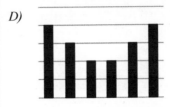

You are looking for the highest standard deviation. A high standard deviation implies that more information is farther from the mean. Since all of the histograms above are symmetrical, you can see that the mean for each is in the center. You can also clearly see in the last histogram the opposite of a spike - a valley. This histogram shows that much of the information is far from the center and that, hence, the data has a high standard deviation.

The correct answer is _D_.

CONTINUE →

Skill 28 Practice Exercises:

▼

Questions 1-2 refer to the following table.

Team 1	10	11	12	12	13	13	14	15
Team 2	10	10	11	12	13	14	15	15

The shoe sizes of the starting 5 players and the first 3 bench players of two basketball teams are listed in the table above.

1

What is the difference between the range of team 1 and the range of team 2?

A) 0

B) 5

C) 10

D) 15

2

Which of the following statements is true about the standard deviations of teams 1 and 2?

A) Team 1 has a higher standard deviation than team 2.

B) Team 1 has a lower standard deviation than team 2.

C) Team 1 and team 2 have the same standard deviation.

D) The standard deviation of either team cannot be calculated.

▲

3

Set A: {5, 5, 5, 5}

Set B: {3, 7, 7, 3}

Given the two sets of data above, which of the following statements is true?

A) Set A has a lower standard deviation.

B) Set B has a lower standard deviation.

C) Set A and Set B have the same standard deviation.

D) The standard deviations cannot be determined.

4

140 bpm   145 bpm   160 bpm   162 bpm

163 bpm   170 bpm   171 bpm   171 bpm

Post-exercise heart rates were taken for a random sample of eight people at a gym exactly one minute after they completed 30-minutes of cardio. If m represents the median heart rate and r represents the range of the sample, what is the value of $m - r$?

A) 130.5

B) 131.0

C) 131.5

D) 132.0

146

CONTINUE ➡

Questions 5-7 refer to the following information.

55, 78, 78, 79, 80, 81, 82, 82, 83, 83, 84, 84, 84, 100

The mid-term exam scores of 14 students in a second year computer aided drafting course are listed above. Two scores are considered outliers.

5

What is the median test score of the class after all outliers are removed?

A) 81.5

B) 82

C) 82.5

D) 83

6

By approximately what percent does the range of test scores decrease if the outliers are removed?

A) 13.3

B) 35.6

C) 51.1

D) 86.7

7

If every number in the list were divided by 5, which of the following would have the greatest percent decrease?

A) Mean

B) Range

C) Standard deviation

D) All of the above would have the same percentage decrease.

8

IQ of Suburban Students

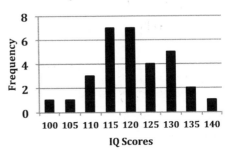

IQ of Urban Students

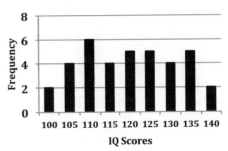

In a recent study, a statistical research group had students in both suburban and urban school systems take a standardized IQ test. The IQ scores were tallied and the data can be seen in the two histograms above. Which of the following statements is supported by the data?

A) Students in suburban school systems have higher IQs on average than students in urban school systems.

B) A student in a suburban school system had the highest IQ recorded in the study.

C) The standard deviation of IQ scores is higher among students from urban school systems.

D) The standard deviation of IQ scores is higher among students from suburban school systems.

CONTINUE

29   *Modifying* Measures of Center and Spread

"Multiplying affects center and spread. Adding or subtracting affects center only."

When you modify a set of data by adding, subtracting, or multiplying by a constant, you have to pay close attention to the effects the modification has on center and on spread.

Multiplying by a Constant:

When you multiply by a constant, the center and spread are affected equally. More precisely, if you have a set of numbers and multiply every number in the set by 4, the center gets multiplied by 4 and the spread becomes 4 times as wide.

Adding or Subtracting a Constant:

If you add or subtract a constant that affects every data point in a set, the center will obviously move up or down according to what has been added or subtracted. However, the spread will remain unaffected. Since each point is receiving the same magnitude of change, being translated up or down, the width of the distribution stays the same.

Example:

A set of 10 different numbers has a range of 20. A second set, Set B, is created by multiplying every number in the original set by 2 and by then adding 5 to each data point. Which of the following is the range of Set B?

A) 20
B) 25
C) 40
D) 45

You know that the original set was modified through multiplication and addition. Since the question is asking about range, you also know that only spread gets affected by the multiplier. So, all you have to do is multiply the original range by the multiplier, 2, and you have arrived at the answer. There is no need to make up a set of numbers and go through a longer process!

$20(2) = 40$ **The correct answer is _C_.**

Skill 29 Practice Exercises:

8, 10, 10, 11, 12, 13, 13, 14, 15

Nine students took part in an IQ test that was based on a scale of 1 to 15. The students were told if they would like to know their exact IQ, they can multiply their score by 10. What is the range of actual IQs among the nine students who took part in the test?

A) 7
B) 12
C) 70
D) 120

2

The average score on a chemistry quiz was 15 out of 20 points. If the teacher decided to scale the test out of one hundred points and then give each student a 5 point curve, what was average of the new set of test scores?

A) 70
B) 75
C) 80
D) 100

CONTINUE

3

$$20 \quad 25 \quad 25 \quad 30 \quad 50$$

If you were to subtract 3 from every number in the list above and then multiply each number by 3, which of the following would be the mean of the modified list of numbers?

A) 81

B) 87

C) 90

D) 99

5

The mean of a list of numbers is x. If every number in the list were to be multiplied by 4 then reduced by 2, the mean would be how much higher than if every number in the list were reduced by 2, then multiplied by 4?

A) 2

B) 3

C) 4

D) 6

6

A large set of test scores has a mean, v, of 1050 and a standard deviation, σ, of 180. If all of the scores were divided by 10 and 5 was added to every number in the set, which of the following gives the correct mean and standard deviation of the new set of scores?

A) $v : 270, \ \sigma : 46$

B) $v : 270, \ \sigma : 36$

C) $v : 110, \ \sigma : 23$

D) $v : 110, \ \sigma : 18$

4

A large group of students' test scores has a mean of 82 and a standard deviation of 4. If every student then receives a 5 point curve on the test, the standard deviation of the new test scores would be which of the following?

A) 4

B) 4.5

C) 9

D) 87

149

CONTINUE

7

Set A consists of 15 different numbers and the median of Set A is equal to the range of Set A. A second set, Set B, is created by multiplying every number in Set A by 4. If m is the median of Set B and r is the range of Set B, which of the following is true?

A) $m = 4r$

B) $m = r$

C) $m = \dfrac{r}{4}$

D) The relationship between m and r cannot be determined.

8

In a list of projected earnings forcasts, after every forcast was increased by 20% and then reduced by $10,000, the standard deviation of the forcasts was $15,000. What was the standard deviation, in dollars, of the original set of projected earnings forcasts?

A) 2,500
B) 12,500
C) 15,000
D) 18,000

Notes:

_____

_____

_____

_____

_____

_____

_____

_____

_____

_____

_____

CONTINUE

30 *Evaluating* Reports to Make Inferences

"It is important to remember, when analyzing data, that you can only make inferences that are appropriate given the type of data that has been collected and the means by which the data has been collected."

As you learned earlier, a sample can be a useful tool for making an inference about a population. You need to be sure to analyze the data carefully and to only make inferences that can be justified given the type of data that was collected. For instance, if your data involves blood samples from middle-aged males, you can make inferences about middle-aged males. You wouldn't want to extend the inference to teenagers or females since you do not have any data on these groups. Furthermore, you must pay attention to bias in sampling. If your sample has a bias, the results will lack meaning. For example, if you have asked your friends face-to-face whether or not they like a shirt that you were wearing, you have sampled with bias. First of all, they are your friends. They may give you the answer that you want to hear, not the truth. In addition, you asked them face-to-face. This may further pressure the people you surveyed to give you favorable responses. Also, sample size is important. You must make sure that a sample is of an appropriate size for making an inference. This is why it is important that a sample is sufficiently large, randomly selected in a uniform fashion, and derived from the full spectrum of the population which you intend to make an inference about.

Example:

In a recent survey, randomly-sampled working adults were asked whether or not they feel that the current federal income taxes are fair. The people surveyed were asked to fill out a questionaire without giving their names and to respond to the question with a simple yes or no. If 75% of the respondents feel that the current federal income taxes are unfair, what can be inferred about the population of working adults

The sampling seems to be fairly well controlled. The sample is random and the people surveyed were not asked to give their names, a measure that facilitated truthful responses. Without getting too involved, you can infer that <u>75% of all working adults believe that the current federal income taxes are unfair</u>.

Skill 30 Practice Exercises:

1

Benny anonymously surveyed a random sample of his classmates at Elmwood High School what they scored on the SAT Math section. After he recieved 3 responses, he calculated the average SAT Math score to be 710. Which of the following statements is correct?

A) Benny can infer that the average score on the SAT Math section from students at Elmwood High is 710.

B) Benny can infer that the average score on the SAT Math section from all SAT test takers is 710.

C) Benny should not have taken a random sample and should have asked only his closest friends. He could have then made an inference about the average score on an SAT Math section for his closest friends.

D) Benny should have continued to randomly sample students at Elmwood High School until his sample was of a more considerable size.

2

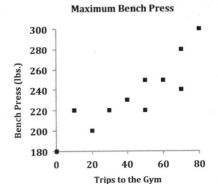

Given the data in the scatterplot above, the owner of a gym can reasonably expect the maximum bench press of a member who visits his gym 50 times to be in which of the following ranges, in pounds?

A) 220-250

B) 230-250

C) 240-280

D) 250-280

CONTINUE

Questions 3-6 refer to the following scatterplot.

Price of a Loaf of Bread

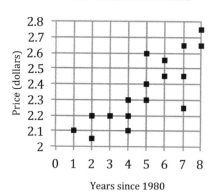

A random sample of 17 loaves of bread over the 8 years following 1980 were selected and their prices were recorded in the scatterplot above.

3

If one were to estimate the price of a loaf of bread in 1986, they would estimate that the price fell within which of the following ranges?

A) $2.30 - $2.60

B) $2.40 - $2.60

C) $2.45 - $2.55

D) $2.25 - $2.65

4

What would be a good estimate of the median sale price of a loaf of bread from the year 1981 to 1988?

A) $2.40

B) $2.45

C) $2.55

D) $2.60

5

If the price data for the 17 loaves of bread were to be estimated with a best fit line, the slope of that line would be closest to which of the following?

A) 0.06

B) 0.1

C) 0.9

D) 1

6

In statistics, a residual in a linear scatterplot is defined as the difference between an observed data point (one that is a part of the actual sample) and the estimated value that results from substituting into the equation for the line of best fit. Which of the following coordinate pairs in the scatterplot would have the greatest residual?

A) $(1, 2.1)$

B) $(2, 2.05)$

C) $(5, 2.6)$

D) $(7, 2.25)$

CONTINUE

7

A television network wanted to conduct a nationwide poll to see which presidential candidate the nation was leaning toward electing as the next president. The network collected a sample by running a commercial that asked viewers to call in and press the number one if they planned to vote for candidate one and press two if they planned to vote for candidate two. Which of the following causes of bias is the strongest reason why the survey results are most likely unreliable?

A) Sample size

B) Sample location

C) Economic status

D) Passion for politics

8

A candy company produces 1000 mystery bars in which the customer has to taste the bar and guess the flavor. 250 bars are grape, 250 bars are sour apple, 250 bars are chocolate, and 250 bars are vanilla. A customer purchases a completely random sample of 250 of the bars and finds that only forty of the bars are sour apple. The customer then infers that only 16% of all the mystery bars are sour apple flavored. What is wrong with the customers sample?

A) It is not properly selected to be representative.

B) It is so large that it changed the probability of getting a sour apple mystery bar in the remaining population.

C) The population is too small and it should be a census.

D) It should have included 25 bars of each flavor.

Notes:

CONTINUE

CONTINUE

Problem Solving and Data Analysis Unit Review:

16. *Understanding* Proportional Relationships, Ratios, and Rates

It is important to have a strong knowledge of all proportional relationships, ratios, and rates so that, when the situation calls for such knowledge, you are ready to proceed without hesitation.

17. *Maintaining* or *Changing* Ratios

When attempting to maintain a ratio or change a ratio, use parts-to-the-whole to create a proportion that sets the modified totals equal to the desired ratio.

18. *Solving* with Percentages

When you are dealing with problems involving percentages, convert the percentages to decimal form. Doing so allows you to solve quickly and efficiently.

19. *Combining* Percentages and Averages

Remember to create a number line between the two given values and to place the combined percentage or average where it belongs. Also remember, the combined percentage or average gets pulled toward the larger quantity.

20. *Solving* with Units and Unit Conversions

Always pay attention to your given units and your target units. Always convert units toward your target units.

CONTINUE

Problem Solving and Data Analysis Unit Review:

21. *Identifying* and *Predicting with* Models That Relate to Scatterplots

You must have a strong understanding of the characteristics of the graphs of each model type. Once these characteristics are memorized, you can quickly recall which model to apply.

22. *Recognizing* Graphical Characteristics of Two-Variable Relationships

Recognize the relationship between the two variables. Recall the characteristics of that relationship's graph and use those characteristics to identify the correct graph.

23. *Identifying* the Strength of Association Between Two Variables

When inspecting scatterplots, you will find that points that seem to closely approximate a line or a curve have a strong association. In general, less scatter means stronger association.

24. *Comparing* Linear Growth with Exponential Growth

If you establish a clear understanding of the context of the problem, you can select the appropriate linear or exponential model and recall its long-run characteristics.

25. *Understanding* Relative Frequency and Conditional Probability in Tables

Pay close attention to row headings, column headings, and margin totals. A question will often conditionally define a margin total that must be considered in a relative relationship.

CONTINUE

Problem Solving and Data Analysis
Unit Review:

26. *Making* Inferences About Population Parameters Based on Sample Data

You must identify the population that any sample was taken from. This population will define the sample group about which you can make inferences.

27. *Calculating* Measures of Center

Although this content is straight-forward, it is important that you know how to identify and calculate Mean, Median, and Mode regardless of the form with which you receive mathematical data.

28. *Comparing* Measures of Spread

Range is the distance between the highest and the lowest data points, and standard deviation is the average distance away from the mean.

29. *Modifying* Measures of Center and Spread

The key point to remember is that multiplying by a constant affects both center and spread, whereas adding or subtracting a constant only affects the center.

30. *Evaluating* Reports to Make Inferences

The population sampled from, the type of sample data collected, and the appropriateness of the sampling method will define whether or not you can make an inference.

CONTINUE

**TURN TO NEXT PAGE FOR
UNIT REVIEW**

CONTINUE

Unit 3 Review - Calculator

55 MINUTES, 38 QUESTIONS

DIRECTIONS

For each question from 1-30, choose the best answer choice provided in the multiple choice bank and fill in the appropriate circle in the provided answer key. Alternatively, for questions **31-38**, answer the problem and enter your answer in the grid-in section of the answer key. Refer to the directions given before question 31 as to how to enter your answers for the grid-in questions. You may complete scratch work in any empty space in your test booklet.

NOTES

A. Calculator usage **is allowed**.
B. Variables, constants, and coefficients used represent real numbers unless indicated otherwise.
C. All figures are created to appropriate scale unless the question states otherwise.
D. All figures are two-dimensional unless the question states otherwise.
E. The domain of any given function is all real numbers x for which the function, $f(x)$, is a real number unless the question states otherwise.

REFERENCE

 $A = \pi r^2$ $C = 2\pi r$

 $A = lw$

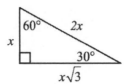 $A = \dfrac{1}{2}bh$

 $c^2 = a^2 + b^2$

 Special Right Triangle

 Special Right Triangle

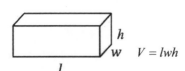 $V = lwh$

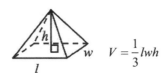 $V = \pi r^2 h$

 $V = \dfrac{4}{3}\pi r^3$

$V = \dfrac{1}{3}\pi r^2 h$

$V = \dfrac{1}{3}lwh$

There are $360°$ in a circle.
There are 2π radians in a circle.
There are $180°$ in a triangle.

159

CONTINUE ➡

1

For all variables y and x, $y = \dfrac{k}{x}$. When y is 16, $x = 4$. What is the value of x when $y = 2$?

A) $\dfrac{1}{2}$

B) 2

C) 16

D) 32

2

At a wedding reception, the ratio of seafood meals to chicken meals is 4:5. There are a total of 72 people at the reception. If 8 additional people arrived at the reception and requested seafood meals, how many additional people would have had to arrive and request chicken meals in order for the initial ratio to have remain the same?

A) 8

B) 9

C) 10

D) 18

3

The final sale price of a book after a 25% discount and 5% sales tax is $9.45. What was the original selling price of the book?

A) $8.00

B) $9.00

C) $10.00

D) $12.00

4

Class A averaged 82 on an AP Physics test. Class B averaged 94 on the same test. If the combined average for both classes was 84 and a combined total of 48 students took the test, how many students were in class B?

A) 6

B) 8

C) 40

D) 42

CONTINUE

5

A large ceramic weight has a density of 187.29 pounds per cubic foot. What is the density of half of the ceramic weight in grams per cubic centimeter?

$(1 \ gm/cm^3 = 62.43 \ lb/ft^3)$

A) 1.5
B) 3.0
C) 4.5
D) 6.0

6

A safe-deposit box is filled with $133,000 in cash. The balance depletes by 25% each year that passes from the initial year that the account was opened, 1980. If the y-axis was labeled *Dollars (in thousands)* and the x-axis was labeled *Years since 1980*, which of the following graphs best depicts the remaining balance in the box as time goes on?

A)
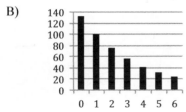

B)
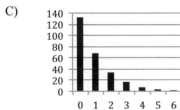

C)
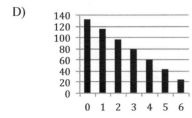

D)

7

Which of the following equations has solutions in only three quadrants of the xy-plane?

A) $f(x) = 2(2)^x - 3$

B) $f(x) = x^2 - 5$

C) $f(x) = 3 - x^2$

D) $f(x) = -3$

8

Which of the following scatterplots shows the strongest association between x and y?

A)
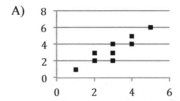

B)
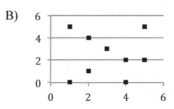

C)
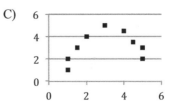

D)
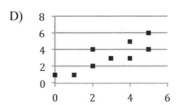

CONTINUE

9

The mass of a 500 kilogram sample of a radioactive isotope decays exponentially following the model $W = 500(0.8)^x$, where W is the mass of the sample in kilograms after x years have passed. A sample of a different radioactive isotope that has an initial mass of 420 kilograms decays linearly following the model $M = -60x + 420$, where M is the mass of the sample in kilograms after x years have passed. For how many years will the mass of the isotope that decays exponentially be less than the mass of the isotope that decays linearly?

A) 0

B) 2

C) 10

D) 20

10

Allan recently conducted a survey. He randomly selected 50 students who worked on their respective high school newspapers, had each student answer a single question on a printed paper without giving any personal information and had all students place the surveys into a single container. Upon analyzing the surveys, Allan discovered that 68% of the random sample of students believed that work on a school newspaper would help in the college application process. Which of the following can Allan most confidently infer?

A) 32% of all students who work on high school newspapers believe that work on a school newspaper *will not* help in the college application process.

B) 68% of all students who work on high school newspapers believe that work on a school newspaper *will* help in the college application process.

C) 32% of all high school students believe that working on a school newspaper *will not* help in the college application process.

D) 68% of all high school students believe that working on a school newspaper *will* help in the college application process.

▼

Questions 11-12 refer to the following table.

	MP1	MP2	MP3	MP4	TOTAL
Algebra	12	4	4	8	28
History	2	7	3	10	22
Spanish	1	3	5	18	27
TOTAL	15	14	12	36	77

A group of 77 students were asked in which class and during which marking period they received their highest grade for a school year. The results were collected in the table above.

11

What percentage of the students who had their highest grade in marking period 1 received that grade in algebra?

A) $\dfrac{4}{5}$

B) $\dfrac{12}{77}$

C) 40

D) 80

12

If a student whose highest grade occured in algebra or history is selected at random, what is the probability that they earned the grade in marking period 4?

A) $\dfrac{18}{77}$

B) $\dfrac{2}{7}$

C) $\dfrac{9}{25}$

D) $\dfrac{36}{77}$

▲

CONTINUE

13

Weight of Cereal Boxes

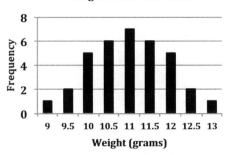

An organic food company is collecting data on the distribution of weight, in grams, of the cereal boxes that it is shipping out to stores. The company would like to use the data to update the label on the box by listing the appropriate mean weight of each box. What weight, in grams, should the manufacturer print on each box?

A) 10.5
B) 11
C) 11.5
D) 12

14

$$A : \{20,40,40,40,60\}$$
$$B : \{20,30,40,50,60\}$$

Which of the the sets of integer values listed above has a lower standard deviation?

A) Set A
B) Set B
C) Set A and set B have the same standard deviation.
D) It *cannot* be determined.

15

A random sample of pH levels taken from 28 points around a lake returned a mean pH level of 8.2 and a standard deviation of 0.6. If every pH level in the sample were to be multiplied by 100 in order to be analyzed on a new scaling system, which of the following would be the values of the mean and the standard deviation in the modified sample?

A) Mean: 820, Standard Deviation: 0.6
B) Mean: 820, Standard Deviation: 6.0
C) Mean: 820, Standard Deviation: 60.0
D) Mean: 8.2, Standard Deviation: 60.0

16

A car is traveling at a constant rate of 62 miles per hour down a long winding road. The odometer shows that the car has traveled a total of 124 miles. If the actual straight-line distance between the car's starting point and end point is 1/2 of the total distance traveled, what is the car's average straight-line rate, in miles per hour, from the starting point to the end point?

A) 31
B) 62
C) 93
D) 124

CONTINUE

17

There are a 42 red jelly beans and 24 green jelly beans in a bowl. If an additional 24 green jelly beans are added to the bowl, how many red jelly beans must be removed in order for the ratio of red jelly beans to green jelly beans to be 1:3?

A) 18

B) 24

C) 26

D) 32

18

A jewelry store is offering a storewide discount of 40% off of all items. If Jennifer has a coupon for 10% off a single item and she receives an additional employee discount of 20% off, excluding tax, how many dollars will Jennifer pay for a necklace that is listed at G dollars?

A) $(.6)(.8)(.9)G$

B) $(.4)(.2)(.1)G$

C) $\dfrac{G}{(.6)(.8)(.9)}$

D) $\dfrac{G}{(.4)(.2)(.1)}$

19

12 ounces of fruit punch that has 5% natural juice is mixed with x ounces of fruit punch that is 100% natural juice to make a fruit punch that is 25% natural juice. What is the value of x?

A) 0.67

B) 1.5

C) 2.25

D) 3.2

20

A cube of model clay measures 8 inches in all directions. If an art teacher plans to give all 8 of her students an equal amount of clay, approximately how many cubic centimeters of clay will each student receive?

(1 inch = 2.54 centimeters)

A) 64

B) 104.9

C) 162.6

D) 1,049

164

CONTINUE

21

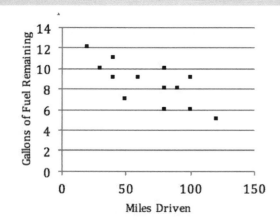

Which of the following equations which defines $G(x)$, the number of remaining gallons of fuel, in terms of x, the number of miles that have been driven, best fits the scatterplot above?

A) $G(x) = 14(.75)^x$

B) $G(x) = 7(.9)^x + 7$

C) $G(x) = -\dfrac{2}{75}x + 14$

D) $G(x) = -\dfrac{1}{25}x + 12$

22

A frisbee is thrown into the air from a height of 4 feet and it does not hit the ground for approximately 7 seconds. If the function $f(x)$ is used to estimate the height of the frisbee in feet, x seconds after it was released, which of the following could be $f(x)$?

A) $f(x) = -x^2 + 14x + 4$

B) $f(x) = -x^2 - 6x + 4$

C) $f(x) = (x-3)^2 + 4$

D) $f(x) = -(x-3)^2 + 13$

23

If the value of rare coin increases by $10 in every odd year and decreases by $2 in every even year, the coin's value will have which of the following associations with time?

A) Strong, positive, linear association

B) Weak, positive, linear association

C) Strong, linear asociation

D) Strong, negative, linear association

24

Two eight-year-old twin brothers were approached by their uncle, who offered them two gift options. He said that he would either put $100 every year on their birthday into each of their savings accounts to help them save for college, or deposit $1 in each account the first year and add double the amount every year until they left for college. Each brother chose a different option. Assuming that the brothers were originally ten years away from entering college, how much more money does the brother who chose the $1 option have than the brother who chose the $100 option?

A) $1,047

B) $100

C) $23

D) He has less money than his brother.

CONTINUE

Questions 25-26 refer to the following table.

	Coupe	Sedan	SUV	TOTAL
Finance	10	6	2	18
Lease	4	8	12	24
TOTAL	14	14	14	42

A survey group recently asked 14 coupe drivers, 14 sedan drivers, and 14 drivers of sports utility vehicles whether they finance or lease their vehicles. The responses are categorized in the table above.

25

Which of the following groups acounts for approximately 38% of all of the people surveyed?

A) Individuals who lease their cars

B) Individuals who finance their cars

C) Individuals who lease, but do not drive sedans

D) Individuals who finance, but do not drive sedans

26

If an individual who leases a vehicle is randomly selected from the surveyed group, what is the probability that they *do not* lease a sedan or a coupe?

A) $\dfrac{1}{21}$

B) $\dfrac{1}{9}$

C) $\dfrac{2}{7}$

D) $\dfrac{1}{2}$

27

In an effort to see what the public response would be to a potential increase in local taxes, a government employee randomly selected 40 town residents that attended a meeting of the town council and asked them to respond to a blind survey about their thoughts on the potential increased taxes. Which of the following factors is the most obvious reason as to why a usable conclusion *cannot* be drawn about the public's response to the potential tax increase?

A) The person who conducted the sample

B) The location of the survey

C) Size of the population

D) Size of the sample

28

If the average test score of a class of 12 students is 50% higher than the average test score of another class of 10 students, then the sum of the test scores in the higher class must be what percent higher than the sum of the test scores in the lower class?

A) 20

B) 80

C) 120

D) 180

CONTINUE

Questions 29-30 refer to the following information.

1420	1450	1450	1480	1490	1500
1510	1510	1510	1530	1550	1600

The final exam scores of 12 students who recently completed an SAT prep course are listed above.

29

The variable r represents the greater of the following two values: the range of the set of test scores if the lowest score is removed or the range of the set of test scores if the greatest score is removed. What is the value of $\frac{r}{2}$?

A) 65
B) 75
C) 150
D) 300

30

If every score in the set was divided by 100 and rounded to the nearest integer, which of the following would be true about the mean of the modified list?

A) $mean > 15$
B) $mean = 15$
C) $mean < 15$
D) The mean of the modified list *cannot* be determined.

CONTINUE

DIRECTIONS

For each question from 31-38, solve and enter your answer in the grid-in section of your answer sheet as described below.

A. Write out your answers in the boxes at the top of each column in order to help you fill in the circles accurately. Remember, you will only receive credit for the circles that are filled in correctly, not for the written answer at the top of the columns.

B. Mark only a single circle in each column.

C. There are no negative answers.

D. If the problem has more than one correct answer, grid only one of the correct answers.

E. When your answer is a **mixed number**, such as $1\frac{1}{2}$, it should be entered as 1.5 or $3/2$. You cannot enter a mixed number because there is no room to fill in a circle that represents a space.

F. If you enter a **decimal answer** with more digits then the grid can handle, the answer may be rounded or truncated, but it absolutely must fill the entire grid.

Answer: 102 - both positions are correct

REMEMBER:
You can begin writing your answers in any column as long as there is enough space. Leave unused columns blank.

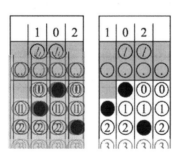

Answer: $\dfrac{8}{21}$ Answer: 6.4

Written answer →

Decimal point →

← Fraction line

The ways to correctly grid $\dfrac{7}{9}$ are:

CONTINUE

31

On a map every inch represents 48 miles. If two cities are exactly 204 miles apart, how many inches separate the two cities on the map?

32

$$(a \times 10\%) + (b \times 20\%) = (b \times 30\%)$$

What is the value of $\dfrac{a}{b}$?

33

Mary Beth has just finished decorating her holiday tree. There are a total of 210 ornaments on her tree and the ratio of blue ornaments to silver ornaments is 5:9. Mary Beth feels that the tree looks quite sparse and hopes that she can remedy the situation by adding more ornaments. If she adds 35 more blue ornaments, how many silver ornaments must she add to the tree in order to maintain the original ratio of blue ornaments to silver ornaments?

34

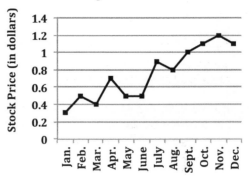

Change in Stock Price over One Year

The line graph above displays the price of a stock on the first of each month over the course of a single year. The approximate linear growth of the penny stock displayed in the graph above can be estimated by the equation $p(s) = 0.3 + 0.07s$ where s represents the number of months that have passed since January 1st and $p(s)$ represents the price of the stock in dollars. What is the absolute difference in dollars between the estimated price of the stock on the first of August and the actual price of the stock on the first of August?

CONTINUE

35

On a game show, two contestants are challenged in different ways. One contestant is given $2,470 to start, but $200 is removed for every ten seconds that the contestant takes to answer a challenge question. The other contestant is haging from a bar that is shaking and receives $10 to start. For every ten seconds that the contestant continues to hang on, this contestant receives double the amount of money earned for the previous ten seconds. For example, if the contestant hangs on the bar for ten seconds, he or she will receive $20 (double $10) for the ten seconds plus the initial $10 for a total of $30. After how many seconds have passed will both contestants have the same amount of prize money?

36

The average weight of 4 bags of thinset morter mix is 28 pounds. If one additional bag is included in the average, the average drops to 26 pounds. What is the weight, in pounds, of the additional bag?

Questions 37-38 refer to the following table.

	6th Grade	7th Grade	8th Grade	Total
Baseball	4	12	8	**24**
Basketball	2	6	10	**18**
Soccer	12	6	4	**22**
Tennis	0	4	6	**10**
Track	0	0	8	**8**
Total	**18**	**28**	**36**	**82**

Eighty-two randomly-selected middle school students were asked their grade level and which sport they preferred with baseball, basketball, soccer, tennis, and track as the options. The data was collected and organized in the two-way table above.

37

What percentage of the students who prefer tennis are in the 7th grade?

38

If a student from the survey that is *not* in 8th grade is randomly selected, what is the probability that the student *does not* prefer baseball, basketball, or soccer??

170

CONTINUE

UNIT 4

Unit 4: Passport to Advanced Math

The main goal of the new SAT is to hold students accountable for mathematics that they will likely see at the collegiate level and beyond. This Passport to Advanced Mathematics unit will discuss many of these extended topics. The most important topics covered will involve a student's ability to analyze, manipulate, and interpret expressions by having a complete understanding of the terms, factors, and coefficients that make up such challenging expressions. The topics will also involve higher-order reasoning skills and the ability to build and interpret functions of a complex nature. This understanding of the building blocks of expressions and of the reasoning skills required to build and interpret higher-order functions is the foundation of the IES "Passport to Advanced Math."

CONTINUE

31   *Creating* Quadratic and Exponential Functions

"Utilize the context of the problem to recall the common non-linear relationships with which you are familiar."

Often, you will be required to create, identify, or even solve a non-linear equation that can be used as a model for a particular contex. Remember the common contexts with which you are famliar from school:

A ball is thrown upward...(Parabolic, $ax^2 + bx + c$)
A bank account accrues interest...(Growth, $a(1+r)^t$)
The half-life of an isotope...(Decay, $a(1-r)^t$)

If you can identify the type of model quickly and are familiar with the structure of that model, you can isolate the correct answer with ease.

Example 1:

A rocket is fired upward from a starting height of 6 feet. The rocket rises, then descends and reaches 6 feet again after 10 seconds have passed. Which of the following equations could be used to model the rocket's height, h, as a function of the time in seconds, t, that has passed since the launch?

A) $h = 2^t + 5$
B) $h = 6 - 2^t$
C) $h = -t^2 + 10t + 6$
D) $h = -2t^2 + 25t + 6$

You know that the rocket is rising and falling over time, and this relationship is remniscent of an inverted parabola. You should thus look for a negative quadratic equation. This eliminates *A* and *B*. You also know that the rocket passes through the points (0,6) and (10,6). Plug these points in to see that the answer is _C_.

Example 2:

A rabbit population doubles every 45 days. If the initial population was 100 rabbits, what is the size of the population after 135 days?

Exponential: $P(t) = 100(2)^{\frac{t}{45}} = 100(2)^3 = 800$

Skill 31 Practice Exercises:

1

Billy has a baseball card collection and he claims that it doubles in size every year. If Billy's baseball card collection currently has 124 cards, which of the following expressions would yield the size of Billy's card collection in two years?

A) $2(124)^2$
B) $124(2)^2$
C) $2(2)^{124}$
D) $248(2)^2$

2

Mary Beth had a total of \$1,280 in a safe under her bed. She decided to take \$1,000 and place it into a savings account that earns 1% interest every year. Which of the following expressions represents the total amount of money in dollars that Mary Beth has *x* years after she opened the savings account?

A) $280(1.01)^x + 1,000$
B) $1,280(.01)^x$
C) $1,280(1.01)^x$
D) $1,000(1.01)^x + 280$

CONTINUE

3

A 500 kilogram log from a fallen tree decomposes at a rate of 50% every 10 years. How many kilograms of the original log remain after two decades have passed?

A) 0

B) 62.5

C) 125

D) 250

5

A petri dish currently contains 240 bacterial colonies. Each time the dish receives a single drop of an anti-bacterial solution, the number of colonies decreases by 25%. Which of the following equations best models the number of bacterial colonies, b, based upon the number of solution drops, t, that have been added to the dish?

A) $b = 240(.25)^t$

B) $b = 240(.75)^t$

C) $b = 240 - .25t$

D) $b = 240 - 25t$

4

A passing submarine makes contact with the chain that attaches a buoy to the ocean floor. The buoy becomes submerged under the water upon the submarine's initial contact with the chain and does not resurface for 6 seconds. If the buoy's vertical height with respect to the ocean's surface follows a parabolic model over time, which of the following equations could give H, the buoy's vertical height x seconds after the submarine struck the chain?

A) $H = (x-6)^2 - 10$

B) $H = -1(x-6)^2 - 12$

C) $H = x^2 - 6x$

D) $H = -x^2 + 36$

6

A catapult fires a boulder over the wall of a fortress. The height of the boulder, h, follows a parabolic model with respect to the time that has passed, t, in seconds. If the boulder was released from the catapult at a height of 10 feet and hit the ground inside the fortress after approximately 8 seconds had passed, which of the following models would best predict the height of the boulder at any time during its flight?

A) $h = t^2 - 8t + 10$

B) $h = -t^2 - 4t + 10$

C) $h = -t^2 + 8t + 10$

D) $h = -2t^2 + 15t + 10$

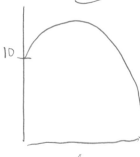

10

8 sec

174

CONTINUE

7

The value of a \$290,000 home increase by 5% every 4 years that pass. Which of the following equations gives that dollar value of the home, D, after x months have passed?

A) $D = 290,000(1.05)^{\frac{x}{48}}$

B) $D = 290,000(1.05)^{\frac{x}{4}}$

C) $D = 290,000(1.05)^{x}$

D) $D = 290,000(1.05)^{4x}$

8

At a certain time during the year, the sun first breaches the horizon in the east at exactly 6:00 am and sets on the horizon in the west at exactly 8:00 pm. If the height of the sun on an unknown vertical scale follows a quadratic model with respect to time in hours and if the quadratic model has a leading coefficient of -1, what is the height of the sun on the unknown vertical scale when it reaches its highest point in the sky?

$(x-6)(x-70)$

A) 49

B) 98

C) 196

D) 392

$x^2 - 20x - 6x + 126$

$x^2 - 26x + 120$

$-x^2 + 26x - 120$

$\frac{-26}{-2}$

$7($

Notes:

CONTINUE

32 | *Creating* Equivalent Expressions with Radicals or Rational Exponents

"Allow your answer choices to guide you toward creating radical expressions or expressions with rational exponents."

With Radicals:

1. Remember that $\sqrt{x}$ and $x^{\frac{1}{2}}$ are always interchangeable. As are $\sqrt[3]{x}$ and $x^{\frac{1}{3}}$, and so on...

2. If you have a radical in the denominator, you can rationalize the expression by multiplying the radical by itself.

With Rational Exponents:

1. The traditional exponent rules apply, whether you are dealing with a fraction or an integer.

2. Basic exponent rules:

$$x^a x^b = x^{a+b} \qquad (xyz)^a = x^a y^a z^a$$

$$\frac{x^a}{x^b} = x^{a-b} \qquad (\frac{x}{y})^a = \frac{x^a}{y^a}$$

$$(x^a)^b = x^{ab}$$

Example 1:

For all values of x, the expression $\dfrac{2x^2}{\sqrt{x}}$ *is equivalent to which of the following?*

A) $2x^2\sqrt{x}$

B) $2x\sqrt{x}$

C) $\dfrac{2\sqrt{x}}{x}$

D) $2x^3$

Your immediate reaction should be to rationalize the expression by eliminating the radical in the denominator. So, multiply the expression by $\frac{\sqrt{x}}{\sqrt{x}}$ **and see that the answer is _B_.**

$$\frac{2x^2}{\sqrt{x}} \bullet \frac{\sqrt{x}}{\sqrt{x}} = \frac{2x^2\sqrt{x}}{x} = 2x\sqrt{x}$$

Example 2:

Which of the following expressions is equivalent to

$$\frac{x^5}{x^{\frac{5}{2}}} \bullet \sqrt{x} \text{, for all values of x?}$$

A) x^{13}

B) x^5

C) x^3

D) x^2

If you look ahead and see that none of the answer choices have radicals, you should immediately convert the radical into exponent form and then carefully follow the exponent rules. The answer is _C_.

$$\frac{x^5}{x^{\frac{5}{2}}} \bullet \sqrt{x} = \frac{x^5}{x^{\frac{5}{2}}} \bullet x^{\frac{1}{2}} = x^{\frac{5}{2}} \bullet x^{\frac{1}{2}} = x^3$$

Example 3:

Which of the following is equivalent to $x^{\frac{3}{2}}$, *for all values of x?*

A) $\sqrt{x^{\frac{1}{2}}}$

B) $\sqrt[3]{x^{\frac{1}{2}}}$

C) $\sqrt[3]{x^2}$

D) $\sqrt{x^3}$

Here, the answer choices are mixed radical expressions. You need to convert toward radicals. The answer here is _D_.

$$x^{\frac{3}{2}} = (x^3)^{\frac{1}{2}} = \sqrt{x^3}$$

CONTINUE

Skill 32 Practice Exercises:

1

The expression $(x^{\frac{1}{16}} \bullet x^{\frac{1}{16}})^4$ is equivalent to which of the following, for all values of x?

A) x^4

B) x^2

C) $\sqrt[4]{x}$

D) $\sqrt{x}$

$\left(x^{\frac{2}{16}}\right)^4$

$\left(x^{-\frac{1}{2}}\right)$

2

The expression $\sqrt[3]{x^2} \bullet \sqrt{x^3}$ is equivalent to which of the following, for all values of x?

A) x

B) $x^{\frac{4}{3}}$

C) $x^{\frac{13}{6}}$

D) x^3

$x^{\frac{2}{3}} \bullet x^{\frac{3}{2}}$

$\frac{4}{6} \cdot \frac{9}{6}$

$\frac{13}{6}$

x

3

$$\frac{12x}{\sqrt{22x^2}}$$

Which of the following expressions is equivalent to the expression above for all positive values of x?

A) $\frac{6\sqrt{22}}{11}$

B) $\frac{6\sqrt{22x^2}}{11}$

C) $\frac{12\sqrt{22}}{11}$

D) $\frac{6x}{11}$

$\frac{12x}{\sqrt{22} \cdot x}$

$\frac{12\sqrt{22}}{22}$

$\frac{6\sqrt{22}}{11}$

4

$$\frac{x^3(x^2 \bullet x^5)^{-2}}{x^0 x^1 x^2 x^{-14}}$$

The expression above is equivalent to which of the following integers?

A) -1

B) 0

C) 1

D) 2

$\frac{x^3(x^7)^{-2} x^{14}}{x^3}$

$\frac{x^3(x^{-14})x^{14}}{x^3}$

x^0

CONTINUE

5

$$5x^2 \cdot \frac{4}{\sqrt{10x^2}} = a\sqrt{10x^2}$$

Given that the equation above shows equivalent forms of an expression, what is the value of a that makes the equation true for all values of x?

A) 2
B) 4
C) 5
D) 10

(handwritten work)
$5 \times \frac{4}{\sqrt{10}} = a \times \sqrt{10}$

$\frac{5 \cdot 4}{\sqrt{10}} = \frac{a\sqrt{10}}{\sqrt{10}}$

$\frac{5 \cdot 4}{\sqrt{10}} \left(\frac{1}{\sqrt{10}} \right)$

$\frac{5 \cdot 4}{10}$

6

$$\frac{x^2}{2\sqrt{x}} - \frac{6}{4\sqrt{x}} = \frac{1}{2\sqrt{x}}$$

The equation above has how many *real* solutions?

A) 0
B) 1
C) 2
D) Infinitely many

(handwritten work)
$\frac{x^{\frac{3}{2}}}{2} - \frac{3}{2x^{\frac{1}{2}}} = \frac{1}{2x^{\frac{1}{2}}}$

$\frac{x^{\frac{3}{2}}}{2} - \frac{4}{2x^{\frac{1}{2}}} = 0$

$\frac{x^2}{2x^{\frac{1}{2}}} -$

7

$$3^x + 3^x + 3^x = 81$$

The equation above is true for what value of x?

A) 1
B) $\frac{3}{2}$
C) 2
D) 3

8

If $121^x = 25b^2$, $11^x = 10bk$, and b is a constant, what value of k makes the system of equations true for all values of x?

A) 0
B) $\frac{1}{2}$
C) 1
D) 2

(handwritten work)
$11^{2x} = 25b^2 = 11^x = 10bk$

$100b^2k^2 = 25b^2$

$100k^2 = 25$

$k^2 = \frac{1}{4}$

178

CONTINUE

33   *Creating* Equivalent Forms of Expressions

"Creating equivalent forms of expressions only requires a strong knowledge of structure and comfort with order of operations"

When creating equivalent forms, you are asked to go with your instincts most of the time. For example, if you see two binomials being multiplied together, you will want to foil, and most likely, the equivalent expression you are looking for is just that.

Example 1:

$$5(2x+1)-(2x+3)$$

Which of the following is equivalent to the expression above?

A) $8x+2$
B) $8x-2$
C) $10x+2$
D) $12x+8$

Well, you want to distribute and combine like terms, so follow exactly these procedures:

$$5(2x+1)-(2x+3)$$
$$10x+5-2x-3$$
$$8x+2$$

The answer is *A*.

Example 2:

$$\frac{14x(x+3)}{7x}$$

What is an expression that is equivalent to the expression above?

$$\frac{14x(x+3)}{7x}=2(x+3)=2x+6$$

Skill 33 Practice Exercises:

1

The expression $(2x-1)+(1-2x)$ is equivalent to which of the following?

A) 0
B) 2
C) $4x$
D) $4x-2$

2

$$(xy-4x^2+2x^2y)-(xy+4x^2-2xy^2)$$

Which of the following is equivalent to the expression above?

$$-8x^2+2x^2y+2xy^2$$

A) $4x^2y$
B) $-8x^2+4x^2y$
C) $2x^2y-8x^2-2xy^2$
D) $2x^2y+2xy^2-8x^2$

CONTINUE

3

$$\frac{4(\frac{1}{4}x^2-1)}{(x+2)(x-2)}$$

Which of the following is equivalent to the expression above, given $x \neq -2$ and $x \neq 2$?

A) $\frac{x^2-1}{x^2-4}$

B) $\frac{x^2+4}{x^2-4}$

C) -1

D) 1

(handwritten: x^2-4 *,* $(x+2)(x-2)$ *,* $(x+2)(x-2)$ *)*

4

$$2x(x-7)(4x+1)$$

Which of the following is equivalent to the expression shown above?

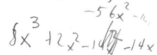

(handwritten: $(2x^2-14x)(4x+1)$ *,* $-56x^2-14$ *,* $8x^3+2x^2-14x-14x$ *)*

A) $8x^3-27x^2-7x$

B) $8x^3-54x^2-14x$

C) $8x^3-27x$

D) $8x^3-54x^2$

5

$$\frac{\left|\frac{2x(-x+1)}{5}\right| \bullet 8x(x-4)}{\left|\frac{2x(-x+1)}{5}\right|}$$

Which of the following expressions is equivalent to the expression above?

A) $\left|\frac{2x(-x+1)}{5}\right|^2 \bullet (8x^2-32x)$

B) $\frac{8x^2-32x}{\left|\frac{2x(-x+1)}{5}\right|^2}$

C) $8x^2-32x$

D) $8x^2-4$

6

$$36a^6-144b^6$$

Which of the following is equivalent to the expression shown above?

A) $(6a^2-12b^2)^3$

B) $(6a^3-12b^3)^2$

C) $(6a^3-12b^3)(6a^3+12b^3)$

D) $(6a^2-12b^2)(6a^2+12b^2)$

CONTINUE

7

$$y = 5x + 1$$

Which of the following is equivalent to the equation above for all values of x, where $x \neq -2$?

A) $y = \dfrac{15x^2 - 27x - 6}{3x + 6}$

B) $y = \dfrac{15x^2 + 33x + 6}{3x + 6}$

C) $y = \dfrac{5x - 1}{-1}$

D) $5y + x = 1$

(handwritten: $5x^2 - 9x - 2$ $5x + 1$ $x - 2$)

8

The equation $y - 3 = (3x + 1)(x - 2)$ can be written in which of the following equivalent forms?

A) $y = 3(x - \dfrac{5}{6})^2 - \dfrac{13}{12}$

B) $y = 3(x - \dfrac{5}{2})^2 + \dfrac{29}{4}$

C) $y = (3x + 1)(x - 1)$

D) $y = 3x^2 - 5x - 5$

(handwritten: $y - 3 = 3x^2 - 6x + x - 2$ $y - 3 = 3x^2 - 5x - 2$ $y = 3x^2 - 5x + 1$ $3(x^2 - \frac{5x}{3} + \frac{1}{3})$)

Notes:

CONTINUE

34   *Solving* Quadratic Equations

"If you can, always choose to factor first. However, remember that the quadratic formula always works."

When solving quadratic equations, manipulate the equation into standard form, attempt to factor, and, if all else fails, use the quadratic formula. Given $y = ax^2 + bx + c$ ...

The Quadratic Formula:

$$\frac{-b \pm \sqrt{b^2 - 4ac}}{2a}$$

If you'd like to know how many solutions a quadradic equation has, use the discriminant. If the discriminant is positive, there are 2 solutions, if it is 0, there is one solution, and if it is negative, there are no *real* solutions.

The Discriminant:

$$b^2 - 4ac$$

Example 1:

What is the lowest value of x that satisfies the equation $0 = 5 + x^2 + 6x$?

In this case, manipulate the equation into standard form, factor, find the roots, and choose the lowest root:

$$0 = x^2 + 6x + 5$$
$$0 = (x+5)(x+1)$$
$$x = -5 \text{ and } x = -1$$

The answer is $x = -5$.

Example 2:

The equation $y = 2x^2 + 4x + 1$ *has how many* real *solutions?*

In this case, use the discriminant:

$$b^2 - 4ac = (4)^2 - 4(2)(1)$$

$$16 - 8 = 8$$

Since the discriminant is positive, the quadratic equation has 2 *real* solutions.

Skill 34 Practice Exercises:

1

For what value of x does the equation $y = x^2 - 12x + 36$ have a y-value equal to 0?

A) 12

B) 6

C) 3

D) 1

2

$$0 = x^2 - 4x - 1$$

Which of the following values of x is a solution to the equation above?

A) $2 + \sqrt{5}$ $4 \pm \sqrt{16 + 4}$

B) $4 - \sqrt{5}$ $4 \pm \sqrt{20}$

C) -1 $4 \pm \sqrt{4}\sqrt{5}$

D) 1 $\dfrac{4 \pm 2\sqrt{5}}{2}$

$2 \pm \sqrt{5}$

CONTINUE

3

How many ordered pairs (x, y) satisfy the equation $0 = 4x^2 + 12x + 9$?

A) 0

B) 1

C) 2

D) Infinitely many

$$144 - 4(4)9$$

4

$$m(m-1) = 2(m+2)$$

What positive value of m makes the equation above true?

A) 1

B) 2

C) 3

D) 4

$$m^2 - n = 2m + 4$$

$$m^2 - 3m + -4 = 0$$

$$(m-4)(x+1) = 0$$

5

Which of the following is the x-coordinate of one of the x-intercepts of the equation $y = 2(x+5)(x-1) - 2$?

A) $-8 - \sqrt{10}$

B) $-8 - 2\sqrt{10}$

C) $-8 - 4\sqrt{10}$

D) $-2 - \sqrt{10}$

$$y = 2(x^2 + 4x - 5) - 2$$

$$y = 2x^2 + 8x - 10 - 2$$

$$y = 2x^2 + 8x - 12$$

$$x^2 + 4x - 6 \qquad 16$$
$$\qquad\qquad +24$$
$$64 - 4(6) \qquad 40$$

$$\frac{-8 \pm \sqrt{64 - 4(6)}}{2}$$

$$-4 \qquad \frac{-4 \pm \sqrt{64 \cdot 11 - 4(6}}{2}$$

$$\frac{-4 \pm \sqrt{40}}{2}$$

6

$$y = -2(x-4)^2 + 1$$

If $(a, 0)$ is the lower x-intercept of the quadratic equation given above, what is the value of a?

A) $4 + \sqrt{2}$

B) $4 - \sqrt{2}$

C) $4 - \dfrac{\sqrt{2}}{2}$

D) $4 + \dfrac{\sqrt{2}}{2}$

$$\sqrt{\tfrac{1}{2}}$$

$$\sqrt{\tfrac{1}{2}} = x - 4$$

$$4 +$$

183

CONTINUE

7

$$7 = (3x+1)(x+1)$$

How many ordered pairs (x, y) satisfy the equation shown above?

$7 = 3x^2 + 3/1x+1$

$0 = 3x^2 + 4x - 6$

$16 - 4(3)(-6)$

$16 + 12(6)$

$16 \uparrow$

A) 0

B) 1

C) 2

D) Infinitely many

8

$$0 = 2(x - \frac{1}{2})^2 + \frac{5}{2}$$

How many ordered pairs (x, y) satisfy the equation shown above?

A) 0

B) 1

C) 2

D) Infinitely many

Notes:

184

CONTINUE

35   *Completing* the Square

"When a situation arises where you need to complete a square, remember to half the constant and square the result. Also, remember whatever you add into an expression or an equation must be accounted for as to not change the overall value of the expression or equation."

Throughout the math section of the new SAT, there are multiple instances where completing the square is the most efficient route and sometimes the only route to attaining an answer. Let's look at some examples of completing the square:

Example 1:

Find the value of x *by completing the square:*

$$x^2 + 6x = 7$$

$$x^2 + 6x + \underline{\quad} = 7 + \underline{\quad}$$

Complete the square by halfing the coefficient in front of the x and squaring the result. Then add the result to both sides of the equation so that it remains balanced...

$$x^2 + 6x + \underline{9} = 7 + \underline{9}$$

$$\downarrow \quad \uparrow \quad \nearrow$$

$$3 \to 9$$

$$(x+3)^2 = 16 \quad \to \quad \sqrt{(x+3)^2} = \sqrt{16} \quad \to \quad x+3 = \pm 4$$

Therefore, $x = 1$ or $x = -7$.

Example 2:

If the equation of a circle defined by the equation $x^2 + 2x + y^2 = 3$ *were converted to the form* $(x-h)^2 + y^2 = r^2$, *what is the radius of the circle?*

$$x^2 + 2x + \underline{\quad} + y^2 = 3 + \underline{\quad} \quad \to \quad (x+1)^2 + y^2 = 4$$

$$\downarrow \quad \uparrow \qquad \nearrow$$

$$1 \to 1 \qquad 1$$

Therefore, $r = 2$.

1

$$x^2 + 8x = 0$$

If the equation above were to be solved by completing the square, what negative value of x would make the equation true?

A) -16
B) -8
C) -4
D) -2

2

$$y = x^2 - 20x$$

If the equation above were to be converted to the form $y = (x-a)^2 + b$, where a and b are integer constants, what would be the value of a?

$$\frac{20}{2}$$

A) -100
B) 5
C) 10
D) 100

CONTINUE

3

If one were to complete the square in the expression $x^2 + hx$ which would result in the expression $(x+b)^2$, which of the following equations gives b in terms of h?

A) $b = \dfrac{h}{2}$

B) $b = (\dfrac{h}{2})^2$

C) $b = h$

D) $b = h^2$

$x^2 + hx = x^2 + 2xb + b^2$

4

$$x^2 - 4x + 2 = (x-a)^2 - 2$$

What positive value of a makes the equation above true for all values of x?

A) 2

B) 4

C) 8

D) 16

$x^2 - 4x + 2 = x^2 - 2ax + a^2 + -2$

$-4x + 4 = -2ax + a^2$

5

If the vertex form of a quadratic equation is $y = (x-h)^2 + k$, where h and k are constants, what is the vertex form of the equation $y = x^2 + 3x + 1$?

A) $y = (x-3)^2 + 10$

B) $y = (x+3)^2 + 10$

C) $y = (x+\dfrac{3}{2})^2 + \dfrac{13}{4}$

D) $y = (x+\dfrac{3}{2})^2 - \dfrac{5}{4}$

$y - (x^2 + 3x + \dfrac{9}{4}) + 1 - \dfrac{9}{4}$

$y = (x + \dfrac{3}{2})^2$

6

$$x^2 + y^2 + 8y = -15$$

If the equation of the circle above is written in the form $x^2 + (y+b)^2 = r^2$, where b and r are both positive integer constants, what is the value of the expression $b+r$?

A) 1

B) 4

C) 5

D) 9

$x^2 + y^2 + 8y + 16 = 1$

$x^2 + (y+4)^2 = 1$

186

CONTINUE

7

Which of the following equivalent forms of the equation $y = x^2 - 11x + 18$ contains the coordinates of the vertex as constants in the equation?

A) $y = (x+9)(x+2)$

B) $y = (x-9)(x-2)$

C) $y = (x-11)^2 - 103$

D) $y = (x - \frac{11}{2})^2 - \frac{49}{4}$

8

$$4x^2 + 8x + 4y^2 + 8y = -4$$

What is the area of the circle defined by the equation above?

$$4(x^2 + 2x + 1) + 4(y^2 + 2y + 1) = 4$$
$$4(x+1)^2 + 4(y+1)^2 = 4$$

A) $\frac{\pi}{4}$

B) π

C) 4π

D) The area cannot be determined.

Notes:

CONTINUE

36   *Creating* Equivalent Forms to Reveal Particular Traits

"Creating equivalent forms to reveal particular traits is as simple as knowing all forms of a particular equation type and what those forms reveal."

Certain questions will ask you to manipulate an expression or an equation to reveal a particular trait in the context of the problem. In most cases, this can be as simple as converting an equation from one form to another. For example, a queston may require a linear function in standard form, $Ax + By = C$, be converted to slope-intercept form, $y = mx + b$, to reveal the slope, m.

Example 1:
$$y - 2 = 4(x - 1)$$
The linear equation above can be rewritten in an equivalent form where the y-intercept appears as a constant in the equation. What is this new form of the equation?

Since the question request a linear equation in a form where the *y*-intercept appears as a constant, one must convert the existing form to slope intercept form, y = mx + b :

$$y - 2 = 4(x - 1)$$
$$y - 2 = 4x - 4$$
$$y = 4x - 2$$

The *y*-intercept is (0, -2).

Example 2:
The equation $y = x^2 - 6x + 8$ can be rewritten in what equivalent form in which the coordinates of the vertex of the parabola appear as constants in the equation?

Quite simply, one must convert from the standard form of a quadratic equation to the vertex form of a quadratic equation by completing the square:

$$y = x^2 - 6x + \_\_ + 8 \ \rightarrow \ y = (x^2 - 6x + 9) + 8 - 9 \ \rightarrow$$
$$y = (x^2 - 6x + 9) - 1 \ \rightarrow \ y = (x - 3)^2 - 1$$

The vertex of the equation is (3, -1).

Skill 36 Practice Exercises:

1

$$2y - x = 12$$

The linear equation above can be rewritten into which of the following forms in which the slope of the line appears as a coefficient in the equation?

A) $x - 2y = -12$

B) $x = 2y - 12$

C) $y = \dfrac{1}{2}x + 6$

D) $2y = x + 12$

2

The equation $y + 1 = 2(x + 1)$ can be written in which of the following equivalent forms in which the *y*-intercept and the slope of the line appear as a constant and a coefficient in the equation?

A) $y = 2x$

B) $y = 2x + 1$

C) $y = 2x + 3$

D) $y - 2x = 1$

CONTINUE

3

$$y = 152(1.08)^{\frac{x}{40}}$$

Which of the following equations is equivalent to the equation above and has the growth percentage of the quantity, which grows by 8% every 40 days, appear as a constant within the equation?

B) $y = 152(\frac{8}{100})^{\frac{x}{40}}$

A) $y = 152(1 + \frac{8}{100})^{x}$

C) $y = 152(1 + \frac{8}{100})^{\frac{x}{40}}$

D) $y = 152(1 + .08)^{\frac{x}{40}}$

4

The equation $y = 587(.65)^{x}$ can be rewritten in which of the following forms where the rate of decay appears as a decimal constant within the equation?

A) $y = 587(1 - .35)^{x}$
B) $y = 587 + (1 - .35)^{x}$
C) $y = (587 - 587(.35))^{x}$
D) $y = 587 - 587(.35)^{x}$

5

Which of the following is an equivalent form of the equation $y = x^2 + 4x - 12$ in which the coordinates of the vertex appear as constants in the equation?

A) $y = (x + 4)^2 - 4x - 28$

B) $y = (x + 2)^2 - 16$

C) $y = (x + 6)(x - 2)$

D) $y = -(x + 6)(-x + 2)$

6

Which of the following is an equivalent form of the equation $y = 2x^2 + 10x - 72$ in which the most basic form of the two binomial factors of the quadratic equation appear in the equation?

A) $y = 2(x + \frac{5}{2})^2 - \frac{169}{2}$

B) $y = 2(x^2 + 5x - 36)$

C) $y = -2(-x - 9)(x - 4)$

D) $y = 2(x + 9)(x - 4)$

CONTINUE

7

$$y + x = (2x+5)(x+4)$$

Which of the following is an equivalent form of the quadratic equation above in which the coordinates of the vertex appear as constants in the equation?

$y+x = 2x^2 + 8x + 26x + 20$

A) $y = 2(x+3)^2 + 2$

B) $y = 2(x+3)^2 + 20$ $y = 2x^2 + 27x + 26$

C) $y = 2x^2 + 12x + 20$

D) $y = 2(x^2 + 6x + 10)$

8

The equation $8x - 3y = 24$ can be written in which of the following equivalent forms where the x-intercept appears as a constant in the equation?

A) $y = \dfrac{3}{8}x - 8$

B) $y = \dfrac{8}{3}x - 8$

C) $x = \dfrac{3}{8}y + 8$

D) $x = \dfrac{3}{8}y + 3$

Notes:

CONTINUE

37 Adding, Subtracting, and Multiplying Polynomial Expressions

"Don't forget to distribute carefully and to combine like terms."

Although the higher order of certain polynomials can be intimidating, adding, subtracting, and multiplying polynomials is as easy as solving equations without any variables at all.

Example 1:

$$(10x^2 + 2x - 6) + (x^3 - 10x^2)$$

What expression is equivalent to the sum of the polynomials given above?

$$(10x^2 + 2x - 6) + (x^3 - 10x^2)$$
$$10x^2 + 2x - 6 + x^3 - 10x^2$$
$$x^3 + 10x^2 - 10x^2 + 2x - 6$$

$$x^3 + 2x - 6$$

Example 2:

$$3x(2x - 3)(3x - 1)$$

What expression is equivalent to the product of the polynomials given above?

$$3x(2x - 3)(3x - 1)$$
$$3x(6x^2 - 11x + 3)$$

$$18x^3 - 33x^2 + 9x$$

Skill 37 Practice Exercises:

1

If the sum of $x^2 + 13$ and $9x - 11$ is written in the form $ax^2 + bx + c$, what is the value of c?

A) -2
B) 2
C) 9
D) 24

2

$$-2(x - 7) - (-4 + x)$$

Which of the following expressions is equivalent to the difference of the polynomials given above?

A) $-3x + 18$
B) $-3x + 10$
C) $-x + 10$
D) $-x - 11$

$-2x + 14 + 4 - x$

$-3x + 18$

CONTINUE

3

$$(xy^2 - x^2y) - (5xy - 3xy^2)$$

Which of the following is equivalent to the expression shown above?

$xy^2 - x^2y - 5xy + 3xy^2$

$4xy^2 - x^2y - 5xy$

A) $-4xy^2 + 2x^2y$

B) $4xy^2 - 6x^2y$

C) $xy^2 - 5xy + 2x^2y$

D) $4xy^2 - 5xy - x^2y$

4

$2x^2y - 2xy^2$

$$(2xy^2 + 3xy + 4x^2y) + (-2x^2y - 3xy - 4xy^2)$$

Which of the following expressions is equivalent to the sum of the polynomials shown above?

$2xy^2 + 3xy + 9$

A) $-2xy^2 + 6xy + 2x^2y$

B) $-2xy^2 + 2x^2y$

C) $2xy^2 - 2x^2y$

D) 0

5

$-2x$

$$(3x + 3) + (2x - x^2) + (3x^2 - 2) + (-2x^2 - 5x)$$

Which of the following is equivalent to the expression above?

A) $-x$

B) $1 - x$

C) 0

D) 1

6

$$(x^2 + x + 1)(x^2 + x + 2)$$

Which of the following expressions is equivalent to the product of the polynomials given above?

A) $2x^2 + 2x + 3$

B) $x^4 + x^2 + 2$

C) $x^4 + 2x^3 + 4x^2 + 3x + 2$

D) $x^4 + 2x^3 + 3x^2 + 2x + 2$

192

CONTINUE

7

$$\frac{2x^3 - 8x + 15x^2 - 11}{2} - \frac{8 - 9x - 10x^2 + 11x^3}{4}$$

Which of the following is equivalent to the expression above?

$4x^3 - 16x + 30x^2 - 11 - 8 + 9x + 10x^2 - 11x^3$

$-7x^3$

A) $\dfrac{-7x^3 + 40x^2 - 7x - 30}{4}$

B) $\dfrac{-7x^3 + 25x^2 + x - 30}{4}$

C) $\dfrac{-9x^3 + 25x^2 + x - 19}{4}$

D) $\dfrac{-4x^3 - 7x^2 + 40x - 33}{4}$

8

$$(2x^3 - 8x)(x - 11x^2)(-2 - x^3)$$

Which of the following is equivalent to the expression above?

A) $22x^8 - 2x^7 - 88x^6 + 44x^5 - 4x^4 - 176x^3 + 16x^2 + 8x$

B) $22x^8 - 2x^7 - 88x^6 + 44x^5 - 4x^4 - 176x^3 + 16x^2$

C) $22x^8 - 2x^7 - 88x^6 + 52x^5 - 4x^4 - 176x^3 + 16x^2$

D) $22x^8 - 2x^7 - 88x^6 + 52x^5 - 4x^4 - 160x^2$

$2x^4 - 22x^5 - 8x^2 + 88x^3$

$(-22x^5 + 2x^4 + 88x^3 - 8x^2)(-2 - x^3)$

$44x^5 - 4x^4 - 176x^3 + 16x^2 + 8x^5$

$22x^8 - 2x^7 - 88x^6 + 8x^4$

Notes:

CONTINUE

38 *Solving* Radical and Rational Equations in One Variable

"You can eliminate radicals by squaring and rationalize by multiplying by the LCM of the denominator. However, don't forget to make sure your answers make sense in light of the original equation."

Solving Radical and Rational Equations is not as difficult as it may appear, so long as you immediately eliminate anything in an equation that makes you uncomfortable.

1. If you see radicals, then square both sides of the equation. Suddenly your radicals vanish.

2. If you need to rationalize an equation, multiply by the LCM of the denominator. Suddenly your fractions disappear.

However, keep an eye out for **extraneous solutions...**

Extraneous Solutions:

At times, when you square radicals to eliminate them or rationalize an equation, you end up with solutions that, when placed back into the original equation, yield answers that do not make any sense or do not exist. For instance, if you are solving a radical equation and end up with a solution that is negative, when you plug that solution back into the original equation it creates an imaginary number. Be aware of these solutions, because the new SAT may require you to identify such extraneous solutions.

Example 1:
Solve the following: $x - 2 = \sqrt{x}$

$$(x-2)^2 = (\sqrt{x})^2$$
$$x^2 - 4x + 4 = x$$
$$x^2 - 5x + 4 = 0$$
$$(x-4)(x-1) = 0$$

The answers are $x = 4$ and $x = 1$. However, $\underline{4}$ is the only solution since 1 is extraneous. Check it.

Example 2:

$$\frac{3}{2x} + \frac{5}{x} = 6.5$$

The equation above is true for which of the following values of x?

A) 1
B) 2
C) 3
D) 4

Your initial reaction should be that you don't want to deal with fractions. So, eliminate them. Find the LCM of the denominator (which is 2x in this case), multiply everything by that LCM, and solve:

$$2x(\frac{3}{2x} + \frac{5}{x} = 6.5)$$
$$\frac{6x}{2x} + \frac{10x}{x} = 13x$$
$$3 + 10 = 13x$$
$$1 = x$$

The answer is $\underline{A}$.

Example 3:
Solve the following for x: $\frac{1}{\sqrt{8x}} = x$

Well, you have a fraction and a radical. Start by eliminating the fraction and then square to get rid of the radical:

$$\sqrt{8x}(\frac{1}{\sqrt{8x}} = x)$$
$$1 = x\sqrt{8x}$$
$$(1)^2 = (x\sqrt{8x})^2$$
$$1 = 8x^3$$
$$\frac{1}{8} = x^3$$
$$\sqrt[3]{\frac{1}{8}} = \sqrt[3]{x^3}$$
$$\frac{1}{2} = x$$

CONTINUE

Skill 38 Practice Exercises:

$$\frac{1}{x}+\frac{1}{x}=1$$

Which of the following is the only value of x that makes the equation above true?

A) 2

B) 1

C) $\frac{1}{2}$

D) $\frac{1}{4}$

2

For what positive value of x is $\sqrt{x}$ equivalent to $2x$?

A) 0

B) $\frac{1}{4}$

C) $\frac{1}{2}$

D) 1

3

Given the equation $\sqrt{x+2}=x$, what value of x is an extraneous solution?

A) 2

B) 1

C) -1

D) -2

$$x+2=x^2$$

$$0=x^2-x-2$$

$$(x-2)(x+1)$$

$$2 \quad , -1$$

4

$$x-6=\sqrt{x}$$

Which of the following gives all values of x that make the equation above true?

A) 3

B) 4

C) 9

D) 4 and 9

CONTINUE

5

If $\dfrac{30}{4x+32} = \dfrac{3}{2x}$, what is the value of $\dfrac{2x}{3}$?

A) $\dfrac{2}{3}$

B) $\dfrac{4}{3}$

C) 3

D) 6

$60x = 12x + 96$

$48x = 96$

$x = 2$

7

What is the solution set to the equation $\sqrt{x} = \sqrt{x^2 - 6}$?

A) $\{-6,1\}$

B) $\{-2,3\}$

C) $\{-2\}$

D) $\{3\}$

$x = x^2 - 6$

$0 = x^2 - x - 6$

$0 = (x-3)(x+2)$

$x = \tilde{?}$

6

$$x - b = \sqrt{x+3}$$

If $b = 3$, what is the solution set of the equation shown above?

A) $\{6\}$

B) $\{3\}$

C) $\{1\}$

D) $\{1,6\}$

$x - 3 = \sqrt{x+3}$

$x^2 - 6x + 9 = x + 3$

$x^2 - 7x + 6 = 0$

$(x-6)(x-1)$

8

If $x \neq 4$ and $x \neq 5$, what value of x makes the equation
$$\dfrac{3}{\dfrac{1}{x-5} + \dfrac{1}{x-4}} = x^2 - 9x + 20 \text{ true?}$$

A) 1

B) 2

C) 3

D) 6

$\dfrac{3(x-5)(x-4)}{x-4 + x-5}$

$\dfrac{3(x-5)(x-4)}{2x-9} = x^2 - 9x + 10$

$3(x-5)(x-1)$

$3 = 2x - 9$

$12 = 2$

CONTINUE

Mid-Unit 4 Review - No Calculator
25 MINUTES, 20 QUESTIONS

DIRECTIONS

For each question from 1-15, choose the best answer choice provided in the multiple choice bank and fill in the appropriate circle in the provided answer key. Alternatively, for questions **16-20**, answer the problem and enter your answer in the grid-in section of the answer key. Refer to the directions given before question 16 as to how to enter your answers for the grid-in questions. You may complete scratch work in any empty space in your test booklet.

NOTES

A. Calculator usage **is not allowed** in this section.
B. Variables, constants, and coefficients used represent real numbers unless indicated otherwise.
C. All figures are created to appropriate scale unless the question states otherwise.
D. All figures are two-dimensional unless the question states otherwise.
E. The domain of any given function is all real numbers x for which the function, $f(x)$, is a real number unless the question states otherwise.

REFERENCE

$A = \pi r^2$
$C = 2\pi r$

$A = lw$

$A = \frac{1}{2}bh$

$c^2 = a^2 + b^2$

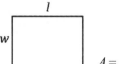
Special Right Triangle

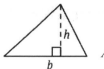
Special Right Triangle

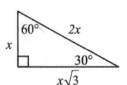
$V = lwh$

$V = \pi r^2 h$

$V = \frac{4}{3}\pi r^3$

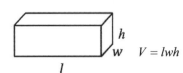
$V = \frac{1}{3}\pi r^2 h$

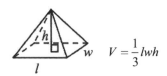
$V = \frac{1}{3}lwh$

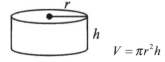

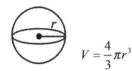

There are $360°$ in a circle.
There are 2π radians in a circle.
There are $180°$ in a triangle.

CONTINUE ➡

1

James bought an old indoor/outdoor table radio for $180 in 1990. Since then, the value of the radio decreased by 10% every year. If James decided to sell the radio at a garage sale for $10 less than its value, 10 years after its purchase, which of the following expressions would yield the final selling price of the radio at the garage sale?

A) $10 - 180(.1)^{10}$

B) $10 - 180(.9)^{10}$

C) $180 - 10(.9)^{10}$

D) $180(.9)^{10} - 10$

$180(.90)^x$

$180(.9)^{10} - 10$

2

The linear equation $-9x + 3y = 54$ can be written in which of the following forms in which the y-intercept of the line appears as a constant in the equation?

A) $y = -3x + 17$

B) $y = 3x + 17$

C) $y = \dfrac{1}{3}x + 18$

D) $y = 3x + 18$

3

$$\dfrac{\sqrt{x^3}}{\sqrt[3]{x}\sqrt[3]{x}}$$

For $x > 0$, the expression above is equivalent to which of the following?

A) $x^{\frac{5}{6}}$

B) $x^{\frac{25}{18}}$

C) x

D) 1

4

$$(4x^2y^2 - 9xy^2 + 3x^2y) - 3x(xy - 2y^2)$$

Which of the following expressions is equivalent to the difference of the polynomials shown above?

A) $4x^2y^2 - 9xy^2 - 2y^2$

B) $4x^2y^2 - 15xy^2$

C) $4x^2y^2 - 3xy^2$

D) $x^2y^2 - 3xy^2 + 3x^2y$

$4x^2y^2 - 9xy^2 + 3x^2y - 3x^2y + 6xy^2$

$4x^2y^2 - 3xy^2$

198

CONTINUE

5

What integer value of x satisfies the equation
$0 = 4x^2 - 19x - 5$?

A) 1

B) 2

C) 4

D) 5 ⟵ (circled)

7

$$y = x^2 - 8x + 2$$

If the equation above were to be written in the form
$y = (x - a)^2 + b$ where a and b are constants, which of the
following would be equivalent to b?

A) −18

B) −14 ⟵ (circled)

C) 14

D) 18

(handwritten: $y = x^2 - 8x + 15 - 14$)

(handwritten: $y = (x - 4)^2 - 14$)

6

$$16a^4 - 24a^2b^2 + 9b^4$$

Which of the following is equivalent to the expression
shown above?

A) $(4a^2 - 3b^2)^2$ ⟵ (circled)

B) $(4a^2 + 3b^2)^2$

C) $(4a^2 + 3b^2)(4a^2 - 3b^2)$

D) $(8a^2 - 9b^2)(2a^2 - b^2)$

8

In an ultimate frisbee match, a frisbee is thrown from one
player to another and its height in feet, h, with respect
to the time that has passed in seconds since its release,
t, follows a parabolic model. If the frisbee was released
from a height of 5 feet and reached its peak height after
4 seconds had passed, which of the following quadratic
equations best models the height of the frisbee over time?

A) $h = \dfrac{1}{2}x^2 - 4x + 5$

(handwritten: 4)

B) $h = -2x^2 + 8x + 5$ ⟵ (circled)

(handwritten: 6)

C) $h = -\dfrac{1}{4}x^2 + 2x + 5$

D) $h = -\dfrac{1}{2}x^2 + 4x$

CONTINUE ➡

9

$$y = 0.65(0.85)^x$$

The equation above can be rewritten in which of the following forms where the decay percentage appears as constant within the equation?

A) $y = 0.65(1 - 0.15)^x$

B) $y = (1 - 0.35)(0.85)^x$

C) $y = \frac{65}{100}\left(\frac{15}{100}\right)^x$

D) $y = \frac{65}{100}\left(1 - \frac{15}{100}\right)^x$

10

$$\frac{-1}{\sqrt{2x}} + \frac{x}{3} = \frac{-3 + \sqrt{2}}{3\sqrt{2x}}$$

What positive value of x makes the equation above true?

A) 1
B) 2
C) 4
D) 8

11

$$5x^2(4x^2 - 3x)(2x - 1)$$

Which of the following is equivalent to the expression shown above?

A) $40x^5 - 20x^4 - 6x^2 + 3x$

B) $40x^5 - 50x^4 + 15x^3$

C) $200x^7 - 150x^6 - 20x^4 + 15x^3$

D) $200x^7 - 250x^6 + 75x^5$

12

The vertex form of a quadratic equation is $y = 2(x - 3)^2 - 6$. Which of the following is a root of the equation?

A) $-3 - \sqrt{3}$

B) $3 + \sqrt{3}$

C) $12 + \sqrt{3}$

D) $12 - 4\sqrt{3}$

CONTINUE

13

If one were to complete the square in the expression $a^2 - 5a$ which would result in an expression in the form $(a-b)^2$, the value of b would be equivalent to which of the following?

A) $-\dfrac{25}{4}$

B) $-\dfrac{5}{2}$

C) $\dfrac{5}{2}$

D) $\dfrac{25}{4}$

14

$$\frac{x-9}{\dfrac{1}{x+1}+\dfrac{1}{x-1}} = 2x^2 - 2$$

What value of x makes the equation above true?

A) -6

B) -3

C) 3

D) 6

(handwritten work:)
$$\frac{x-9(x+1)(x-1)}{2x} = 2(x^2-1)$$
$$x - 9 = 4x$$
$$-9 = 3x$$
$$x = -7$$

15

Which of the following is an equivalent form of the equation $y = \dfrac{1}{3}x^2 + x + 6$ in which the coordinates of the vertex appear as constants in the equation?

A) $y = \dfrac{1}{3}(x+3)^2 + 6$

B) $y = \dfrac{1}{3}(x+3)^2 - 3$

C) $y = \dfrac{1}{3}(x+\dfrac{3}{2})^2 + \dfrac{21}{4}$

D) $y = \dfrac{1}{3}(x+2)(x+1)$

(handwritten work:)
$$\frac{1}{3}\left(x^2 + 3x + 18\right)$$
$$\frac{1}{3}\left(x^2 + 3x + \frac{9}{4}\right) + 18 - \frac{9}{4})$$

CONTINUE

DIRECTIONS

For each question from 16-20, solve and enter your answer in the grid-in section of your answer sheet as described below.

A. Write out your answers in the boxes at the top of each column in order to help you fill in the circles accurately. Remember, you will only receive credit for the circles that are filled in correctly, not for the written answer at the top of the columns.

B. Mark only a single circle in each column.

C. There are no negative answers.

D. If the problem has more than one correct answer, grid only one of the correct answers.

E. When your answer is a **mixed number**, such as $1\frac{1}{2}$, it should be entered as 1.5 or $3/2$. You cannot enter a mixed number because there is no room to fill in a circle that represents a space.

F. If you enter a **decimal answer** with more digits then the grid can handle, the answer may be rounded or truncated, but it absolutely must fill the entire grid.

Answer: $\frac{8}{21}$ Answer: 6.4

Written answer →
Decimal point →
← Fraction line

The ways to correctly grid $\frac{7}{9}$ are:

Answer: 102 - both positions are correct

REMEMBER:
You can begin writing your answers in any column as long as there is enough space. Leave unused columns blank.

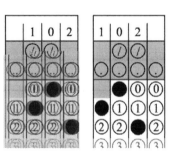

CONTINUE →

16

$$\frac{4x^2}{\sqrt{2x}}$$

The expression above can be written in the form $ax\sqrt{2x}$. What is the value of a?

$$\frac{4x^2\sqrt{2x}}{2x}$$

$$2x\sqrt{2x}$$

②

17

$$\frac{(-x^2+x)-(3-x^2)}{7x-21}$$

The expression above can be simplified to what value, given $x \neq 3$?

$-x^2+x-3+x^2$

$x+3$

$7(x-3)$

$\boxed{\frac{1}{7}}$

18

The sum of the expressions $-2x^2+3$ and $-7x^2-5x+12$ can be written in the form ax^2+bx+c. What is the sum of a, b, and c?

$-9 \quad -5 \quad 15$

①

19

$$4-x = \sqrt{k+x}$$

If $k = 68$, the equation above is true for $x = -p$. What is the value of p?

$4+p = \sqrt{68-p}$

$16+8p+p^2 = 68-p$

$p^2+7p-52 = 0$

68
-16
52

-13

203

CONTINUE

20

$$\frac{1}{2}\left(x-\frac{1}{4}\right)^2 = \frac{3}{2}x^2 + \frac{3}{64}$$

The equation above is true for how many *real* values of x?

$$\frac{1}{2}\left(x^2 - \frac{1}{2}x - \frac{1}{16}\right) = \frac{3}{2}x^2 + \frac{3}{64}$$

$$\frac{1}{2}x^2 - \frac{1}{4}x - \frac{1}{32} = \frac{3}{2}x^2 + \frac{3}{64}$$

$$x^2 + \frac{1}{4}x \neq \frac{5}{64}$$

$$\frac{-\frac{1}{4}}{2}$$

$$-\frac{1}{4}$$

CONTINUE

39   *Solving* Mixed Systems

"Just set the equations equal to each other."

Solving any system of equations is as simple as finding a point of intersection. This can be accomplished by setting the equations equal to each other and solving, regardless of the equation type. Also remember, if the question asks for the number of solutions, use the discriminant.

Example 1:

$$y = 3x - 1$$
$$y = x^2 - 11$$

What positive value of x is a solution to the system of equations given above?

$$3x - 1 = x^2 - 11$$
$$0 = x^2 - 3x - 10$$
$$0 = (x - 5)(x + 2)$$
$$x = 5 \text{ and } x = -2$$

The positive value of x is 5.

Example 2:

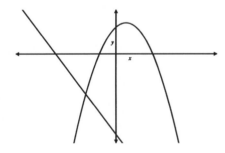

The equations $y = -3x - 9$ and $y = -2x^2 + 2x + 3$ are graphed in the xy-plane above. The two equations reach their minimum point of intersection at what value of x?

$$-3x - 9 = -2x^2 + 2x + 3$$
$$2x^2 - 5x - 12 = 0$$
$$(2x + 3)(x - 4) = 0$$
$$x = -\tfrac{3}{2} \text{ and } x = 4$$

The minimum point of intersection occurs at 4.

Skill 39 Practice Exercises:

1

What is the lowest value of x at which the line $y = 5$ intersects the function $y = (x - 6)(x - 2)$?

A) 0
B) 1
C) 4
D) 7

(handwritten):
$$5 = x^2 - 8x + 12$$
$$0 = x^2 - 8x + 7$$
$$0 = (x - 7)(x - 1)$$

2

For what positive value of x does $f(x) = g(x)$ when $f(x) = -x^2 + 64$ and $g(x) = -3x + 10$?

A) 0
B) 3
C) 6
D) 9

(handwritten):
$$-x^2 + 64 = -3x + 10$$
$$0 = x^2 - 3x - 54$$

CONTINUE

3

The line $y = \dfrac{5}{2}$ intersects the quadratic function $y = x^2$ at the x-values a and b. What is the sum of a and b?

A) -5

$-1.58113\,4$

B) $-\dfrac{5}{2}$

C) 0

D) 5

4

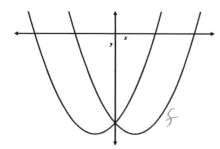

f

The functions $f(x) = x^2 - 2x - 8$ and $g(x) = x^2 + 2x - 8$ are graphed in the xy-plane above. What is the value of $f(x)$ at the x-value where $f(x) = g(x)$?

A) -8 $(x-4)(x+2)$

B) -4

C) -2

D) 0

5

$$y = 5x + 3$$
$$y = x^2 - 3x + 19$$

How many ordered pairs (x, y) satisfy the system of equations shown above?

A) 0

B) 1

C) 2

D) Infinitely many

$y - 76$

$x^2 - 8x + 16$

$64 - 4$

6

$$y = 3x - 5$$
$$y = 2x^2 - 5x + 3$$

If the ordered pair (x, y) is the only solution to the system of equations above, what is the value of x?

A) 8 $2x^2 - 8x\,18$

B) 7

C) 4

D) 2

$x^2 - 4x + 4$

206

CONTINUE

7

$$x = \frac{1}{2}y + 9$$
$$y = 3(x-7)(x-8)$$

How many ordered pairs (x, y) satisfy the system of equations shown above?

A) 0

B) 1

C) 2

D) Infinitely many

(handwritten work)
$$x - 9 = \frac{1}{2}y$$
$$2x - 18 = y$$
$$2x - 18 = 3(x^2 - 15x + 56)$$
$$2x - 18 = 3x^2 - 45x + 168$$
$$0 = 3x^2 - 47x + 186$$

8

If the line $y = -\frac{1}{2}x + \frac{3}{2}$ intersects the parabola

$y = x^2 + \frac{1}{2}x - \frac{9}{2}$ at the points A and B, what is the average

of the y-values of points A and B?

A) -1

B) $-\frac{1}{2}$

C) $\frac{7}{4}$

D) $\frac{7}{2}$

(handwritten) 3

Notes:

CONTINUE

40   *Simplifying* Rational Expressions and Polynomial Expressions

"For rational expressions and polynomials, all of the basic rules of adding, subtracting, multiplying, and dividing still apply, such as using common denominators, distributing, and canceling."

Adding and Subtracting:

Regardless of variable type, when adding or subtracting, one can efficiently reach a simplified expression by cross-multiplying, adding or subtracting, and combining like terms to create the numerator and multiplying across to create the denominator. (*See Example 1.*)

Multiplying:

When multiplying with rational expressions, your basic rules of distribution still apply.

Dividing:

When you are dividing, particularly with polynomial expressions, your first instinct should be to factor and cancel common expressions. However, sometimes it is difficult to factor, and you should understand how to apply long division to polynomials or how to use synthetic division when necessary.

Example 1:

Simplify the following expression: $\dfrac{5}{x} - \dfrac{1}{x+3}$

Just remember to cross multiply, subtract, and combine like terms for the numerator, and to multiply across for the denominator:

$\dfrac{5}{x} \searrow \dfrac{1}{x+3}$ yields $5(x+3)$.

$\dfrac{5}{x} \nearrow \dfrac{1}{x+3}$ yields x.

$x \rightarrow x+3$ yields $x(x+3)$.

$\dfrac{5}{x} - \dfrac{1}{x+3} = \dfrac{5(x+3)-x}{x(x+3)}$

$\dfrac{5(x+3)-x}{x(x+3)} \quad \rightarrow \quad \dfrac{4x+15}{x^2+3x}$

Example 2:

Simplify the following: $(x^3 + 3x^2 + 3x + 1) \div (x+1)$

For this example, using long division to solve:

$$x+1\overline{)x^3 + 3x^2 + 3x + 1}$$

$$
\begin{array}{r}
x^2 + 2x + 1 \\
x+1{\overline{)x^3 + 3x^2 + 3x + 1}} \\
-(x^3 + x^2) \\
\hline
2x^2 + 3x \\
-(2x^2 + 2x) \\
\hline
x + 1 \\
-(x+1) \\
\hline
0
\end{array}
$$

The answer is $x^2 + 2x + 1$.

Alternately, using synthetic division to solve:

$$(x^3 + 3x^2 + 3x + 1) \div (x+1)$$

Remember to use the root of the dividing factor...

$$
\begin{array}{r|rrrr}
-1 & 1 & 3 & 3 & 1 \\
& & & & \\
\hline
& & & &
\end{array}
$$

$$
\begin{array}{r|rrrr}
-1 & 1 & 3 & 3 & 1 \\
& & -1 & -2 & -1 \\
\hline
& 1 & 2 & 1 & 0
\end{array}
$$

1, 2, and 1 are the values of a, b, and c in the standard form of a quadratic: $y = ax^2 + bx + c$

The remainder is the last number on the end. In this case, there is no remainder.

Therefore, the answer is $x^2 + 2x + 1$.

CONTINUE ➔

Skill 40 Practice Exercises:

1

$$\frac{x}{3} - \frac{3}{x}$$

Which of the following expressions is equivalent to the expression above?

A) $\dfrac{x^2 - 3}{3x}$

B) $\dfrac{x - 9}{3x}$

C) $\dfrac{x^2 - 9}{9x}$

D) $\dfrac{(x+3)(x-3)}{3x}$

(handwritten work) $\dfrac{x^2}{3x} - \dfrac{9}{3x}$ $\dfrac{x^2 - 4}{3x}$

2

$$\frac{x^2 - 3x - 28}{x - 7}$$

Which of the following expressions is equivalent to the expression above, given $x \neq 7$?

A) $x + 4$

B) $x - 4$

C) $x + 7$

D) $\dfrac{(x+7)(x-4)}{x-7}$

(handwritten work) $x - 7 \,(x + 4)$

3

$$\frac{6}{x+1} + \frac{2}{x-1}$$

Which of the following expressions is equivalent to the expression above?

A) $\dfrac{4x - 6}{x^2 - 1}$

B) $\dfrac{4x - 4}{x^2 - 1}$

C) $\dfrac{8x - 6}{x^2 - 1}$

D) $\dfrac{8x - 4}{x^2 - 1}$

(handwritten work) $\dfrac{6x - 6 + 2x + 2}{x^2 - 1}$ -4 $8x - 4$

4

$$x - 5 \overline{\smash{)}\, x^3 - 8x^2 + 19x - 20}$$

Which of the following expressions is equivalent to the expression above?

A) $x^2 + 3x + 2$

B) $x^2 + 4x - 3$

C) $x^2 - 3x + 4$

D) $x^2 - 4x - 5$

(handwritten work)
$5 \,|\, 1 \quad -8 \quad 19 \quad -20$
$ \quad 5 \quad -15 \quad 20$
$1 \quad -3 \quad 4 \quad 0$

$x^2 - 3x + 4$

CONTINUE

5

The expression $\dfrac{-8x-7}{x+1}$ is equivalent to which of the following?

A) $-8-\dfrac{15}{x+1}$

B) $-8+\dfrac{1}{x+1}$

C) $-8+\dfrac{15}{x+1}$

D) -15

(handwritten: $x^4+x^3-13x^2-26x-8=$)

6

If $x>0$, which of the following is equivalent to

$\dfrac{15x+36}{\dfrac{2}{x+2}+\dfrac{3}{x+3}}$?

A) $3x^2+15x+18$

B) $5x^2+25x+30$

C) $\dfrac{3}{x^2+5x+6}$

D) $\dfrac{3(x^2+5x+6)}{5x+12}$

(handwritten: $(x+2)(x+3)$ $15x+36$ / $2(x+3)+3(x+2)$ / $2x+6+3x+6$ / $5x+12$ / $3(x+2)(x+3)$ / $3(x^2$)

7

$$x^2+3x+1\overline{)x^4+x^3-13x^2-26x-8}$$

If the remainder of the quotient above is written in the form $\dfrac{b}{x^2+3x+1}$, what is the value of b?

A) -16

B) 0

C) $-22x-8$

D) $32x+12$

(handwritten long division: x^2-2x+1 over $x^2+3x+1\overline{)x^4+x^3-13x^2-26x-8}$; $x^4+3x^3+x^2$; $-2x^3-14x^2-26x$; $-2x^3-6x^2-2x$; $-8x^2-24x-8$; $8x^2+24x+8$; $x-16$)

8

$$\frac{8x^2+16x-3}{kx+3}=4x+2-\frac{9}{kx+3}$$

The equation above is true for all values of x where $x\neq-\dfrac{3}{k}$ and k is a constant. What is the value of k?

A) -4

B) -2

C) 2

D) 4

(handwritten: $(4x+2)(kx+3)-9$ / $4kx^2+12x+2kx+6-9$ / $12+2k=16$ / $k=2$)

CONTINUE

41 — Interpreting Non-Linear Expressions or Equations

"When interpreting non-linear expressions or equations, pay close attention to the context of the problem and recall the meanings of variables and constants in that form."

Non-Linear Forms:

Quadratic:

$ax^2 + bx + c$, where a is the vertical stretch, $-\frac{b}{2a}$ defines the x-coordinate of the vertex, and c represents the y-intercept.

Exponential Growth:

$a(1+r)^t$, where a is the initial value, r is the growth rate, and t represents the number of times the growth factor occurs.

Exponential Decay:

$a(1-r)^t$, where a is the initial value, r is the decay rate, and t represents the number of times the decay factor occurs.

Example:

Angela opened a savings account with $2,300 and the value of her account closely follows the expression $2,300(1.02)^y$, where y represents the number of years that have passed since she initially opened the account. Which of the following can we conclude?

A) Angela's account value increases by $2,300 per year.
B) Angela's account value increases by .02% per year.
C) Angela's account value increases by 2% per year.
D) Angela's account value will double within 10 years.

The expression that represents Angela's savings account value follows an exponential growth model. Since the rate is .02 over 1, you know that the account is growing by .02 or 2% per year.

The correct answer is _C_.

Skill 41 Practice Exercises:

1

$$-x^2 + 4x + 5$$

A young girl tosses a stone into the air, and the stone's height can be calculated from the expression above, where x represents the number of seconds that have passed since the stone was thrown. What does the constant 5 represent in the context of this situation?

A) The amount of time it takes the stone to hit the ground after it has been thrown

B) The amount of time it takes the stone to rise and descend to the original height from which it was thrown

C) The maximum height that the stone reaches while in flight

D) The initial height from which the stone left the girl's hand

2

Helina opened a bank account that accrues 3 percent interest compounded annually. She initially opened the account with $350, and uses the expression $350(a)^t$ to find the value of the account t years after the initial deposit. What is value of a in the expression?

A) 1.03
B) 1.3
C) 2.3
D) 4

CONTINUE

3

Denise bought a laptop computer with a built in tablet for a final sale price of $1,295(1-p)(1.07)$ dollars. If the computer was originally \$1,295 and Denise paid 7% sales tax, what is the most likely meaning of the variable p in the expression?

A) The number of dollars that Denise saved below the computer's list price

B) The percentage of discount that Denise received off the list price of the computer

C) The percentage discount out of 100 that Denise received off the list price of the computer

D) The percentage of the computer that Denise paid for

4

$$p(t) = 5,000(0.95)^t$$

The population in the city of Saundersburg was 5 million people in the year 2000. The population has been diminishing since then and can be calculated using the equation above, where t represents the number of years that have passed since the year 2000. Which of the following statements is true?

A) The population of Saundersburg diminishes by 95% per year.

B) $p(t)$ represents the number of people residing in Saundersburg, in thousands, t years after the year 2000.

C) The population of Saundersburg will reach half its size in 2000 within 5 years.

D) The population of Saundersburg decreases by 0.5% per year.

5

Resha throws a ball into the air and the height of the ball in feet, $h(x)$, x seconds after it has left her hand is given by the equation $h(x) = -2(x-3)^2 + 25$. What is the meaning of the constant 25 in the equation?

A) The ball starts at an initial height of 25 feet.

B) The ball is in the air for 25 seconds.

C) The ball reaches its maximum height after 25 seconds have passed.

D) The ball reaches a maximum height of 25 feet.

6

$$p(x) = 8(2)^{\frac{x}{4}} + 102$$

The equation above is used to calculate the size of a population of rabbits that doubles every 4 months, x months from January 1st, 2010. Which of the following statements is correct about the initial population of rabbits on January 1st, 2010?

A) The initial population was 8 rabbits.

B) The initial population was 102 rabbits.

C) The initial population was 110 rabbits.

D) The initial population was 116 rabbits.

CONTINUE

7

The remaining mass in grams of an 850 gram sample of a radioactive isotope t years after it was initially weighed can be calculated using the equation $M_t = 850(1 - \frac{1}{2})^{\frac{t}{52}}$. What is the meaning of the expression $1 - \frac{1}{2}$ within the equation?

A) The fraction of the isotope that remains after $\frac{t}{52}$ years

B) The fraction of the isotope that has decayed after t years

C) The percentage of the isotope that remains after $\frac{t}{52}$ years

D) The percentage of the isotope that has decayed after t years

8

In the last orbit of a hammer throw, before the ball is released, the ball's height in feet, $h(x)$, with respect to time in deciseconds, x, is given by the equation $h(x) = 4(x - 1.5)^2 + 0.5$. What do the constants 1.5 and 0.5 represent in the equation?

A) The time and height of the ball, respectively, at the highest point in its orbit

B) The time and height of the ball, respectively, at the lowest point in its orbit

C) The height and time of the ball, respectively, at the highest point in its orbit

D) The height and time of the ball, respectively, at the lowest point in its orbit

Notes:

CONTINUE

42 — *Understanding* Zeros and the Factors of Polynomials

"**Always remember that the zeros, or roots, of polynomials are *x*-intercepts. So, if *b* is a root of a polynomial, when *b* is put into the polynomial, the output will be zero.**"

Some important things to note:

1. Zeros, or roots, of polynomials are *x*-intercepts.

2. Knowing how to factor and foil interchangeably and knowing your special cases of factoring are important. For example, if you know that $(x-b)$ is the only factor of a quadratic equation, you also know that the quadratic equation follows the form $x^2 - 2bx + b^2$.

3. If an *x*-value of *b* gives a *y*-value of zero when input into a polynomial, then $(x-b)$ is a factor of the polynomial

4. If an *x*-value of *b* gives a *y*-value that is not zero when input into a polynomial, then $(x-b)$ is a factor that has a remainder of the returned *y*-value.

Example 1:

If we know that $(x+2)$ is the only factor of the quadratic expression $x^2 + mx + m$, what is the value of m?

Recognize the special case and proceed...

$$x^2 + mx + m = (x+2)(x+2) = x^2 + 4x + 4$$

You can see that *m* is equal to 4.

Example 2:

If we know that $f(2) = 4$, what do we know about the factor $(x-2)$ in regards to the polynomial defined by $f(x)$?

If $(x-2)$ were a factor of the polynomial, it would have given 0. So, since it returns a *y*-value of 4, you know that if you divide $f(x)$ by $(x-2)$, you will get a remainder of 4.

Skill 42 Practice Exercises:

1

If we are given the quadratic equation $y = 2x^2 + bx + c$ and we know that $(2x+1)$ is one of the factors of the equation, which of the following could be the other factor if *c* is equal to 7?

A) $x+7$

B) $4x+7$

C) $x+3$

D) $x-7$

2

If $p(5) = 0$ and $p(x)$ is a quadratic equation, which of the following is a factor of $p(x)$?

A) $x+5$

B) x

C) $x-5$

D) $5x$

214

CONTINUE

3

x	0	3	6	7	9
$G(x)$	-12	-5	0	3	4

The function G is defined by a polynomial. The table above displays some values of x and $G(x)$. Which of the following must be a factor of $G(x)$?

A) $x-12$
B) $x-6$
C) $x+5$
D) $x+12$

4

$$(x+2)(x+4) = x^2 + abx + 8$$

If a and b are positive integers which of the following could *not* be the value of b?

A) 1
B) 2
C) 3
D) 4

5

For a polynomial $m(x)$, the value of $m(2)$ is 3. Which of the following must be true about $m(x)$?

A) $x+5$ is a factor of $m(x)$.
B) $x+3$ is a factor of $m(x)$.
C) $x-3$ is a factor of $m(x)$.
D) The remainder when $m(x)$ is divided by $x-2$ is 3.

6

$$(x+a)(x+b) = x^2 + cx + 12$$

If a, b, and c are positive integers, which of the following could be the value of c?

A) 4
B) 6
C) 7
D) 9

215

CONTINUE

7

x	-4	-2	0	2	4
$H(x)$	-8	0	1	0	1

The function H, presented in the table above, is defined by a polynomial. Which of the following must be a factor of the polynomial?

A) $x^2 - 4$

B) x

C) $x + 6$

D) $x + 8$

8

The polynomial $f(x)$ has only positive constants and coefficients and it intersects the x-axis at only one point. If $f(-5) = 0$, which of the following must be true about $f(x)$?

A) $x - 5$ is the only binomial factor of $f(x)$

B) $x + 5$ is the only binomial factor of $f(x)$

C) $x - 5$ and $x + 5$ are both factors of $f(x)$

D) None of the above *must* be true.

Notes:

_____

_____

_____

_____

_____

_____

_____

_____

_____

_____

_____

_____

CONTINUE

43 *Identifying* Non-Linear Equations and Their Graphs

"When you are dealing with non-linear equations and their graphs or characteristics, it is most important to have a strong understanding of those characteristics, both algebraic and graphical."

Quadratic Equations:

1. Have parabolic shapes.
2. Are symmetric about their vertices.
3. May or may not have x-intercepts.
4. In the form $y = ax^2 + bx + c$, a represents the vertical stretch. If a is greater than one, the graph appears narrow, and if a is less than one, the graph appears wider. If a is negative, the graph is inverted. c is the y-intercept of the graph. $-\frac{b}{2a}$ is the x-coordinate of the vertex.
5. In the form $y = a(x-h)^2 + k$, a represents the vertical stretch. If a is greater than one, the graph appears narrow, and if a is less than one, the graph appears wide. (h,k) is the vertex of the parabola.

Exponential Equations:

1. Follow curved shapes, but never turn back on themselves.
2. Do *not* have x-intercepts unless translated downward.
3. In the form $y = ab^x$, a represents the y-intercept, or initial value. b is the growth or decay factor. If b is greater than one, the graph will curve upward and continually get steeper and steeper, but will never reach 90 degrees. If b is less than one, the graph will decrease less and less steeply from left to right, but will never reach 0.

\

Example 1:

The graph of a particular function crosses the x-axis at the points $(2,0)$ and $(4,0)$. It reaches a minimum value at the point $(3,-1)$. Which of the following equations is represented by this graph?

A) $y = -1(x-3)^2 + 1$
B) $y = (x-3)^2 + 1$
C) $y = x^2 - 6x + 8$
D) $y = x^2 + 6x + 8$

Since the graph has two x-intercepts and a minimum value located between them, the graph is a parabola that is opening upward. This eliminates choice A. The roots are $(2,0)$ and $(4,0)$, so the factors must be $(x-2)$ and $(x-4)$. If you multiply these factors, <u>C</u> becomes the clear answer.

Example 2:

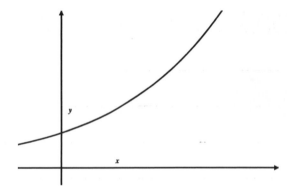

Which of the following equations could be graphed in the xy-plane above?

A) $y = x^2$
B) $y = x^3$
C) $y = 0.5^x$
D) $y = 1.5^x$

As you can see from the graph, the function rises from left to right and never turns back on itself. These are the characteristics of an exponential growth function. The only exponential growth equation given in the answer choices is <u>D</u>.

CONTINUE

Skill 43 Practice Exercises:

1

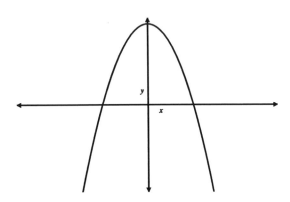

Which of the following equations has most likely been graphed in the *xy*-plane above?

A) $y = 25 - x^2$

B) $y = -x^2$

C) $y = -x^2 + 2x + 3$

D) $y = 2(0.5)^x$

2

Carly created a scatterplot marking her savings account balance for every week that had passed since she opened the account. She noticed that her account balance started at $2,000 and soon after decreased substantially. However, as she became more and more aware of her spending, she spent less and less money each week. Which of the following could be a best-fit model for Carly's savings account balance, $f(x)$, given the number of weeks that have passed, x, since she opened the account?

A) $y = 2,000(1.02)^x$

B) $y = 2,000(0.85)^x$

C) $y = 2,000 - 150x$

D) $y = 2,000 - 2x^2$

3

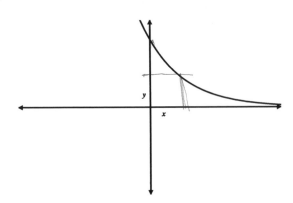

Given that the *x* and *y*-axes both share the same scale, which of the following equations has most likely been graphed on the *xy*-plane above?

A) $y = 3(0.5)^x$

B) $y = 3(0.99)^x$

C) $y = -3(0.99)^x$

D) $y = -3(0.5)^x$

4

While inspecting the points in a scatterplot, a statistics student took note of three points that closely followed the center of the data's trend. The three points that he recorded were $(2,153)$, $(3,51)$, and $(4,17)$. If the student were to calculate a best fit model for the data, which of the following constants would most likely appear in the equation?

A) 3

B) 1

C) $\frac{1}{2}$

D) $\frac{1}{3}$

CONTINUE

5

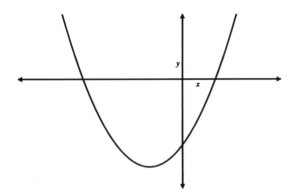

Given the graph is *not* drawn to scale, which of the following quadratic functions could be graphed in the *xy*-plane above?

A) $y = x^2 - 6x + 8$
B) $y = x^2 - 2x - 8$
C) $y = x^2 + 2x - 8$
D) $y = x^2 + 6x + 8$

6

An engineer graphed the height of a pendulum over time and noticed that the pendulum attained a height of 6 feet twice in its first pass, at 1.2 seconds and again at 3.4 seconds. If the engineer were to calculate a quadratic equation in vertex form that approximates the height of the pendulum in feet over time in seconds during the pendulum's first pass, which of the following constants would appear in the equation?

A) 1.2
B) 2.3
C) 3.4
D) 6

7

Which of the following types of equations has the characteristic where in the first quadrant of the *xy*-plane its slope continually increases from left to right?

A) Linear equation with a positive slope
B) Exponential growth equation
C) Exponential decay equation
D) Both B and C

8

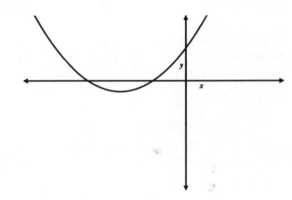

Given the graph is *not* drawn to scale, which of the following quadratic functions could be graphed in the *xy*-plane above?

A) $y = x^2 - 6x + 8$
B) $y = -\dfrac{1}{2}x^2 - 6x - 8$
C) $y = 2x^2 + 16x + 24$
D) $y = \dfrac{1}{2}x^2 - 4x + 6$

$(y-4)(x-2)$

219

CONTINUE

44   *Working* with Function Notation

"If you are given a rule, $f(x)$, remember that $f(a) = b$ tells you two things."

Working with function notation algebraically:

When working with function notation, you have to have a clear understanding that what is inside the parenthesis is the input, and whatever $f(x)$ equals is the output.

When $f(x)$ is defined, you can consider it a rule. For example, $f(x) = 2x + 3$ would be considered a rule in which you take the input value, x, multiply it by 2, and then add 3. So, if the question states that $f(a) = 5$, you know two things: $f(a) = 5$ and $f(a) = 2a + 3$. You thus know the value of $f(a)$ and know what a returns when it is plugged into the rule. This is important to remember because you can substitute 5 for $f(a)$ and continue to solve. Also, remember that your input, a, can be an entire expression, even one defined by another function notation. You can consider this "composition."

Working with function notation graphically:

Remember your shifting rules with function notation. When you add or subtract *outside* of the function, the graph shifts *vertically* and moves *exactly* as the change implies. When you add or subtract *inside* of the function, the graph shifts *horizontally* and moves *opposite* to what the change implies. Also, make sure that you can identify the minimum and maximum x and y-values of a graphed function. For example, if a maximum occurs at $f(2) = 7$, the x-value is 2 and the value of $f(x)$, the y-value, is 7.

Example 1:

If $f(x) = x + 3$ and we know that $f(b + 2) = 8$, what is the value of b?

Remember that $f(b + 2)$ tells you two things:

$$f(b + 2) = 8 \text{ and } f(b + 2) = (b + 2) + 3$$

Substituting:
$$8 = (b + 2) + 3$$
$$8 = b + 5$$
$$3 = b$$

Example 2:

If $g(x) = x^2$ and $f(x) = 5x - 10$, which of the following equations, $h(x)$, is equivalent to $g(f(x))$?

A) $h(x) = 25x^2 - 100x + 100$
B) $h(x) = x^2 - 4x + 4$
C) $h(x) = 5x^2 - 10$
D) $h(x) = 5x^2 - 100$

You are looking for $g(f(x))$, which means that you want to put the $f(x)$ function inside of the $g(x)$ function as if it were an input:

$$g(x) = x^2$$
$$f(x) = 5x - 10$$
$$g(f(x)) = (5x - 10)^2$$

$$g(f(x)) = 25x^2 - 100x + 100$$

The correct answer is $\underline{A}$.

Example 3:

If the function $f(x)$ were to be modified to become $f(x + 3) - 2$, which of the following best describes the translations that would affect its graph?

A)   *Right 3, Down 2*
B)   *Left 3, Down 2*
C)   *Right 2, Up 3*
D)   *Left 2, Up 3*

The rule states that the outside change is *vertical* and *exactly* as it implies: Down 2. The inside change is *horizontal* and *opposite* to what it implies: Left 3.

The answer is Left 3, Down 2, which is $\underline{B}$.

CONTINUE

Skill 44 Practice Exercises:

1

If $h(x) = 5 - x^2$ and $h(a) = 1$, what is the value of $2a$ if a is a positive integer?

A) 1
B) 2
C) 4
D) 8

2

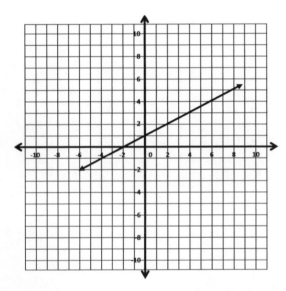

The function $f(x)$ is graphed in the xy-plane above. If $h(x) = f(x+1) - 3$, which of the following quadrants contain all of the coordinate solutions to the function $h(x)$?

A) III only
B) I and III
C) I, II, and III
D) I, III, and IV

3

If $a(x) = \sqrt{x}$ and $b(x) = x^2 + 6x + 9$, which of the following expressions is equivalent to $a(b(x))$?

A) $x + 6\sqrt{x} + 9$

$x + 3$

B) $x + \sqrt{6x} + 3$

C) $x + 3$

D) $\sqrt{x^2 + 6x} + 3$

4

If $m(x) = x^2 - 4$ and $m(k+1) = 0$, what is the positive value of k that satisfies the equation?

A) 1
B) 2
C) 3
D) 4

221

CONTINUE

5

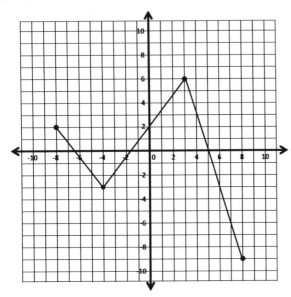

The complete graph of the function g is shown in the xy-plane above. For what value of x is the value of $g(x)$ at its maximum?

A) -4

B) 3

C) 5

D) 8

6

If $h(x) = -5x + 7$, which of the following is equivalent to $h(-3x + 1)$?

A) $15x^2 - 5x + 7$

B) $15x + 2$

C) $-15x + 2$

D) $-15x + 8$

$15x - 5 + 7$

$15 + 2$

7

$$c(x) = 12 + bx^2$$

For the function c defined above, $c(8) = 44$ and b is a constant. What is the value of $c(2)$?

A) 14

B) 16

C) 20

D) 24

8

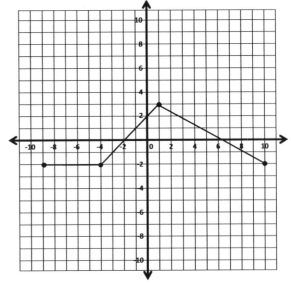

The complete graph of the function f is shown in the xy-plane above. Which of the following are equivalent to -2?

    I. $f(-7)$

    II. $f(-4)$

    III. $f(10)$

A) I only

B) I and II only

C) II and III only

D) I, II, and III

CONTINUE

45 — *Isolating* a Variable

"**You can always utilize simple variables to represent large expressions in order to make a complicated equation easy to work with.**"

Isolating a variable seems like an easy enough task. So, why is it covered in the Passport to Advanced Math unit? Well, occassionally the SAT will ask you to isolate a variable in an incredibly complicated equation. This can seem like a daunting task, but pay attention to the large expressions. Often times, you will be multiplying by or dividing by these large expressions, in which case you can substitute simple variables for the large expressions and manipulate the equation in a more basic form.

Example:

$$Q = \frac{\left|\frac{x^2 - 20}{\sqrt{x}}\right| - F}{\left|\frac{2x - 12}{x^2 - 4x - 12}\right|}$$

Given the equation above, what is the value of F in terms of Q and x?

The equation appears to be complicated, but you only need to solve for F, which is already somewhat isolated on the right hand side. If you use some variables to represent the larger expressions, you can solve for F much more easily:

$$A = \left|\frac{x^2 - 20}{\sqrt{x}}\right|$$

$$B = \left|\frac{2x - 12}{x^2 - 4x - 12}\right|$$

So, $Q = \dfrac{A - F}{B}$ and therefore $-QB + A = F$

The answer is...

$$-Q\left|\frac{2x - 12}{x^2 - 4x - 12}\right| + \left|\frac{x^2 - 20}{\sqrt{x}}\right| = F$$

1

The line $y = mx + b$, where m and b are constants, contains the point (a, c). If a and c do not equal 0, what is the slope of the line in terms of a, b, and c?

A) $\dfrac{b - c}{a}$

B) $\dfrac{b - a}{c}$

C) $\dfrac{a - b}{c}$

D) $\dfrac{c - b}{a}$

$(0, b)$

(a, c)

$\dfrac{b - c}{a}$

2

$$F = \left(\frac{4\pi df}{c}\right)^2$$

The free space path loss of a radio signal, F, can be calculated from d, the distance from the receiver to the transmitter, f, the frequency of the radio signal, and c, the speed of light in a vacuum. Which of the following gives the speed of light in a vacuum in terms of F, d, and f?

A) $c = \dfrac{4\pi df}{F^2}$

B) $c = \dfrac{4\pi df}{\sqrt{F}}$

C) $c = \sqrt{\dfrac{4\pi df}{F^2}}$

D) $c = \sqrt{\dfrac{4\pi df}{F^2}}$

$c^2 = \dfrac{4\pi^2 d^2 f^2}{F}$

223

CONTINUE

3

The equation $B = I(1+r)^t$ gives the balance of a savings account, B, that accrues $100r$ % interest each year, t years after the account was opened with an initial deposit of I dollars. Which of the following gives r in terms of B, I, and t?

A) $r = \sqrt[t]{\dfrac{B}{I}} - 1$

B) $r = \dfrac{\sqrt[t]{\dfrac{B}{I}} - 1}{100}$

C) $r = (\dfrac{B}{I})^t - 1$

D) $r = \dfrac{(\dfrac{B}{I})^t - 1}{100}$

Handwritten work:
$\dfrac{B}{I} = (1+r)^t$
$\dfrac{B}{I} = \#$
$\log_{1+r} \dfrac{B}{I} = \#$
$\log \dfrac{B}{I} = T \log(1+r)$
$\dfrac{1}{t} \log \dfrac{B}{I} = \log(1+r)$
$\log(\dfrac{B}{I})^{\frac{1}{t}}$
$(\dfrac{B}{I})^{\frac{1}{t}} - 1 = r$

4

$$\frac{M}{(2s+5)} = \frac{\sqrt{x+1} \bullet (x^2+8)}{T}$$

Which of the following equations gives T in terms of M, s, and x?

Handwritten: $TM =$

A) $T = \dfrac{\sqrt{x+1} \bullet (x^2+8)}{M(2s+5)}$

B) $T = M(2s+5) \bullet \sqrt{x+1} \bullet (x^2+8)$

C) $T = \dfrac{(2s+5) \bullet \sqrt{x+1} \bullet (x^2+8)}{M}$

D) $T = \dfrac{M(2s+5)}{\sqrt{x+1} \bullet (x^2+8)}$

5

$$\frac{H}{x^2+5x+4} = \sqrt{\frac{x^3-8}{L}} \bullet B$$

Which of the following equations gives L in terms of H, B, and x?

A) $L = \dfrac{(x^2+5x+4)(x^3-8)B}{H}$

B) $L = \dfrac{HB}{(x^2+5x+4)(x^3-8)}$

C) $L = \dfrac{(x^3-8) \bullet B}{(x^2+5x+4)^2 \bullet H^2}$

D) $L = \dfrac{(x^2+5x+4)^2 \bullet (x^3-8) \bullet B^2}{H^2}$

6

$$E = \frac{S}{S+U}$$

At a parts manufacturer, an employee's efficiency rating, E, can be calculated based on the number of working parts he produces, S, and the number of non-working parts he produces, U. Which of the following expresses the number of working parts the employee produces in terms of the other variables?

A) $S = \dfrac{U}{E-1}$

B) $S = \dfrac{U}{1-E}$

C) $S = \dfrac{EU}{1-E}$

D) $S = \dfrac{EU}{E-1}$

Handwritten work:
$SE + UE = S$
$SE - S + UE = 0$
$S(E-1) = -UE$
$S = \dfrac{-UE}{E-1}$

224

CONTINUE

7

$$y = (a-6)(b-2)$$

If the equation above is a quadratic equation in factored form in which $a = b$, which of the following gives the lowest root of the equation in terms of the other variables?

A) $b = 2 - \dfrac{y}{a-6}$

B) $b = \dfrac{y}{a-6} + 2$

C) $a = \dfrac{y}{b-2} - 6$

D) $a = \dfrac{y}{b-2} + 6$

8

$$y = a(x-h)^2 + k$$

The equation above is the vertex form of a quadratic equation. Which of the following gives the x-coordinate of the vertex in terms of the other variables, given $x > h$?

A) $h = x - \sqrt{\dfrac{y-k}{a}}$

B) $h = \sqrt{\dfrac{y-k}{a}} - x$

C) $k = a(x-h)^2 - y$

D) $k = y - a(x-h)^2$

Notes:

CONTINUE

CONTINUE

Passport to Advanced Math
Unit Review:

31. *Creating* Quadratic and Exponential Functions

Utilize the context of the problem to recall the common non-linear relationships with which you are familiar.

32. *Creating* Equivalent Expressions with Radicals or Rational Exponents

Allow your answer choices to be your guides. They will tell you whether or not to convert a radical to a rational exponent, or vice-versa.

33. *Creating* Equivalent Forms of Expressions

In order to manipulate the form of an expression, you must have a strong knowledge of the structure of the expression and of the order of operations.

34. *Solving* Quadratic Equations

Whenever possible, always choose to factor first. However, remember the quadratic formula and that it always works as a safety net.

35. *Completing* the Square

When a situation arises where you need to complete a square, remember to half the constant and square the result. Also, remember that the equation must remain balanced!

CONTINUE ➡

Passport to Advanced Math
Unit Review:

36. *Creating* Equivalent Forms to Reveal Particular Traits

When creating equivalent forms to reveal particular traits, you have to know the equivalent forms of expressions and equations that have the requested traits.

37. *Adding*, *Subtracting*, and *Multiplying* Polynomial Expressions

As with any type of simplifying, don't forget to distribute with care and to combine like terms.

38. *Solving* Radical and Rational Equations in One Variable

You can eliminate radicals by squaring both sides of an equation and you can rationalize by multiplying by the LCM of the denominator, but be aware of extraneous solutions.

39. *Solving* Mixed Systems

Solving mixed systems is as easy as solving a system of linear equations. Just set the equations equal to each other and solve.

40. *Simplifying* Rational Expressions and Polynomial Expressions

Remember that all of your basic rules of adding, subtracting, multiplying, and dividing still apply, such as effective use of common denominators, distributing, and canceling.

CONTINUE

Passport to Advanced Math
Unit Review:

41. *Interpreting* Non-Linear Expressions or Equations

When interpreting non-linear expressions or equations, pay close attention to the context of the problem and recall the meanings of the variables and constants in that form.

42. *Understanding* Zeros and the Factors of Polynomials

Always remember that the zeros, or roots, of polynomials are x-intercepts. So, if b is a root of a polynomial, when b is input into the polynomial, the output will be zero.

43. *Identifying* Non-Linear Equations and Their Graphs

It is important to have a strong prior understanding of the characteristics of non-linear equations, both algebraically and graphically.

44. *Working* with Function Notation

If you are given a rule, $f(x)$, and the question states that $f(a) = b$, that statement actually tells you two things, which will ultimately allow you to solve.

45. *Isolating* a Variable

You can always utilize simple variables to represent large expressions in order to make a complicated equation easy to work with.

CONTINUE ➡

**TURN TO NEXT PAGE FOR
UNIT REVIEW**

CONTINUE

Unit 4 Review - Calculator

55 MINUTES, 38 QUESTIONS

DIRECTIONS

For each question from 1-30, choose the best answer choice provided in the multiple choice bank and fill in the appropriate circle in the provided answer key. Alternatively, for questions **31-38**, answer the problem and enter your answer in the grid-in section of the answer key. Refer to the directions given before question 31 as to how to enter your answers for the grid-in questions. You may complete scratch work in any empty space in your test booklet.

NOTES

A. Calculator usage **is allowed**.
B. Variables, constants, and coefficients used represent real numbers unless indicated otherwise.
C. All figures are created to appropriate scale unless the question states otherwise.
D. All figures are two-dimensional unless the question states otherwise.
E. The domain of any given function is all real numbers x for which the function, $f(x)$, is a real number unless the question states otherwise.

REFERENCE

$A = \pi r^2$
$C = 2\pi r$

$A = lw$

$A = \dfrac{1}{2}bh$

$c^2 = a^2 + b^2$

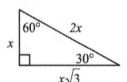
Special Right Triangle

Special Right Triangle

$V = lwh$

$V = \pi r^2 h$

$V = \dfrac{4}{3}\pi r^3$

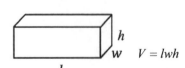
$V = \dfrac{1}{3}\pi r^2 h$

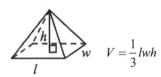
$V = \dfrac{1}{3}lwh$

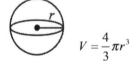
There are $360°$ in a circle.
There are 2π radians in a circle.
There are $180°$ in a triangle.

CONTINUE ➤

1

Angelo has an ant farm that he initially started with 60 ants. If the population grows by 15% each month, which of the following expressions would give the number of ants in Angelo's ant farm one year after he first set up the farm?

A) $1.15(60)^1$

B) $1.15(60)^{12}$

C) $60(1.15)^1$

D) $60(1.15)^{12}$

2

$$4x - 8y = 24$$

The linear equation above can be rewritten into which of the following forms in which the slope of the line appears as a coefficient in the equation?

A) $x - 2y = 6$

B) $y = \frac{1}{2}x - 3$

C) $y = 2x - 3$

D) $y = -2x + 3$

(handwritten work: $-8y$, $4x - 24 = 8y$, $\frac{1}{2}x - 3 = y$)

3

The expression $(x^3 x^2)^{\frac{1}{2}}$ is equivalent to which of the following, for all values of x?

A) x^3

B) $\sqrt{x^{11}}$

C) $\sqrt{x^5}$

D) $\sqrt{x}$

4

$$(2a^2b^2 + 4a^4) - (4b^4 - 2a^2b^2) + (4a^4 + 4a^2b^2)$$

Which of the following is equivalent to the expression above?

A) $8a^4 + 8a^2b^2 - 4b^4$

B) $4a^4 + 8a^2b^2 - 8b^4$

C) $8a^4 - 4b^4$

D) $4a^4 - 8b^4$

232

CONTINUE

5

$$y = 2x^2 - 4x + 1$$

Which of the following is the least value of x that is a solution to the equation above?

A) $1 - \dfrac{\sqrt{2}}{2}$

B) 1

C) $1 + \dfrac{\sqrt{2}}{2}$

D) $1 + \sqrt{2}$

$$\frac{4 - \sqrt{16 - 4(2)}}{4}$$

$$1 - \sqrt{16 - 8}$$

$$1 - \sqrt{\frac{8}{4}}$$

$$1 - \frac{2\sqrt{2}}{4}$$

6

If the sum of $x^2 + 3x$, $x^2 + 8x + 1$, and $-7x + 6$ is written in the form $ax^2 + bx + c$, what is the product of a, b, and c?

A) 2

B) 4

C) 13

D) 56

$$2x^2 + 4x + 7$$

7

$$\sqrt{x + 5} = x + 3$$

Which of the following values of x is an extraneous solution to the equation above?

A) 4

B) 1

C) -1

D) -4

$$x + 5 = x^2 + 6x + 9$$

$$0 = x^2 + 5x + 4$$

$$(x + 4)(x + 1)$$

8

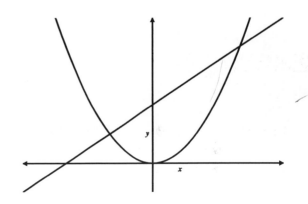

The functions $f(x) = x^2$ and $g(x) = x + 2$ are graphed in the xy-plane above. What is the value of $f(x)$ at the positive x-value where $f(x) = g(x)$?

A) 1

B) 2

C) 4

D) 6

$$x^2 = x + 2$$

$$x^2 - x - 2 = 0$$

$$(x - 2)(x + 1) = 0$$

CONTINUE

9

$$\frac{x+7}{3} - \frac{5}{x+1}$$

Which of the following expressions is equivalent to the expression above?

A) $\dfrac{x^2+8x-8}{3x+3}$

B) $\dfrac{x^2+8x+7}{3x+1}$

C) $\dfrac{-2x+16}{3x+3}$

D) $\dfrac{-2x+26}{3x+1}$

11

If $f(-6)=0$ and $f(x)$ is a quadratic equation, which of the following is a factor of $f(x)$?

A) $-6x$

B) x

C) $x-6$

D) $x+6$

10

$$1,200(1.03)^x$$

A money market account at a local bank accrues interest annually and the account value can be calculated using the expression given above, where x represents the number of years that have passed since the initial deposit was made to the account. The constant 1,200 in the expression most likely represents which of the following?

A) The growth rate of the account in dollars per year

B) The initial amount of money deposited in the account

C) The account value at the end of the first year

D) The amount of additional money deposited each year

12

Which of the following types of equations must have a graph that only has solutions in Quadrant III and Quadrant IV of the xy-plane?

A) Linear equation with a slope of 0

B) Exponential decay equation with a negative y-intercept

C) Quadratic equation with a negative leading coefficient and no real roots

D) Both B and C

234

CONTINUE

13

If $f(x) = 3 - (x+1)$ and $f(k+1) = 13$, what is the value of $-3k$?

A) 14

B) 18

C) 36

D) 42

(handwritten work:)
$3 - (k+1+1) = 13$
$3 - (k+2) = 11$
$3 - k - 2 = 13$
$1 - k = 13$
$-k = 12$
$k = -12$

14

$$\frac{\sqrt{M}}{(x^2 + 3x - 1)} = \frac{D - |5 - x|}{(x-11)^2}$$

Which of the following equations gives M in terms of D and x?

A) $M = \dfrac{D - |5 - x|}{(x^2 + 3x - 1)(x - 11)^2}$

B) $M = \dfrac{(D - |5 - x|)^2}{(x^2 + 3x - 1)^2(x - 11)^4}$

C) $M = \dfrac{(D - |5 - x|)(x^2 + 3x - 1)}{(x - 11)^2}$

D) $M = \dfrac{(D - |5 - x|)^2(x^2 + 3x - 1)^2}{(x - 11)^4}$

(handwritten work:)
$\sqrt{M} =$
$\sqrt{A} \qquad D$
$C \qquad D^2$
$\sqrt{mk}$
$\sqrt{AD} = (D)$
$\sqrt{A} = \frac{CD}{B^2}$
$A =$

15

An 800 gram sample of a radioactive isotope has a half-life of 50 years. Which of the following equations best models the mass of the radioactive isotope remaining t years after the sample was taken?

A) $M = 800 - \frac{1}{2}t$

(handwritten:) $800($

B) $M = 800 - \frac{1}{50}t^2$

C) $M = 800(50)^{\frac{1}{2}t}$

D) $M = 800\left(\frac{1}{2}\right)^{\frac{t}{50}}$

16

$$y = 2x + 1$$

Which of the following is an equivalent form of the equation above in which the x- and y-coordinates of a point that lies on the line appear as constants in the equation?

A) $2y = 4x + 2$ *(handwritten:)* $1 = 2x - y$

B) $y - 3 = 2(x - 1)$

C) $2x - y = -1$

D) $-2x + y = 1$

CONTINUE

17

$$\frac{1}{\sqrt{2}} + \frac{3}{2\sqrt{2}}$$

Which of the following expressions is equivalent to the expression above?

C) $\dfrac{3\sqrt{2}}{4}$

B) $\dfrac{5\sqrt{2}}{4}$

D) $2\sqrt{2}$

A) $3\sqrt{2}$

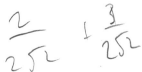

18

$$9a^2 - 49b^{10}$$

Which of the following is equivalent to the expression shown above?

A) $(3a + 7b^5)(3a - 7b^5)$

B) $(3a - 7b^5)(3a + 7b^2)$

C) $(3a - 7b^5)^2$

D) $(3a^{\frac{2}{5}} - 7b^2)^5$

19

$$0 = (x - 5)^2 + \frac{1}{2}$$

How many ordered pairs (x, y) satisfy the equation shown above?

A) 0

B) 1

C) 2

D) Infinitely many

20

$$(x + 1)^2 (x + 1)^2$$

Which of the following expressions is equivalent to product shown above?

A) $x^2 + 2x + 1$

B) $x^3 + 3x^2 + 3x + 1$

C) $x^4 + 4x^3 + 6x^2 + 4x + 1$

D) $x^5 + 5x^4 + 10x^3 + 10x^2 + 5x + 1$

236

CONTINUE

21

If $\dfrac{1}{x+1}+\dfrac{2}{x+2}=1$, what positive value of x makes the equation true?

A) 1

B) $\sqrt{2}$

C) $\sqrt{6}$

D) 4

$x+2+2(x+1)=1$

$x+2+2x+2=1$

22

$$y = 4x^2 - 15x$$
$$y = 5x - 25$$

If the ordered pair (x, y) is the only solution to the system of equations above, what is the value of x?

A) $\dfrac{2}{5}$

B) 2

C) $\dfrac{5}{2}$

D) 5

$4x^2 - 15x = 5x - 25$

$4x^2 - 15x = 5x - 25$

$4x^2 - 20x + 25 = 0$

$20 \pm \sqrt{400 - 4(25)4}$

23

If the remainder when $x^3 - 8x^2 + 4x + 1$ is divided by $x+5$ is written in the form $\dfrac{b}{x+5}$, what is the value of b?

A) -346

B) -344

C) -56

D) -54

24

$$y = -(x+1)(x-7)$$

An object is set in motion and its distance from a midline, y, is calculated based on x, the number of seconds that have passed. Positive values of y occur when the object is to the left of the midline and negative values of y occur when the object is to the right of the midline. What does the negative sign in front of the multiplied binomials imply?

A) The object will begin moving to the left, cross the midline, and later return to the right.

B) The object will begin moving to the right, cross the midline, and later return to the left.

C) The object will continually move to the left.

D) The object will continually move to the right.

CONTINUE

25

For a polynomial $g(x)$, $g(8) = 6$. Which of the following must be true about $g(x)$?

A) $x + 8$ is a factor of $g(x)$.

B) $x - 8$ is a factor of $g(x)$.

C) $x - 6$ is a factor of $g(x)$.

D) The remainder when $g(x)$ is divided by $x - 8$ is 6.

26

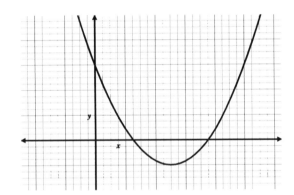

Which of the following equations could correspond to the graph in the *xy*-plane above?

A) $y = x^2 - 4x + 3$

B) $y = x^2 + 4x + 3$

C) $y = 3(0.25)^x$

D) $y = (0.5)^x$

27

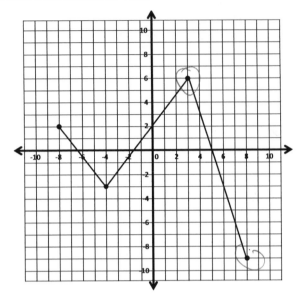

The complete graph of the function f is shown in the *xy*-plane above. If t is the *x*-value at which $f(x)$ yields its maximum value and v is the *x*-value at which $f(x)$ yields its minimum value, what is the value of $t - v$?

A) -5

B) -1

C) 1

D) 5

$6 + 9$

$3 - 8$

28

$$F = \frac{Q + M}{Q} + T$$

In the equation above, which of the following gives Q in terms of F, M, and T?

A) $Q = \dfrac{M}{F - T}$

B) $Q = \dfrac{M}{F - T - 1}$

C) $Q = F - M - T$

D) $Q = \sqrt{F - M - T}$

$F - T = \dfrac{Q + M}{Q}$

$Q(F - T) = Q + M$

$Q(F - T) - Q = M$

$Q(F - T')$

CONTINUE

29

A shot put is released from a height of 6 feet and travels through the air for 4 seconds before it reaches the ground. If the height of the shot put in feet follows a quadratic model with respect to time in hours and if the quadratic model has a leading coefficient of -2, what is the height in feet of the shot put when it reaches its highest point during its flight?

A) $\dfrac{13}{8}$

B) 8

C) $\dfrac{361}{32}$

D) 16

(handwritten work)

$\dfrac{169}{4}$

$-\dfrac{169}{2}t$

$-2x^2+6x+6$

$-2(16)+b4+6 = 0$

$-32+b4+6=0$

$b4-26=0$

$4b=26$

$\dfrac{26}{4}$ $\dfrac{13}{2}$

$-\dfrac{b}{2a}$

$x\dfrac{b}{c}$

$\dfrac{b}{4}$

30

$$y = 2x^2 - x + 8$$

Which of the following is an equivalent form of the quadratic equation above in which the coordinates of the vertex appear as constants in the equation?

A) $y = 2(x^2 - \dfrac{1}{2}x + 4)$

B) $y = 2(x-2)^2 + 8$

C) $y = 2(x - \dfrac{1}{4})^2 + \dfrac{63}{8}$

D) $y = 2(x - \dfrac{1}{2})^2 + \dfrac{127}{16}$

(handwritten work)

$y = 2\left(x^2 - \dfrac{1}{2}x + 4\right)$

$y = 2\left(\left(x^2 - \dfrac{1}{2}x + \dfrac{1}{4}\right) + 4\right)$

6.5

$-\dfrac{13}{2}\left(\dfrac{1}{4}\right)$

$\dfrac{13}{8}$

239

CONTINUE

DIRECTIONS

For each question from 31-38, solve and enter your answer in the grid-in section of your answer sheet as described below.

A. Write out your answers in the boxes at the top of each column in order to help you fill in the circles accurately. Remember, you will only receive credit for the circles that are filled in correctly, not for the written answer at the top of the columns.

B. Mark only a single circle in each column.

C. There are no negative answers.

D. If the problem has more than one correct answer, grid only one of the correct answers.

E. When your answer is a **mixed number**, such as $1\frac{1}{2}$, it should be entered as 1.5 or $3/2$. You cannot enter a mixed number because there is no room to fill in a circle that represents a space.

F. If you enter a **decimal answer** with more digits then the grid can handle, the answer may be rounded or truncated, but it absolutely must fill the entire grid.

Answer: $\frac{8}{21}$

Answer: 6.4

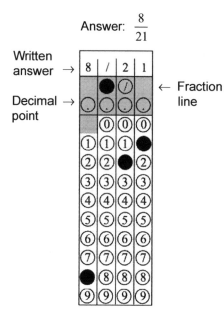

Written answer →
Decimal point →
← Fraction line

The ways to correctly grid $\frac{7}{9}$ are:

Answer: 102 - both positions are correct

REMEMBER:
You can begin writing your answers in any column as long as there is enough space. Leave unused columns blank.

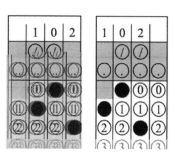

CONTINUE ➤

31

$$\frac{(x^3x^4)^5(x^3x^4)^5}{\left(\left(x^3\right)^4\right)^5}$$

The expression above simplifies to the form x^a. What is the value of a?

33

$$\sqrt{x} = x - 2$$

What is the value when the extraneous solution to the equation above is subtracted from the actual solution to the equation above?

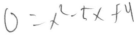

$$x = (x-2)(x-2)$$
$$x = x^2 - 4x + 4$$
$$0 = x^2 - 5x + 4$$
$$(x-4)(x-1)$$
$$4, 1$$

32

$$x^2 + 2ax = 4 - a^2$$

If a is a constant and one were to solve the equation by completing the square on the left hand side of the equation, what is the positive value of $x + a$?

$$x^2 + 2ax + a^2 = 4 - a^2 + a^2$$
$$(x + a)^2 = 4$$

34

$$x - 2 \overline{\smash{\big)}\, x^2 + 17x - 38}$$

If the remainder of the quotient given above has the form $\frac{b}{x-2}$, what is the value of b?

$$4$$

241

CONTINUE

35

$$(x+a)(x+b) = x^2 + mx + 14$$

If a and b are positive integers, what is one possible value of m?

9

36

If $g(x) = 10 - x^2$ and $g(a+5) = -134$, what is the positive value of a that satisfies the equation?

─────────── ▼ ───────────

Questions 37-38 refer to the following information.

$$f(x) = x^2 - 4$$
$$g(x) = x + 2$$

It had been many years since the value of a home was assessed. However, in 2010 an assessment was made which valued the home at $310,000. Two different companies had been estimating the value of the home for years. These estimations relative to the actual assessed value of the home in 2010 can be modeled by the equations above where x represents the number of years from 2010 and $f(x)$ and $g(x)$ represent the estimated value of the home in thousands of dollars relative to the assessed value of the home in 2010.

37

What is one of the years that both companies estimate the value of the home to be the same?

38

For how many years did the company using the linear model estimate the value of the home to be higher than the value estimated by the company using the quadratic model?

CONTINUE ➡

UNIT 5

Unit 5: Additional Topics in Math

Along with the extensive range of topics considered in the previous units, the redesigned SAT covers additional material outside of the realm of algebra, advanced algebra, and data analysis. These topics include important geometric and trigonometric skills, as well as the pythagorean theorem. While useful on its own, this subject matter becomes extremely powerful when it is used in connection with the major topics you have encountered thus far. These concepts will be covered in this unit, "Additional Topics in Math."

CONTINUE ➡

46 *Calculating* Volume for Standard Solids

"In order to calculate volume, you must identify or solve for all missing dimensions and appropriately substitute these quantities into the given formula."

When dealing with volume, one extremely helpful hint is to know all of the volume formulas, as well as all of your area formulas, in advance. Even though the formulas are given to you within certain questions and on the reference sheet, having a prior knowledge of the formulas will increase your efficiency and accuracy in application. Occasionally, the question will give you the area of a single face; from there you will have to determine the side lengths in order to calculate volume. (This is why it is important to know the area formulas as well.) Here is a list of some common area and volume equations with which you should be familiar:

Area:

Square: s^2

Rectangle: lw

Triangle: $\frac{1}{2}bh$

Circle: πr^2

Volume:

Cube: s^3

Rectangular Solid: lwh

Cylinder: $\pi r^2 h$

Sphere: $\frac{4}{3}\pi r^3$

The Rule of One Third:

Any time you are working with a solid that comes to a point, such as a cone or a pyramid, the volume of the cone or pyramid is exactly one third the volume of the respective solid that does *not* come to a point. For example:

1. $V_{cone} = \frac{1}{3}V_{cylinder}$ *(with same base radius and height)*
2. $V_{pyramid} = \frac{1}{3}V_{prism}$ *(with congruent base and height)*

Example 1:

The area of one face of a cube is $16\,in^2$. What would be the volume of a stack of four of these cubes?

A) 16
B) 64
C) 128
D) 256

You have to pay close attention to what you are looking for. In this case, you are looking for $4s^3$. In order to find $4s^3$, you must first calculate the length of one side, s, and then plug into the target expression:

$$s^2 = 16$$
$$s = 4$$
$$4s^3 = 4(4)^3 = 256$$

The answer is <u>D</u>.

Example 2:

A cone is being carved from a cylindrical block of marble that has a base radius of 3 inches and a height of 8 inches. If the volume of the cone is given by the expression $B\pi$, what is the value of B?

A) 12
B) 24
C) 36
D) 72

In this case, you will need to find the volume of a cone given a cylinder. Remembering the rule of one third, find the volume of the cylinder and multiply by one third. The calculation is that simple:

$$V_{cylinder} = \pi r^2 h = \pi(3)^2(8) = 72\pi$$

Using the Rule of One Third:

$$\frac{1}{3}(72\pi) = 24\pi$$

The answer is <u>B</u>.

CONTINUE

Skill 46 Practice Exercises:

1

A circular pool measures 20 feet across the water's surface and has a constant depth of 5 feet. What is the volume of water required to fill the pool, in cubic feet?

A) 500
B) 2000
C) 500π
D) 2000π

2

A large block of ice measuring 12 inches tall by 24 inches wide by 6 inches deep is broken into 3 congruent pieces. What is the volume, in cubic inches, of one of the congruent ice blocks?

A) 576
B) 864
C) 1728
D) 3456

3

The solid wooden cone shown above has a volume of 27π. What is the volume of a cylinder that has the same base radius, but is twice the height of the cone?

A) 27π
B) 81π
C) 162π
D) 243π

4

The surface area of a cube is 120 square inches. Which of the following is the volume of the cube, in cubic inches?

A) $40\sqrt{5}$
B) $80\sqrt{5}$
C) 120
D) 200

246

CONTINUE

5

A spherical storage container fits perfectly inside of a cubic box, touching the box on all sides. If the surface area of the box is $600\,ft^2$, the spherical container has how many cubic feet of storage space?

A) $\dfrac{25\pi}{3}$

B) $\dfrac{100\pi}{3}$

C) $\dfrac{125\pi}{3}$

D) $\dfrac{500\pi}{3}$

6

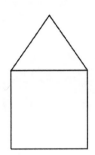

The diagram above shows the profile view of a cone sitting atop a cylinder. The height of the cone is half the height of the cylinder and the cone has a volume of 5π cubic inches. If the volume of the cylinder is written in the form $\dfrac{K}{2}\pi$, what is the value of K?

A) 120

B) 60

C) 30

D) 15

7

If the volume of the cylinder above is 144π cubic units, what is the area of the bottom face of the cylinder in square units?

A) 4π

B) 8π

C) 9π

D) 16π

8

What is the volume in cubic inches of the smallest cylinder that can fully contain a sphere with a volume of 36π cubic inches?

$(V_{sphere} = \dfrac{4}{3}\pi r^3)$

A) 27π

B) 54π

C) 162π

D) 324π

247

47   *Calculating* Volume for Non-Standard Solids

"Whenever you are presented with a solid shape that is unfamiliar to you, immediately break the shape into smaller shapes that you are familiar with or identify the larger shape from which it came."

Often, you will be asked to calculate the volume of a non-standard solid. In such a case, you will have to make a decision, visually and mentally, as to what occured to create the object in the first place. For example, if you are attempting to find the volume of a wedge of cheese, you should visualize that it came from an entire wheel of cheese, which generally has the shape of a cylinder. Calculate the volume of the whole cylinder, then use the degree measure to discover what part of the entire cylinder is represented by the volume that you desire.

Example:

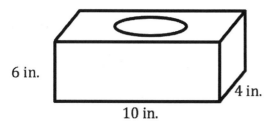

6 in.

10 in.

4 in.

A hole with a diameter of two inches has been drilled completely through the rectangular solid shown above. What is the volume of the object?

A) $40 - \pi$
B) $240 - \pi$
C) $240 - 6\pi$
D) $480 - 24\pi$

After inspecting the object presented in the problem, you should realize that the rectangular solid with a hole drilled through it can be mathematically calculated by removing a cylinder from a rectangular prism. Don't forget that you have been given a diameter, not a radius:

$$prism - cylinder = (6)(10)(4) - \pi(1)^2(6) = 240 - 6\pi$$

The answer is *C*.

Skill 47 Practice Exercises:

1

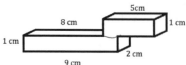

What is the volume, in cubic centimeters, of the solid pictured above?

A) 23
B) 26
C) 28
D) 52

2

A rectangular swimming pool has a width of 15 feet and a length of 20 feet. The depth of the pool is 5 feet at one end and consistently declines to 10 feet at the opposite end of its length. What is the volume of water, in cubic feet, required to fill the pool?

A) 300
B) 1500
C) 2250
D) 3000

CONTINUE

3

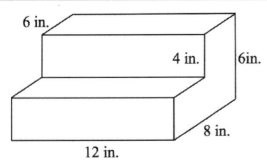

What is the volume, in cubic inches, of the prism pictured above?

A) 480

B) 528

C) 576

D) 672

4

Standard dice measure $\frac{5}{8}$ of an inch in all directions. A store sells a pack of 27 dice that are packaged in the shape of a larger cube. What is the volume of that larger cube in cubic inches?

A) $\frac{125}{512}$

B) $\frac{675}{512}$

C) $\frac{1125}{512}$

D) $\frac{3375}{512}$

5

A grain silo stands 30 feet tall at its center, and has a base radius of 8 feet. The conical top section has the same height as the cylindrical base section. How many square feet of grain can the silo hold?

A) 1280π

B) 1440π

C) 1920π

D) 2560π

6

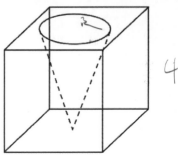

A conical hole has been drilled into a cubic metal block as shown above. If the volume of the cubic metal block was originally $64in^3$ and the diameter of the conical hole's base is 3 inches, what is the volume of the block, in cubic inches, after the hole has been drilled?

A) $16-3\pi$

B) $16+9\pi$

C) $64-9\pi$

D) $64-3\pi$

CONTINUE

$\frac{3}{8} \cdot \frac{1}{2}$

7

An aluminum spacer is created by boring a hole with a $\frac{3}{8}$ *in.* diameter drill bit vertically through a cylindrical aluminum spacer blank that measures $\frac{1}{2}$ *in.* across and 2 *in.* tall. What is the volume in cubic inches of a finished aluminum spacer?

A) $\frac{7}{256}\pi$

B) $\frac{7}{128}\pi$

C) $\frac{23}{256}\pi$

D) $\frac{23}{128}\pi$

$(.25)^2 \pi (2) - \left(\left(\frac{3}{8}\right)/2\right)^2 2 \pi$

$\frac{1}{16} \quad \frac{1}{8}\pi - \left(\frac{3}{16}\right)^2 2 \pi$

$\frac{1}{8} - \frac{9}{256}\left(2\right)\pi$

$\frac{1}{8} - \frac{9}{128}\pi$

$\frac{16}{128} - \frac{9}{128}\pi$

8

A rectangular prism has a square base and stands 2 inches tall. The four vertices of the top of the prism are labeled A, B, C, and D. A saw is used to cut through the prism from the midpoint of edge AB to the midpoint of edge DA. If the triangular prism that was removed has a triangular base with an area of 32 square inches, what is the volume, in cubic inches, of the pentagonal prism that remains?

A) 224

B) 448

C) 480

D) 512

Notes:

CONTINUE

48 — Working with 3D-Ratios

"When you are given the ratios of objects in different dimensions, you can use powers and roots to efficiently move between dimensions."

If you know the ratio between two objects in a certain dimension, there is no need to make up lengths, areas, or volumes in order to algebraically and geometrically manipulate the results to find a ratio. The ratios can simply be identified through the use of powers and roots. Look at the table below:

	Object A	Object B
1D (Length, Width, Circumference)	x	y
2D (Area, Surface Area)	x^2	y^2
3D (Volume, Mass)	x^3	y^3

<u>Note</u>: **When converting from 3D to 2D, it is best to convert down to 1D first, then back up to 2D.**

Example 1:

A large and a small equilateral triangle have side lengths that are in a ratio of 5:3. What is the ratio of their areas?

A) 5:3
B) 5:9
C) 25:3
D) 25:9

	Large	Small
1D	5	3
2D	25	9

Create a small table and square the ratio to get from 1D (side length) up to 2D (area).

The answer is <u>*D*</u>.

Example 2:

The areas of rectangle A and rectangle B are in a ratio of 1:4. What is the ratio of the length of one of rectangle A's diagonals to the length of one of rectangle B's diagonals?

Well, area is in 2D and any length is in 1D. So, simply take the square root of both sides of the ratio. The ratio of the diagonal lengths is $\sqrt{1}:\sqrt{4}$, or <u>1:2</u>.

<u>**Skill 48 Practice Exercises:**</u>

1

Circle *A* has a diameter that measures 8 inches in length. Circle *B* has a diameter that measures 4 inches in length. What is the ratio of the area of circle *A* to the area of circle *B*?

A) 1:4
B) 1:2
C) 2:1
D) 4:1

2

The volume of a cylinder is 216 cubic centimeters and the volume of a smaller cylinder is 64 cubic centimeters. What is the ratio of the radius of the base of the smaller cylinder to the radius of the base of the larger cylinder?

A) 1:3
B) 4:9
C) 2:3
D) 3:2

CONTINUE

3

A large equilateral triangle has sides that measure 4 inches each. An equilateral triangular pyramid has a volume of 27 cubic inches. What is the ratio of the surface area of the equilateral triangular pyramid to the area of the large equilateral triangle?

A) 4:3

B) 3:4

C) 9:16

D) 27:64

4

The ratio of volume of sphere A to the volume of sphere B is $2\sqrt{2}:1$. What is the ratio of the area of a circle with the same radius as sphere A to the area of a circle with the same radius as sphere B?

A) $\sqrt{2}:1$

B) $2:1$

C) $\sqrt{8}:1$

D) $4:1$

Questions 5-6 refer to the following triangle.

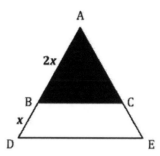

In the triangle above, the length of $\overline{AB}$ is equivalent twice the length of $\overline{BD}$.

5

What is the ratio of the shaded area to the unshaded area in the triangle above?

A) 4:5

B) 4:9

C) 2:1

D) 2:3

6

If triangle ABC has an area of $4\sqrt{3}$, what is the area of triangle ADE?

A) 5

B) $5\sqrt{3}$

C) 9

D) $9\sqrt{3}$

CONTINUE

7

The surface area of sphere A is π square centmeters. The surface area of sphere B is 36π. Which of the following is equivalent to the volume of sphere B divided by the volume of sphere A?

A) 216

B) 27

C) 9

D) 3

8

Two cylinders are similar and one has a diameter that is 3 times the diameter of the other. If the volume of the larger cylinder is 9π, what is the volume of the smaller cylinder?

A) $\frac{1}{3}\pi$

B) π

C) 3π

D) 9π

Notes:

_____

_____

_____

_____

_____

_____

_____

_____

_____

_____

CONTINUE

49 *Using* Trigonometric Ratios

"Do you remember Soh-Cah-Toa? If you do, you have your trigonometry under control."

One big change from the former version of the SAT is that the new SAT will incorporate questions that require an understanding of trigonometric ratios. As you first learned, these ratios can be memorized simply by knowing the term Soh-Cah-Toa. Beyond that, the remaining three trigonometric ratios, which would be helpful to memorize (Cotangent, Secant, and Cosecant), are simply the reciprocals of Sine, Cosine, and Tangent:

$$Soh => \operatorname{Sin} A = \frac{opposite}{hypotenuse}$$

$$Cah => \operatorname{Cos} A = \frac{adjacent}{hypotenuse}$$

$$Toa => \operatorname{Tan} A = \frac{opposite}{adjacent}$$

$$\operatorname{Cotan} A = \frac{adjacent}{opposite}$$

$$\operatorname{Sec} A = \frac{hypotenuse}{adjacent}$$

$$\operatorname{Csc} A = \frac{hypotenuse}{opposite}$$

Important Note:

When working with trigonometric ratios, remember to place yourself at the angle in question. Above all else, you want to make sure that, as you look for opposite, adjacent, and hypotenuse, you are looking out from the correct position. This is easy to address. For example, if the question asks for $\operatorname{Sin} A$, immediately draw a star on angle A and plant yourself in that location.

Example 1:

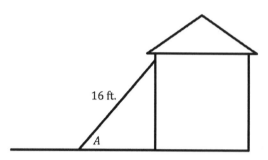

A 16-foot ladder is leaning against the side of a house and forms an angle, A, with the ground. If the Sine of Angle A is $\frac{3}{4}$, what is the elevation, in feet, at which the ladder makes contact with the side of the house?

A) *12*
B) *15*
C) *20*
D) *21.3*

The first step is to put a star on Angle A and look for the relationship associated with Sine (Soh). If opposite over hypotenuse is 3 over 4, then the height you are solving for over 16 is the same as 3 over 4:

$$\operatorname{Sin} A = \frac{opposite}{hypotenuse} = \frac{3}{4} = \frac{h}{16}$$

$$4h = 3(16)$$
$$h = 12 \, feet$$

The answer is _A_.

Example 2:

Given that angle B is an acute angle in a right triangle and that $\operatorname{Tan} B = 1$, what is the measure of angle B, in degrees?

You know that Tangent is $\frac{opposite}{adjacent}$; if Tangent is equivalent to 1, then opposite and adjacent are the same. Hence, the right triangle must be isosceles, so the angle measure must be $45°$.

The answer is _45_.

CONTINUE

Skill 49 Practice Exercises:

1

A certain right traingle has a shortest side that measures 6 inches and a longest side that measures 10 inches. What is the Sine of the smallest angle in the triangle?

A) $\dfrac{3}{5}$

B) $\dfrac{3}{4}$

C) $\dfrac{4}{5}$

D) $\dfrac{5}{4}$

2

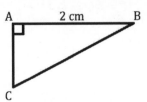

In the right triangle shown above, $\cos B = \dfrac{4}{5}$. What is the length of BC, in centimeters?

A) 2.5

B) 4

C) 5

D) 5.5

3

In a right triangle, the tangent of one of the acute angles is $\dfrac{1}{\sqrt{3}}$. What is the measure, in degrees, of the larger acute angle in the triangle?

A) 30

B) 45

C) 60

D) 75

4

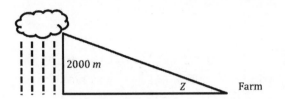

A farmer is at his farm, looking up at a storm cloud in the distance. The cloud is at an altitude of 2000 meters. If the farmer knows that the Cotangent of Angle Z is 4, how many meters away is the closest farmland that is receiving rainwater?

A) 500

B) 1000

C) 4000

D) 8000

CONTINUE

5

In a right triangle, one angle measures $a°$, where $\cos a° = \dfrac{3}{5}$. What is $\sin(90° - a°)$?

A) $\dfrac{4}{3}$

B) $\dfrac{4}{5}$

C) $\dfrac{3}{4}$

D) $\dfrac{3}{5}$

6

Triangle XYZ has a right angle at Y. Side YZ measures 12, and side XZ measures 13, what is the value of $\cos Z$?

A) $\dfrac{5}{13}$

B) $\dfrac{5}{12}$

C) $\dfrac{12}{13}$

D) $\dfrac{12}{5}$

7

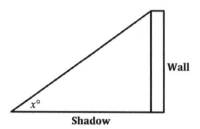

Wall

Shadow

If the 8 foot wall pictured above casts a shadow that is 5 yards long, what is the value of $\tan x°$?

A) $\dfrac{15}{8}$

B) $\dfrac{8}{15}$

C) $\dfrac{5}{8}$

D) $\dfrac{8}{5}$

8

In a right triangle, the cosine of one of the acute angles that measures $a°$ is equal to the sine of the other acute angle that measures $b°$. If $a = 18x - 1$ and $b = 11x + 4$, what is the value of x?

A) 2.4

B) 3

C) 3.2

D) 6.1

CONTINUE

50 — *Using* the Pythagorean Theorem

"Remember, in a right triangle, $a^2 + b^2 = c^2$ always."

Pythagorean Theorem:

$$a^2 + b^2 = c^2$$

The Pythagorean Theorem happens to be one of the easiest theorems in mathematics to memorize, as well as one of the most useful. Just remember that a crucial requirement is that the triangle must be a right triangle.

In addition, in order to save time, it cannot hurt to memorize your special Pythagorean Triples:

3-4-5 (or any multiples of 3-4-5)
5-12-13 (or any multiples of 5-12-13)
8-15-17 (or any multiples of 8-15-17)

Example:

The hypotenuse of a right triangle measures $12\sqrt{2}$ inches. If both legs of the triangle have the same measure, what is the measure of one of those legs, in inches?

A) 6
B) $6\sqrt{2}$
C) 12
D) $12\sqrt{2}$

Since the problem states that the triangle is right, you should use the Pythagorean Theorem. Also, remember that the two legs have the same measure. So, $a^2 = b^2$:

$$a^2 + b^2 = c^2$$
$$(a)^2 + (a)^2 = (12\sqrt{2})^2$$
$$2a^2 = 288$$
$$a^2 = 144$$
$$a = 12$$

The answer is _C_.

Skill 50 Practice Exercises:

1

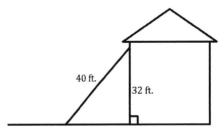

A 40-foot-tall fallen tree is leaning against a building. The tree makes contact with the building at a height of 32 feet. How far is the base of the tree from the base of the building?

A) 18 feet
B) 24 feet
C) 32 feet
D) 48 feet

2

Which of the following sets of side lengths *do not* form a right triangle?

A) 10, 24, 26
B) 8, 15, $\sqrt{285}$
C) 4, 8, $4\sqrt{5}$
D) 6, 8, 10

CONTINUE

3

Malcolm wants to suspend a perforated hose diagonally above his garden to serve as a misting device for his plants. If his garden measures 5 yards wide by 10 yards long, how many feet of perforated hose will he need to cover the diagonal?

A) $5\sqrt{5}$

B) $5\sqrt{3}$

C) $15\sqrt{5}$

D) $15\sqrt{3}$

4

Which of the following sets of side lengths forms a right triangle?

A) 8, 10, 12

B) 9, 16, 25

C) 25, 60, 75

D) 16, 30, 34

5

A competition swimming pool measures 25 meters wide and 50 meters long. If a swimmer were to swim diagonally across the pool, how many meters would the swimmer swim?

A) $25\sqrt{5}$

B) $20\sqrt{5}$

C) 625

D) 3125

6

The points $A(3,1)$, $B(9,1)$, and $C(9,9)$ define the vertices of a triangle in the xy-plane. What is the perimeter of triangle ABC?

A) 10

B) 12

C) 18

D) 24

CONTINUE

7

One end of a board is resting on the ground and the other end is resting on a cylinder whose circular base has an area of 20.25π square inches. If the board makes contact with the cylinder 22 inches from the end that is touching the ground, approximately how many inches is that end of the board from the center of the cylinder?

A) 22

B) 22.10

C) 22.46

D) 22.77

8

A 14 foot ladder is resting against a building and its base is 8 feet from the base of the building. If the ladder rests against the building $\frac{A}{3}\sqrt{33}$ feet above the ground, what is the value of A?

A) $\frac{2}{3}$

B) 2

C) 6

D) 24

Notes:

CONTINUE

51 *Working with* Complex Numbers

"When you see complex numbers, mainly when you see the letter *i*, your first thoughts should be either $i^2 = -1$ or to multiply by the conjugate."

Complex numbers are any numbers that can be written in the form $a + bi$, where *a* and *b* are real numbers and *i*, which is equivalent to $\sqrt{-1}$, serves as the imaginary part of the expression. It is of the utmost importance that you are able to perform basic operations on mplex numbers, such as addition, subtraction, multiplication, and division. Generally, such operations can be as basic as combining like terms. However, multiplying complex binomials or even rationalizing expressions with complex denominators, your work can become a bit more tricky. The following examples demonstrate important points to anticipate when dealing with complex numbers:

Example 1:

The expression $(3-2i)-(-1-i)$ is equivalent to what expression of the form $a+bi$?

$$(3-2i)-(-1-i)$$
$$3-2i+1+i$$
$$4-i$$

Example 2:

If the expression $(2+3i)(3-2i)$ is written in the form $a+bi$, what is the value of b?

$$6-4i+9i-6i^2 \rightarrow 6-4i+9i-6(-1) \rightarrow 12+5i$$
$$b=5$$

Example 3:

$$\frac{1}{3+2i}$$

If the expression above were to be rewritten in the form $a+bi$, what is the value of b?

$$\frac{1}{3+2i} \bullet \frac{(3-2i)}{(3-2i)} = \frac{3-2i}{9-4i^2} = \frac{3-2i}{13} = \frac{3}{13} - \frac{2}{13}i$$
$$b = -\frac{2}{13}$$

Skill 51 Practice Exercises:

1

Given that $i = \sqrt{-1}$, which of the following expressions is equivalent to the sum of $2+3i$ and $-3+2i$?

A) $-2i$

B) $4i$

C) $-1+i$

D) $-1+5i$

2

Multiplying $3+4i$ by which of the following expressions results in a value of 50? ($i = \sqrt{-1}$)

A) $3-4i$

B) $3-2i$

C) $6-8i$

D) $6+2i$

CONTINUE

3

For $i = \sqrt{-1}$, what is the sum $(-3-2i)+(5-4i)$?

A) $-8-6i$

B) $-8+2i$

C) $2-6i$

D) $2-2i$

4

$$\frac{1+i}{2-i}$$

If the expression above is converted to the form $a+bi$, where a and b are positive numbers, what is the value of a?

A) $\dfrac{1}{5}$

B) $\dfrac{2}{5}$

C) $\dfrac{3}{5}$

D) $\dfrac{4}{5}$

5

$$y = \frac{8}{1+i} + 4i$$

If $i = \sqrt{-1}$, given the equation above, y is equivalent to which of the following positive integer values?

A) 2

B) 4

C) 8

D) 16

6

$$(9+8i)-(2+4i)+(6-4i)$$

Which of the following is equivalent to the expression above?

A) $1+8i$

B) $13+8i$

C) 1

D) 13

CONTINUE

7

Which of the following expressions in the form $a+bi$ is equivalent to $\dfrac{2+5i}{3+2i}$? (Note: $i=\sqrt{-1}$)

A) $-\dfrac{16}{13}-\dfrac{11}{13}i$

B) $\dfrac{16}{13}+\dfrac{11}{13}i$

C) $\dfrac{2}{3}-\dfrac{5}{2}i$

D) $\dfrac{2}{3}+\dfrac{5}{2}i$

8

$$(6-5i)(4-3i)(2-i)$$

If the product above is simplified to the form $a+bi$, in which a and b are integers, what is the value of $a+b$?

A) -105

B) -69

C) 29

D) 65

Notes:

CONTINUE

52 Converting Between Degrees and Radians

"Just remember three things when converting between degrees and radians: $\frac{\pi}{180}$ **,** $\frac{180}{\pi}$ **, and the numbers that measure angles in degrees are larger than the numbers that measure angles in radians."**

There are 360 degrees in a circle and there are 2π radians in a circle. Given these facts, you can proportionally determine radians from degrees or degrees from radians.

$$\frac{2\pi}{360} = \frac{\pi}{180}$$

$$1 \text{ radian} = \frac{180}{\pi} \text{ degrees}$$

$$1 \text{ degree} = \frac{\pi}{180} \text{ radians}$$

To convert to radians, multiply the angle measure, in degrees, by $\frac{\pi}{180}$ **.**

To convert to degrees, multiply the angle measure, in radians, by $\frac{180}{\pi}$ **.**

Example 1:

What is the measure of a 45 degree angle in radians?

Just multiply by $\frac{\pi}{180}$ **:**

$$45 \bullet \frac{\pi}{180} = \frac{\pi}{4}$$

Example 2:

The central angle of an arc measures 0.4 radians. What is the measure of the arc in degrees?

Just multiply by $\frac{180}{\pi}$ **:**

$$0.4 \bullet \frac{180}{\pi} = \frac{72}{\pi} \text{ or } 22.9 \text{ degrees}$$

Skill 52 Practice Exercises:

1

An angle that measures 210 degrees measures how many radians?

A) π

B) $\frac{7\pi}{6}$

C) $\frac{5\pi}{4}$

D) $\frac{4\pi}{3}$

2

An angle that measures $\frac{\pi}{6}$ radians measures how many degrees?

A) 30
B) 45
C) 60
D) 75

263

CONTINUE

3

Three angles measure $\frac{\pi}{2}$ radians, 45 degrees, and $\frac{\pi}{3}$ radians. What is the sum of all three angles in degrees?

A) 120

B) 150

C) 165

D) 195

4

How many radians are in a 540 degree arc?

A) 2

B) 3

C) 2π

D) 3π

5

One of the angles in an equilateral triangle measures $(39x-18)^\circ$. An angle that measures x°, would measure how many radians?

A) $\frac{\pi}{180}$

B) $\frac{\pi}{120}$

C) $\frac{\pi}{90}$

D) $\frac{\pi}{60}$

6

The four angles of a quadrilateral measure π radians, $2x+1$ radians, $3x+2$ radians, and $11x-3$ radians. What is the measure, in degrees, of an angle that measures x radians?

A) $\frac{45}{4}$

B) $\frac{45}{3}$

C) $\frac{45}{2}$

D) 45

CONTINUE

7

The measure of the largest angle in an isosceles triangle is 7 times the size of the smallest angle. If the triangle has one obtuse angle, what is the measure, in radians, of the largest angle in the triangle?

A) $\dfrac{7\pi}{18}$

B) $\dfrac{7\pi}{9}$

C) $\dfrac{\pi}{18}$

D) $\dfrac{\pi}{9}$

8

The sum of the interior angles of a particular polygon is 6π radians. What is the polygon?

A) Pentagon

B) Hexagon

C) Octagon

D) Nonegon

Notes:

265

CONTINUE

**TURN TO NEXT PAGE FOR
MID-UNIT REVIEW**

CONTINUE

Mid-Unit 5 Review - No Calculator

25 MINUTES, 20 QUESTIONS

DIRECTIONS

For each question from 1-15, choose the best answer choice provided in the multiple choice bank and fill in the appropriate circle in the provided answer key. Alternatively, for questions **16-20**, answer the problem and enter your answer in the grid-in section of the answer key. Refer to the directions given before question 16 as to how to enter your answers for the grid-in questions. You may complete scratch work in any empty space in your test booklet.

NOTES

A. Calculator usage **is not allowed** in this section.

B. Variables, constants, and coefficients used represent real numbers unless indicated otherwise.

C. All figures are created to appropriate scale unless the question states otherwise.

D. All figures are two-dimensional unless the question states otherwise.

E. The domain of any given function is all real numbers x for which the function, $f(x)$, is a real number unless the question states otherwise.

REFERENCE

$A = \pi r^2$
$C = 2\pi r$

$A = lw$

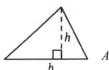
$A = \dfrac{1}{2}bh$

$c^2 = a^2 + b^2$

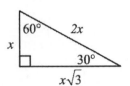
Special Right Triangle

Special Right Triangle

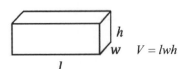
$V = lwh$

$V = \pi r^2 h$

$V = \dfrac{4}{3}\pi r^3$

$V = \dfrac{1}{3}\pi r^2 h$

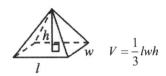
$V = \dfrac{1}{3}lwh$

There are $360°$ in a circle.
There are 2π radians in a circle.
There are $180°$ in a triangle.

CONTINUE ➡

1

A cylindrical shaped pool has a depth of 6 feet. If the bottom surface of the pool has an area of 49π square feet, what is the volume of water, in cubic feet, required to fill the pool?

A) $\dfrac{49}{6}\pi$

B) 42π

C) 294π

D) 343π

2

A right triangle has one leg that measures 5 centimeters and another leg that measures $5\sqrt{3}$ centimeters. What is the cosine of the smallest angle in the triangle?

A) $\dfrac{1}{2}$

B) $\dfrac{\sqrt{3}}{2}$

C) $\dfrac{2\sqrt{3}}{3}$

D) $\sqrt{3}$

3

Which of the following sets of side lengths *does not* form a right triangle?

A) 45, 108, 117

B) 45, 60, 75

C) 16, 30, 36

D) 10, 24, 26

4

A square-shaped bolt is created by drilling a threaded hole with a half-inch diameter through the center of a steel block that measures one inch by one inch, by one-half inch. What is the volume of the bolt in cubic inches?

A) $\dfrac{1}{2} - \dfrac{\pi}{32}$

B) $\dfrac{1}{2} - \dfrac{\pi}{16}$

C) $\dfrac{1}{2} - \dfrac{\pi}{4}$

D) $\dfrac{1}{2} - \dfrac{\pi}{2}$

CONTINUE

5

$$(-2+5i)-(2-8i)$$

For $i = \sqrt{-1}$, which of the following is equivalent to the expression above?

A) $-3i$

B) $13i$

C) $-4+3i$

D) $-4+13i$

7

The length of the diagonal on the square base of a rectangular prism is 10 centimeters. What is the volume of the rectangular prism, in cubic centimeters, if it stands 20 centimeters tall?

A) 250

B) 500

C) 750

D) 1000

6

An arc is defined by an angle that measures $\dfrac{\pi}{36}$ radians. What is the measure of the central angle that defines the arc in degrees?

A) 5

B) 10

C) 12

D) 18

8

The three angles in a triangle measure $\dfrac{3\pi}{5}$ radians, 52 degrees, and x radians. What is the value of x?

A) $\dfrac{\pi}{18}$

B) $\dfrac{\pi}{9}$

C) 20

D) 20π

CONTINUE

9

In right triangle ABC, where the right angle occurs at vertex B, $\sin A$ is equivalent to $\dfrac{\sqrt{2}}{2}$. What is the value of $\dfrac{\cos A}{\sin A}$?

A) $\dfrac{1}{2}$

B) $\dfrac{\sqrt{2}}{2}$

C) 1

D) 2

10

In a right triangle, the sine of one of the acute angles that measures $a°$ is equal $\dfrac{1}{2}$ and the other acute angle measures $b°$. If $a = 11x - 3$ and $b = 22x - c$, what is the value of c?

A) 2

B) 3

C) 4

D) 6

11

$$(3+i)(2-i)(1+i)$$

Which of the following is equivalent to the expression above?

A) $6 + 6i$

B) $6 + 8i$

C) $8 + 6i$

D) $8 + 8i$

12

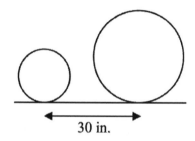

Figure not drawn to scale.

A circle with a diameter of 15 inches and a circle with a diameter of 40 inches are drawn as pictured above. If the midlines of both circles are 30 inches apart, what is the distance, in inches, between the centers of the two circles?

A) 32.5

B) 36.0

C) 39.1

D) 42.4

CONTINUE

13

A block of cheese is in the shape of a rectangular prism. If the prism has a square base with an area of 144 square inches and the height of the prism is 6 inches, what is the volume, in cubic inches, of the largest cylindrical wheel of cheese that can be cut from the block?

A) 72π

B) 216π

C) 512π

D) 864π

14

$$y + 2 = \frac{10}{2+i} + 2(2+i)$$

Given the equation above where $i = \sqrt{-1}$, what is the value of y?

A) 6

B) $6 + 4i$

C) $8 + 4i$

D) 10

15

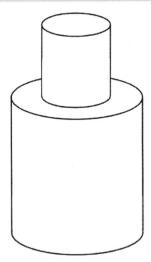

A hard rubber slider for the leg of a couch is formed in the shape of two stacked cylinders. If the volume of the bottom cylinder is 32π cubic millimeters and every dimension of the top cylinder is half of the bottom cylinder, what is the volume, in cubic millimeters, of the entire slider?

A) 16π

B) 36π

C) 40π

D) 48π

CONTINUE

DIRECTIONS

For each question from 16-20, solve and enter your answer in the grid-in section of your answer sheet as described below.

A. Write out your answers in the boxes at the top of each column in order to help you fill in the circles accurately. Remember, you will only receive credit for the circles that are filled in correctly, not for the written answer at the top of the columns.

B. Mark only a single circle in each column.

C. There are no negative answers.

D. If the problem has more than one correct answer, grid only one of the correct answers.

E. When your answer is a **mixed number**, such as $1\frac{1}{2}$, it should be entered as 1.5 or 3/2. You cannot enter a mixed number because there is no room to fill in a circle that represents a space.

F. If you enter a **decimal answer** with more digits then the grid can handle, the answer may be rounded or truncated, but it absolutely must fill the entire grid.

Answer: $\frac{8}{21}$

Written answer →
Decimal point →
← Fraction line

Answer: 6.4

The ways to correctly grid $\frac{7}{9}$ are:

Answer: 102 - both positions are correct

REMEMBER:
You can begin writing your answers in any column as long as there is enough space. Leave unused columns blank.

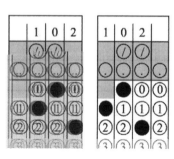

CONTINUE

16

The sum of three angles that measure $\dfrac{\pi}{x}$ radians, $\dfrac{\pi}{2x}$ radians, and $\dfrac{\pi}{4x}$ radians is 7. What is the measure, in degrees, of an angle that measures x radians?

17

In right triangle ABC, if the $\sin A$ equals $\dfrac{4}{5}$ and angle C measures 90 degrees, what is the $\cos B$?

18

A 25-foot fallen telephone pole is leaning against a fence, 10 feet above the ground. If the base of the telephone pole is $2F\sqrt{21}$ feet from the fence, what is the value of F?

19

What is the surface area, in square feet, of a cube that circumscribes a sphere with a volume of 288π cubic feet? $\left(V_{sphere} = \dfrac{4}{3}\pi r^3\right)$

CONTINUE

20

$$\frac{5-8i}{8+5i}$$

If the expression above were written in the form $a+bi$, what is the value of a? (Note: $i=\sqrt{-1}$)

CONTINUE

53 — *Using* Radians to Determine Arc Length

"Radians measure the number of radii in an arc. So, all you have to do is multiply the measure of a circle's radius by the radian measure of the arc."

Measuring arc length is actually much easier when using radians, since radians measure the number of radii in an arc. Remember, you can always convert degrees to radians for an easy alternative to measuring arc length.

Example 1:

The central angle that defines an arc in a circle with a radius of 5 inches measures 0.8 radians. What is the length of the arc in inches?

Remember, if you have the measure of an arc in radians and you know the radius, just multiply the radius by the radian angle measure to get the arc length.

$$5(0.8) = 4$$

Example 2:

A circle with a radius that measures π units contains a 120 degree arc. What is the measure of the arc?

Try finding the arc length by converting to radians:

$$120° \cdot \frac{\pi}{180} = \frac{2\pi}{3}$$

$$\frac{2\pi}{3} \cdot \pi = \frac{2\pi^2}{3} \, units$$

1

A 135 degree arc is defined in a circle that has a radius of 10 centimeters. What is the length of the arc in centimeters?

A) 7.5π
B) 15π
C) 22.5π
D) 100π

2

Points A and B lie on circle O. If the area of the circle is 36π and $\overset{\frown}{AB}$ is defined by an angle that measures 3 radians, what is the length of $\overset{\frown}{AB}$?

A) 2

B) 18

C) 108

D) $\frac{480}{\pi}$

CONTINUE

3

A circle has a radius that measures π units. A major arc that has a central angle that measures $\dfrac{15}{\pi}$ radians is defined in the circle. What is the length of the arc?

A) 0.0625
B) 0.2
C) 5
D) 15

4

Points C and D lie on circle Q. If the area of the circle is 121π and the measure of $\overset{\frown}{CD}$ is 27.5 inches, what is the radian measure of $\angle CQD$?

A) $\dfrac{1}{4}$

B) 2

C) $\dfrac{5}{2}$

D) $\dfrac{450}{\pi}$

5

What is the length of an arc in the unit circle, $x^2 + y^2 = 1$, that is defined by an angle that measures 2 radians?

A) π

B) 2

C) 1

D) $\dfrac{1}{\pi}$

6

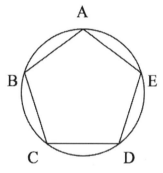

If pentagon $ABCDE$ is regular and is inscribed in a circle with an area of 25π square centimeters, what is the length, in centimeters, of $\overset{\frown}{ABC}$?

A) $\dfrac{\pi}{5}$

B) $\dfrac{2\pi}{5}$

C) 2π

D) 4π

CONTINUE

7

If an arc between two points on a circle measures 5 inches in length and the arc is defined by an angle that measures 2 radians, what is the area of the circle in square inches?

A) $\dfrac{25\pi}{4}$

B) $\dfrac{25}{4}$

C) $\dfrac{4}{25}$

D) $\dfrac{4\pi}{25}$

8

$$aN = 2\pi$$

The formula above relates the radian measure, a, of an exterior angle of a regular polygon to the number of sides, N, of the polygon. If the measure of an exterior angle of a regular polygon is greater than or equal to $\dfrac{\pi}{3}$ radians, what is the least measure of an arc between two vertices of the polygon if it is inscribed in a circle with a radius of 3?

A) $\dfrac{\pi}{6}$

B) $\dfrac{\pi}{3}$

C) π

D) 2π

Notes:

_____

_____

_____

_____

_____

_____

_____

_____

_____

_____

CONTINUE

54 | *Using* Trigonometric Functions of Radian Measure

"It is a good idea to know the trigonometric ratios of standard angles and to know the radian measures of those angles."

If you have a strong understanding of standard angles, the radian measures of those angles, and the corresponding trigonometric ratios, you can answer a great number of questions accurately and efficiently. Remember, if the angles are larger than 2π, you can subtract 2π or any multiple of 2π to find a reference angle with which you are familiar.

Standard Angles and Trigonometric Ratios:

Angle	Radians	Sin	Cos	Tan
0°	0	0	1	0
30°	$\pi/6$	$1/2$	$\sqrt{3}/2$	$\sqrt{3}/3$
45°	$\pi/4$	$\sqrt{2}/2$	$\sqrt{2}/2$	1
60°	$\pi/3$	$\sqrt{3}/2$	$1/2$	$\sqrt{3}$
90°	$\pi/2$	1	0	Und.
180°	π	0	-1	0
270°	$3\pi/2$	-1	0	Und.
360°	2π	0	1	0

Example:

What is the cosine of an angle that measures $\frac{\pi}{6}$ radians?

A) 0
B) 1
C) $\frac{1}{2}$
D) $\frac{\sqrt{3}}{2}$

According to the table above, the answer is _D_.

1

An angle that measures $\frac{\pi}{3}$ radians defines an arc in the unit circle. What is the cosine of the angle?

A) 0

B) $\frac{1}{2}$

C) $\frac{\sqrt{3}}{2}$

D) 1

2

If the $\sin x = \frac{\sqrt{3}}{2}$ and x is the radian measure of an angle, what is the $\cos x$?

A) 0

B) $\frac{1}{2}$

C) $\frac{\sqrt{3}}{2}$

D) 1

CONTINUE

3

If x is the radian measure of an angle and the $\cos x = \dfrac{\sqrt{2}}{2}$, what is the $\sin(\dfrac{\pi}{2} - x)$?

A) 0

B) $\dfrac{1}{2}$

C) $\dfrac{\sqrt{2}}{2}$

D) 1

4

What is the sine of an angle that measures 3π radians?

A) 0

B) $\dfrac{1}{2}$

C) $\dfrac{\sqrt{3}}{2}$

D) 1

5

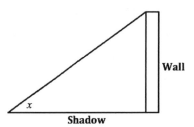

A 12-foot wall casts a shadow that measures $144\sqrt{3}$ inches. If x is the radian measure of the angle that the light makes with the ground behind the wall, what is the cosine of an angle that measures $(\dfrac{\pi}{2} - x)$ radians?

A) $\dfrac{1}{2}$

B) $\dfrac{4}{5}$

C) $\dfrac{\sqrt{3}}{2}$

D) 1

6

If x is the radian measure of an angle and the $\sin x = \dfrac{1}{2}$, what is the value of $\dfrac{\pi}{2} - x$?

A) $\dfrac{\pi}{6}$

B) $\dfrac{\pi}{4}$

C) $\dfrac{\pi}{3}$

D) $\dfrac{\pi}{2}$

CONTINUE

7

A metal beam is used to support a radio tower and forms an angle that measures $\frac{\pi}{4}$ radians with the ground. What is the tangent of the angle that the tower forms with the support beam?

A) -1

B) 0

C) $\frac{1}{2}$

D) 1

8

A kite is flying 200 feet above the ground. If the kite's string makes an angle that measures $\frac{\pi}{6}$ radians with the ground, how many feet of kite string have been let out?

A) 200

B) $200\sqrt{2}$

C) $200\sqrt{3}$

D) 400

Notes:

CONTINUE

55   *Applying* Theorems About Circles

"The only two things you need to know about circles are the area formula and the circumference formula. A sector is just a part of the area and an arc is just a part of the circumference."

Circles are fairly simple to work with because you only really need to know that the area of a circle is calculated using the expression πr^2 and that the circumference is calculated using the expression $2\pi r$. There are other formulas that relate to circles, but it is usually easier to remember these other formulas as relationships derived from the two formulas above. For example:

Area of a Sector: $\dfrac{\theta}{360} \bullet \pi r^2$

An easier way to think of the formula above is to think,

"The area of a sector is just part of the area of the entire circle. What fraction of the whole?"

Length of an Arc: $\dfrac{\theta}{360} \bullet 2\pi r$

An easier way to think of the formula above is to think,

"The length of an arc is just part of the circumference. What fraction of the whole?"

Length of a Chord: $2r \bullet \text{Sin}\dfrac{\theta}{2}$

The length of a chord is an exception to the concept of finding a relationship to the two major circle formulas. In most cases, it is easiest to just memorize the formula for chord length given the radius and the angle that defines the chord length.

Example 1:

The length of a 45° arc in a circle measures 2π inches. Which of the following values is the length of the radius of the circle in inches?

A) 4
B) 8
C) 12
D) 16

You should think, "2π is part of the circumference. What part? 45 out of 360, or one-eighth of the circumference." Once you know this, solving for the radius should be simple:

$$2\pi = \frac{1}{8}2\pi r$$

$$1 = \frac{1}{8}r$$

$$8 = r$$

The answer is _B_.

Example 2:

Given that the length of arc ab *measures* $\dfrac{\pi}{2}$ *and that the radius of the circle above is 3, what is the area of the defined sector?*

You can use the relationship between the given arc length and the circumference of the circle to proportionally define the relationship between the area of the sector and the area of the entire circle:

Circumference $= 2\pi r = 2\pi(3) = 6\pi$

$\dfrac{\pi}{2}$ is $\dfrac{1}{12}$ of the circumference 6π.

So, the sector must be $\dfrac{1}{12}$ of the area of the circle.

Area of Circle $= \pi r^2 = \pi(3)^2 = 9\pi$

So, $\dfrac{1}{12} \bullet 9\pi = \dfrac{3}{4}\pi$

CONTINUE

Skill 55 Practice Exercises:

1

If a circle with a circumference of 12π is cut into 12 equivalent pieces, what is the area of one piece?

A) π
B) 2π
C) 3π
D) 4π

2

An arc is defined by an angle that measures 1.25 radians. If the radius of the circle is 4 inches, what is the length of the defined arc, in inches?

A) 3.33
B) 4
C) 5
D) 5.2

3

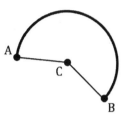

If the length of segment AC is 6 and the area of the enclosed sector ACB is 24π, what is the measure, in degrees, of the major angle, $\angle ACB$?

A) 120
B) 135
C) 225
D) 240

4

Arc FG is defined by a 60-degree angle. If the radius of the circle is 4 centimeters, what is the length of the chord that runs from F to G, in centimeters?

A) 2
B) 4
C) $4\sqrt{2}$
D) 8

CONTINUE

5

An extra large pizza has a diameter of 20 inches. If the pizza is cut traditionally into 8 slices and the area of a single slice, in inches, is given by the expression $G\pi$, what is the value of G?

A) 12.5
B) 25
C) 37.5
D) 50

6

Two points, A and B, are on circle O. If the length of $\overline{AB}$ is $\sqrt{2}$ centimeters and the circumference of circle O is 2π, what is the degree measure of $\angle AOB$?

A) 90
B) 60
C) 45
D) 30

7

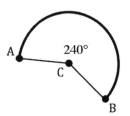

A raven is flying along a circular path around a central point. If the distance from this central point to the raven's starting point is 99 meters and the raven flies along the arc from A to B, what is the distance, in meters, that the raven has traveled?

A) 33π
B) 60π
C) 66π
D) 132π

8

What is the absolute difference in the length of each individual arc that is created when a regular octagon is inscribed in a circle with an area of $\frac{9}{4}\pi$ and the length of each individual arc created when an equilateral triangle is inscribed in the same circle?

A) π

B) $\dfrac{5\pi}{8}$

C) $\dfrac{\pi}{2}$

D) $\dfrac{3\pi}{8}$

CONTINUE

56 — *Understanding* Congruence and Similarity

"When dealing with similar figures, always remember that corresponding side lengths are proportional."

If two figures share common angle measures throughout, they are considered similar. Similar figures have side lengths that are proportional.

If two similar figures have equal side lengths, then they are congruent, or the same.

Similar:

Congruent Angles and Proportional Side Lengths

Congruent:

Congruent Angles and Congruent Side Lengths

Important Note:

When dealing with similar figures, remember that the proportional sides have to be in corresponding positions. For example, if the angle measures of two similar triangles are 50, 60, and 70 degrees, the side that runs between the 50- and 60-degree angles is proportional to the side of the other figure that runs between the 50- and 60-degree angles.

Example:

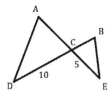

In the figure above, $\angle DAC = \angle EBC$ and $\angle ADC = \angle BEC$. If BE measures 7 units, what is the measure of AD?

Since $\angle ACD$ is vertical to $\angle BCE$, you know that the angles are congruent. This makes the two triangles similar, so you know that the sides are proportional. Since CE is 5 and CD is 10, you also know the ratio of side lengths is 1:2. So, if BE is 7, since AD is in a corresponding position, AD is <u>14</u>.

Skill 56 Practice Exercises:

1

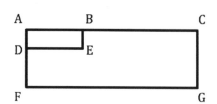

ABED and ACGF are similar rectangles. If the ratio of AD to DF is 1:3 and the length of BC is 9 centimeters, what is the length of AB in centimeters?

A) 1
B) 3
C) 6
D) 9

2

Two squares in the *xy*-plane are congruent and have side lengths of 8 inches. If the two squares are placed adjacent to each other in the *xy*-plane, what is the area of the resulting rectangle, in square inches?

A) 256
B) 128
C) 64
D) 16

CONTINUE

3

In the figure above, the hypotenuses of both right triangles are parallel and the ratio of the smaller hypotenuse to the larger hypotenuse is 3:5. If the length of the longer leg of the larger right triangle is 12.5 feet, what is the absolute difference in length between the two longer legs of the two right triangles?

A) 2 feet

B) 4 feet

C) 5 feet

D) 7.5 feet

4

If a cube with a volume of 216 cubic inches were to be divided into 27 congruent smaller cubes, what would be the surface area of one of these smaller cubes in cubic inches?

A) 1

B) 6

C) 8

D) 24

5

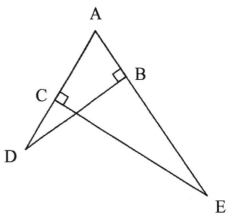

In the diagram above, $\overline{AC} = 2\overline{AB}$. What is the length of $\overline{AD}$ in inches if $\overline{AE}$ measures 1.5 inches?

A) .75

B) 1

C) 1.5

D) 3

6

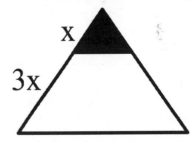

A pyramid shaped container stands 24 inches tall. The container has a solid pyramid-shaped top. What is the height in inches of the tallest object that can be placed vertically inside of the storage container?

A) 6

B) 16

C) 18

D) 24

CONTINUE

7

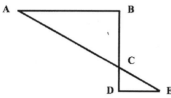

Barry, *B*, lives directly across the street from David, *D*. Angela, *A*, lives 200 feet west of Barry and Eric, *E*, lives 50 feet east of David. If Barry lives exactly 150 feet from Charlie, *C*, how many feet does Eric live from Charlie?

A) 62.5

B) 100

C) 112.5

D) 250

8

The furthest distance between two vertices of a regular hexagon is 16 centimeters. If a similar hexagon is drawn with dimensions that measure half of the length of the original hexagon's dimensions and that hexagon is divided into 6 congruent equilateral triangles, what is the area of one of those triangles?

A) $16\sqrt{3}$

B) 24

C) 12

D) $4\sqrt{3}$

Notes:

CONTINUE

<table>
<tr><td>

57

Utilizing Similarity and Trigonometry in Right Triangles

</td></tr>
</table>

"When attempting to identify side lengths and angle measures in right triangles, make sure to remember the proportional relationships of similar triangles, as well as Soh-Cah-Toa."

It is vital not only that you know the relationships represented by Soh-Cah-Toa, but also that you memorize the particular trigonometric ratios that pair with standard angle measurements. A list of these angle measures and trigonometric ratios can be found on page 120. (Skill #49)

Also, remember that trigonometric ratios are just that, ratios. So, if you identify a relationship (such as Sine in a particular right triangle), the same ratio can be applied to any other right triangle that may be similar to the original triangle.

Example:

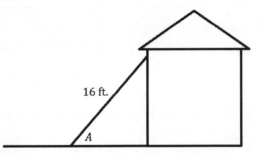

16 ft.

A

Suppose that a 16-foot ladder is leaning against a house and forms an angle, A, with the ground. The measure of Angle A is $30°$. *If a man climbs 6 feet up the length of the ladder, how high above the ground will the man be, in feet?*

If you know that the angle measures $30°$, **you can recall that** $\text{Sin}\,30°$ **is equivalent to** $\frac{1}{2}$. **If you visualize a smaller, similar right triangle, one where the hypotenuse is 6 feet long, you can use the proportional relationship to calculate the man's height above the ground.**

$$\text{Sin}\,30° = \frac{1}{2} = \frac{x}{6\,feet}$$ **The measure of** x **is <u>3 feet</u>.**

1

A right triangle has two legs that measure 18 and 24 inches. What is sine of the smallest angle in the triangle?

A) $\frac{3}{5}$

B) $\frac{3}{4}$

C) $\frac{4}{5}$

D) 1

2

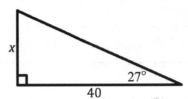

x

$27°$

40

Which of the following expressions is equivalent to the value of x?

A) $40\,\text{Tan}\,27°$

B) $\dfrac{40}{\text{Tan}\,27°}$

C) $40\,\text{Sin}\,27°$

D) $\dfrac{40}{\text{Sin}\,27°}$

CONTINUE

3

The shortest side of a right triangle measure 9 inches and the hypotenuse measures 15 inches. Which of the following is equivalent to the sine of the second largest angle in the triangle?

A) $\dfrac{3}{5}$

B) $\dfrac{4}{5}$

C) $\dfrac{5}{4}$

D) $\dfrac{5}{3}$

4

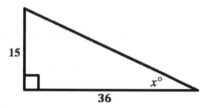

Which of the following is equivalent to $\cos(90-x)$?

A) $\dfrac{12}{5}$

B) $\dfrac{12}{13}$

C) $\dfrac{5}{12}$

D) $\dfrac{5}{13}$

5

An isosceles right triangle has a hypotenuse that measures 8 inches in length. What is the tangent of one of the acute angles of a similar triangle that has side lengths that measure half of the length of the original triangle?

A) 2

B) 1

C) $\dfrac{\sqrt{2}}{2}$

D) $\dfrac{1}{2}$

6

A stabilizing rope is tied to the top of a tent and staked into the ground a few feet from the tent. If the rope is 72 inches long and forms a $60°$ angle with the ground, how far is the stake from the tent, in feet?

A) 36

B) 18

C) 6

D) 3

CONTINUE

7

Jonathan is standing on the roof of his house and looking down at a ball that is lying on his back lawn. If the angle of depression between Jonathan's sightline and the ball is $45°$ and if the ball is exactly 32 feet from him, how many feet will Jonathan have to travel to get to the ball if he climbs down the side of the house and walks across the yard to reach it?

A) $16\sqrt{2}$

B) 32

C) $32\sqrt{2}$

D) 64

8

Annabelle, Bernice, and Cassandra are standing in the form of a right triangle where the right angle occurs at Cassandra's position. Annabelle is standing exactly $4\sqrt{3}$ meters from Bernice. If A, B, and C represent the positions of Annabelle, Bernice, and Cassandra, and $\sec \angle ABC = 2$. how many meters apart are Annabelle and Cassandra?

A) 3

B) $3\sqrt{3}$

C) 6

D) $6\sqrt{3}$

Notes:

CONTINUE

58 — *Creating* and *Solving* Circle Equations in Two Variables

"When working with circle equations, always utilize the form $x^2 + y^2 = (radius)^2$ in order to solve or identify the attributes of the graphs of circles."

When you are creating or solving the equations of circles, it is extremely valuable to understand the form of a circle's equation and how the constants relate to the graph of the circle. Here are some important facts about the equations of circles:

Unit Circle:
$$x^2 + y^2 = 1$$

The unit circle is centered at $(0,0)$ and has a radius of 1.

Standard Form of a Circle:
$$(x-a)^2 + (y-b)^2 = r^2$$

a is the horizontal shift of the circle's graph. Remember, since the form of the equation has a minus sign in the parentheses, you perform a horizontal shift that is opposite to how the constant appears. If the equation states $(x-3)^2$, the circle horizontally shifts 3 units to the *right*. However, if the equation states $(x+3)^2$, the circle shifts 3 units to the left.

b is the vertical shift of the circle's graph. This will dictate how far up or down the circle's center will translate in relation to the origin. As with the horizontal shift, the vertical shift is opposite to how the constant appears.

(a,b) defines the coordinate of the center of the circle's graph.

r is the radius of the circle.

Example 1:

$$x^2 + (y-2)^2 = 36$$

If the area of the circle defined by the equation above is given by the expression $A\pi$, what is the value of A?

A) 6
B) 12
C) 36
D) 72

After recognizing the standard form of the circle equation, you should notice that 36 is equivalent to the square of the radius. Since we know that the radius is 6, we can use the radius to find the area of the circle:

$$\pi r^2 = \pi(6)^2 = 36\pi$$

The answer is *C*.

Example 2:

A circle has a radius of 5 and is centered at the point $(1,-1)$. Which of the following equations defines the circle?

A) $(x-1)^2 + (y+1)^2 = 25$
B) $(x+1)^2 + (y-1)^2 = 25$
C) $(x-1)^2 + (y+1)^2 = 5$
D) $(x+1)^2 + (y-1)^2 = 5$

According to the standard form of the circle equation, $(x-a)^2 + (y-b)^2 = r^2$, the center is defined as (a,b) and the radius is *r*. All you have to do is substitute the given data into the standard form, and you will be able to identify the correct equation:

$$(x-a)^2 + (y-b)^2 = r^2$$
$$(x-(1))^2 + (y-(-1))^2 = (5)^2$$

$$(x-1)^2 + (y+1)^2 = 25$$

The answer is *A*.

CONTINUE

Skill 58 Practice Exercises:

1

$$(x+1)^2 + (y-6)^2 = 169$$

Which of the following points lies on the circle defined by the equation above?

A) $(5,12)$

B) $(11,5)$

C) $(4,6)$

D) $(-6,18)$

2

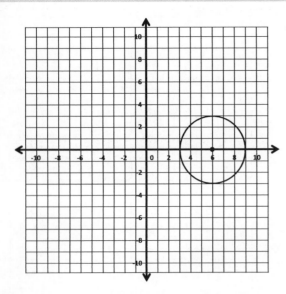

Which of the following equations defines the circle pictured in the xy-plane above?

A) $(x+6)^2 + y^2 = 3$

B) $(x+6)^2 + y^2 = 9$

C) $(x-6)^2 + y^2 = 9$

D) $x^2 + (y-6)^2 = 9$

3

$$x^2 + (y-4)^2 = 64$$

What is the radius of the circle that is defined by the equation above?

A) 8

B) $\sqrt{68}$

C) $\sqrt{80}$

D) 64

4

Which of the following is the equation of a circle in the xy-plane with center $(2,0)$ and a radius with endpoint $(2,5)$?

A) $(x-2)^2 + y^2 = 25$

B) $(x+2)^2 + y^2 = 25$

C) $(x-2)^2 + y^2 = 5$

D) $(x+2)^2 + y^2 = 5$

CONTINUE

5

$$x^2 + 6x + y^2 + 2y = 6$$

The equation of a circle in the *xy*-plane is shown above. Which of the following coordinate points is the center of the circle?

A) $(6,2)$

B) $(3,1)$

C) $(-3,-1)$

D) $(-6,-2)$

6

If every coordinate in the unit circle is multiplied by 2, which of the following changes would occur to the equation of the unit circle?

A) The only constant would double.

B) The only constant would quadruple.

C) The circle would shift vertically and horizontally by positive 2 units.

D) The equation would no longer define a circle.

7

$$3x^2 + 6x + 3y^2 + 3y = \frac{33}{4}$$

What is the radius of the circle defined by the equation above?

A) $\dfrac{\sqrt{11}}{2}$

B) 2

C) $\dfrac{\sqrt{33}}{2}$

D) 4

8

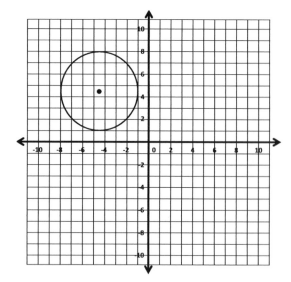

The equation of the circle above is
$(x-a)^2 + (y-b)^2 = 12.25$. If the constant *a* is increased by 10 and the constant *b* is decreased by 5, all of the solutions to the equation fall in which of the following quadrants?

A) I only

B) III only

C) I and II

D) I and IV

CONTINUE

Additional Topics in Math
Unit Review:

46. *Calculating* Volume for Standard Solids

The process for calculating volume for standard solids involves identifying the missing dimensions and substituting the appropriate quantities into the correct formula.

47. *Calculating* Volume for Non-Standard Solids

When calculating volume for a non-standard solid, you must rely on your visualization skills. You have to be able to break the solid into smaller, more identifiable shapes and then find those volumes separately.

48. *Working With* 3D-Ratios

When you are given the ratios of objects in different dimensions, you can use powers and roots to efficiently move between dimensions.

49. *Using* Trigonometric Ratios

The extent of trigonometry on the new SAT is not especially deep. If you have a solid understanding of Soh-Cah-Toa, you have a high chance of success.

50. *Using* the Pythagorean Theorem

The Pythagorean Theorem is as easy to use as when you first learned it; it also appears quite often. Just remember, $a^2 + b^2 = c^2$.

CONTINUE

Additional Topics in Math
Unit Review:

51. *Working with* Complex Numbers

It is important to remember that i is equivalent to $\sqrt{-1}$. It is even more important, however, to understand that you cannot have a complex number in the denominator of a fraction. Remember to rationalize using the Difference of Squares.

52. *Converting* Between Degrees and Radians

Converting between degrees and radians, and the other way around, can easily be accomplished by multiplying by $\frac{\pi}{180}$ or $\frac{180}{\pi}$. To choose the correct multiplier, remember that degrees are larger than radians.

53. *Using* Radians to Determine Arc Length

Radians measure the number of radii in an arc. So, when calculating arc length, you should simply multiply the measure of a circle's radius by the radian measure of its arc.

54. *Using* Trigonometric Functions of Radian Measure

It is a good idea to know the trigonometric ratios of standard angles and to also know the radian measures of those angles.

55. *Applying* Theorems About Circles

For circles, make sure that you memorize the formulas for the circumference and the area of a circle. An arc length is just a part of the circumference and a sector is just a part of the area.

CONTINUE

Additional Topics in Math
Unit Review:

56. *Understanding* Congruence and Similarity

When dealing with similar figures, always remember that corresponding side lengths are proportional to each other.

57. *Utilizing* Similarity and Trigonometry in Right Triangles

When attempting to identify side lengths and angle measures in right triangles, you should keep in mind the proportional relationships of similar triangles and the ratios defined by Soh-Cah-Toa.

58. *Creating* and *Solving* Circle Equations in Two Variables

The biggest factors that determine success with circle equations are understanding the form of the standard circle equation and understanding how the constants and coefficients affect the circle's graph.

CONTINUE

**TURN TO NEXT PAGE FOR
UNIT REVIEW**

CONTINUE ➡

Unit 5 Review - Calculator

55 MINUTES, 38 QUESTIONS

DIRECTIONS

For each question from 1-30, choose the best answer choice provided in the multiple choice bank and fill in the appropriate circle in the provided answer key. Alternatively, for questions **31-38**, answer the problem and enter your answer in the grid-in section of the answer key. Refer to the directions given before question 31 as to how to enter your answers for the grid-in questions. You may complete scratch work in any empty space in your test booklet.

NOTES

A. Calculator usage **is allowed**.
B. Variables, constants, and coefficients used represent real numbers unless indicated otherwise.
C. All figures are created to appropriate scale unless the question states otherwise.
D. All figures are two-dimensional unless the question states otherwise.
E. The domain of any given function is all real numbers x for which the function, $f(x)$, is a real number unless the question states otherwise.

REFERENCE

$A = \pi r^2$
$C = 2\pi r$

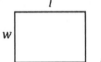
$A = lw$

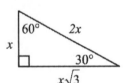
$A = \frac{1}{2}bh$

$c^2 = a^2 + b^2$

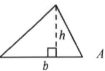
Special Right Triangle

Special Right Triangle

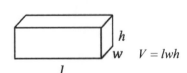
$V = lwh$

$V = \pi r^2 h$

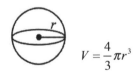
$V = \frac{4}{3}\pi r^3$

$V = \frac{1}{3}\pi r^2 h$

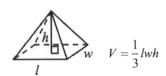
$V = \frac{1}{3}lwh$

There are $360°$ in a circle.
There are 2π radians in a circle.
There are $180°$ in a triangle.

CONTINUE →

1

A cylindrical beverage container stands approximately 8 inches tall and has a base with a circumference of 3π inches. The container can hold approximately how many cubic inches of liquid?

A) 8π

B) 12π

C) 18π

D) 24π

2

If the sine of a certain angle in a right triangle equals $\dfrac{4}{5}$, what is the cosine of the same angle?

A) 1

B) $\dfrac{4}{5}$

C) $\dfrac{3}{5}$

D) 0

3

Which of the following sets of side lengths forms a right triangle?

A) $8, 12, 4\sqrt{13}$

B) $8, 10, 12$

C) $4, 7, \sqrt{53}$

D) $4, 5, 7$

4

Given that $i = \sqrt{-1}$, which of the following expressions is equivalent to the sum of $(8-7i)$, $(2-6i)$, and $(-10+17i)$?

A) -4

B) 0

C) $-4i$

D) $4i$

298

CONTINUE

5

The measure of a single exterior angle of a regular polygon is $\frac{\pi}{5}$ radians. What is the measure of the angle in degrees?

A) 30

B) 32

C) 36

D) 45

6

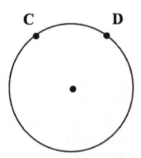

Points C and D lie on a circle with a radius that measures 16 centimeters. If the length of $\overset{\frown}{CD}$ is $\frac{8\pi}{3}$ centimeters, what is the radian measure of the angle that defines the arc?

A) $\frac{\pi}{6}$

B) $\frac{\pi}{3}$

C) $\frac{2\pi}{3}$

D) $\frac{3\pi}{2}$

7

A small box contains 7 bouillon cubes which have a total volume of $\frac{7}{8}$ cubic inches. What is the length in inches of one side of one of the bouillon cubes?

A) $\frac{1}{8}$

B) $\frac{1}{4}$

C) $\frac{1}{2}$

D) 1

8

A right triangle has one angle that measures $\frac{\pi}{6}$. What is the cosine of the second largest angle in the triangle?

A) 0

B) $\frac{1}{2}$

C) $\frac{\sqrt{3}}{2}$

D) 1

CONTINUE

9

An equilateral triangle is inscribed in a circle with a radius that measures 5 inches in length. What is the length in inches of a chord that runs between two of the vertices of the triangle?

A) $\dfrac{5}{2}$

B) $\dfrac{5}{2}\sqrt{3}$

C) 5

D) $5\sqrt{3}$

10

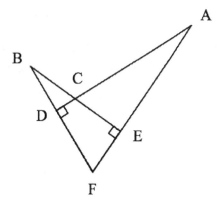

In the diagram above, $\overline{EF} = \dfrac{2}{3}\overline{DF}$. If $\overline{AD} = 36$ and $\overline{DF} = 15$, what is the length of $\overline{BF}$?

A) 10

B) 24

C) 26

D) 32

11

$$x^2 + 4x + y^2 = -3$$

Which of the following values is equivalent to the radius of the circle defined by the equation above?

A) -3

B) 1

C) 2

D) $i\sqrt{3}$

12

In a right triangle, the two legs measure 8 inches and 15 inches. What is the sine of the smallest angle in a similar triangle with side lengths that are one-quarter of the length of the original triangle?

A) $\dfrac{2}{17}$

B) $\dfrac{2}{15}$

C) $\dfrac{8}{17}$

D) $\dfrac{8}{15}$

CONTINUE

13

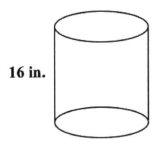

16 in.

The cylinder above has a diameter that is half of its height and is made of solid brass. If a milling machine were to carve the cylinder into a cone with a congruent base and height, what is the volume, in cubic inches, of the amount of brass that is carved away by the milling machine?

A) $\dfrac{256}{3}\pi$

B) $\dfrac{512}{3}\pi$

C) 256π

D) $\dfrac{2048}{3}\pi$

14

In a right triangle, $\sin(36°)$ is equivalent to $\cos(x°)$.
What is the value of x?

A) 36

B) 45

C) 54

D) 72

15

Given that $i = \sqrt{-1}$, which of the following is equivalent to the product $(2+3i)(2-3i)$?

A) -5

B) 13

C) $-5-12i$

D) $-5+6i$

16

The central angle of a major arc is defined by an angle that measures 5 radians. If the measure of the arc's defining angle, in degrees, is given by the expression $\dfrac{J}{\pi}$, what is the value of J?

A) 180

B) 360

C) 540

D) 900

301

CONTINUE

17

A circle with a radius of 5 millimeters contains an arc that is defined by an angle that measures $\frac{\pi}{5}$ radians. What is the length of the arc, in millimeters?

A) π

B) 2π

C) 4π

D) 5π

18

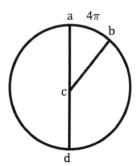

In circle c, given that the length of segment ad is 40 meters, what is the area, in square meters, of sector abc?

A) 40π

B) 50π

C) 100π

D) 400π

19

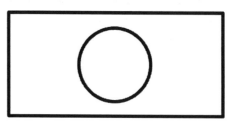

The diagram above displays an overhead view of a rectangular prism with a hole cut through its center. The prism measures 6 feet in length, 18 feet in width, and 2 feet in depth. If the diameter of the circle is two thirds of the length of the rectangular prism and the volume of the prism, in feet, can be written in the form $A - B\pi$, what is the value of $A - B$?

A) 98

B) 100

C) 208

D) 212

20

A baseball bat is leaning against a batting cage and makes an angle that measures $\frac{\pi}{3}$ radians with the ground. What is the cosine of the smallest acute angle in the triangle that the bat makes with the cage and the ground?

A) $\frac{1}{2}$

B) $\frac{\sqrt{3}}{2}$

C) $\frac{12}{13}$

D) 1

CONTINUE

21

A cube has sides that measure 3 inches in length. Another cube has faces with areas that measure 4 square inches. What is the ratio of the volume of the larger cube to the volume of the smaller cube?

A) 3:2

B) 27:16

C) 9:4

D) 27:8

22

$$x^2 - 8x + y^2 - y = -\frac{1}{4}$$

The equation of a circle in the xy-plane is shown above. Which of the following is equivalent to the length of the radius of the circle?

A) 1

B) 2

C) $\sqrt{\dfrac{31}{2}}$

D) 4

23

The longest diagonal of a cube measures 36 inches. What is the surface area of the cube in square inches?

A) 144

B) 432

C) 864

D) 2592

24

A radio tower stands 132 feet tall and has a stabilizing cable bolted to the ground x yards from the base of the tower. If the cable makes an angle with the ground that measures $\dfrac{\pi}{4}$ radians, what is the value of x?

A) 44

B) $44\sqrt{2}$

C) 132

D) $132\sqrt{2}$

CONTINUE

25

What is the volume in cubic centimeters of the smallest sphere that can fully contain a cube with a longest diagonal that measures 12 centimeters in length?

$(V_{sphere} = \dfrac{4}{3}\pi r^3)$

A) 48π

B) 288π

C) 576π

D) 864π

26

In a right triangle, $\sin((2x+1)^\circ) = \cos((3x+4)^\circ)$. What is the value of x?

A) 17

B) 34

C) 35

D) 55

27

A right triangle has two legs that measure 25 inches and 60 inches in length. What is the perimeter of the triangle?

A) 30

B) 65

C) 98

D) 150

28

$$\dfrac{2+3i}{5-i}$$

If the expression above is written in the form $a+bi$, where a and b are positive fractions, what is the value of $a+b$?

A) $\dfrac{7}{26}$

B) $\dfrac{5}{13}$

C) $\dfrac{17}{26}$

D) $\dfrac{12}{13}$

CONTINUE

29

The three angles of a theoretical triangle measure $x-2$ radians, $2x-5$ radians, and $3x+7$ radians. What is the measure, in degrees, of an angle that measures x radians?

A) 30
B) 45
C) 60
D) 90

30

A cylinder has a volume of 64π cubic inches. If the cylinder has a diameter that is twice its height, what is the volume in cubic inches of a cube with sides that measure the same length as the radius of the cylinder's base?

A) 8
B) 64
C) 216
D) 512

CONTINUE

DIRECTIONS

For each question from 31-38, solve and enter your answer in the grid-in section of your answer sheet as described below.

A. Write out your answers in the boxes at the top of each column in order to help you fill in the circles accurately. Remember, you will only receive credit for the circles that are filled in correctly, not for the written answer at the top of the columns.

B. Mark only a single circle in each column.

C. There are no negative answers.

D. If the problem has more than one correct answer, grid only one of the correct answers.

E. When your answer is a **mixed number**, such as $1\frac{1}{2}$, it should be entered as 1.5 or 3/2. You cannot enter a mixed number because there is no room to fill in a circle that represents a space.

F. If you enter a **decimal answer** with more digits then the grid can handle, the answer may be rounded or truncated, but it absolutely must fill the entire grid.

Answer: $\frac{8}{21}$

Written answer →
Decimal point →
← Fraction line

Answer: 6.4

The ways to correctly grid $\frac{7}{9}$ are:

Answer: 102 - both positions are correct

REMEMBER:
You can begin writing your answers in any column as long as there is enough space. Leave unused columns blank.

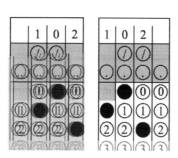

CONTINUE

31

In a right triangle, $\sin x$ is equivalent to $\frac{1}{2}$. If x is the radian measure of an angle in the form $\frac{\pi}{a}$, what is the value of a?

32

A paintball arena has been created on a rectangular plot of land that has the dimensions 48 yards by 64 yards. If a player were to fire a paintball from one corner of the arena diagonally across to the farthest corner, how many feet would the paintball travel? (1 yard = 3 feet)

33

The larger of two similar triangles has sides that measure 3 meters, 5 meters, and $\sqrt{34}$ meters in length. If the longest side length of the smaller triangle measures $\frac{\sqrt{34}}{2}$ inches, what is the sum of the two shorter side lengths of the smaller triangle, in inches?

34

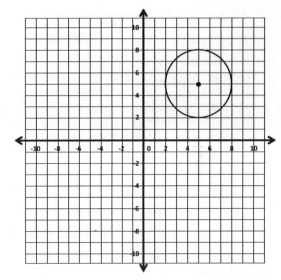

The equation of the circle graphed on the xy-plane above is $(x-a)^2 + (y-b)^2 = c$. What is the value of the product of a, b, and c?

307

CONTINUE

35

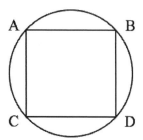

Square *ABDC* has an area of 16 square inches and is inscribed in a circle. What is the length, in centimeters, of $\overset{\frown}{ABC}$?

(Round your answer to the nearest tenth.)

36

Jennifer made a pizza that she plans to split evenly among her friends who will be sleeping over and herself. Jennifer invited 4 friends, but one of them may not be able to make it. If the pizza has a diameter of $\dfrac{60}{\sqrt{\pi}}$ inches, each slice will have how many additional square inches if only 3 friends arrive for the sleepover as opposed to all 4 friends arriving?

---- ▼ ----

Questions 37-38 refer to the following information.

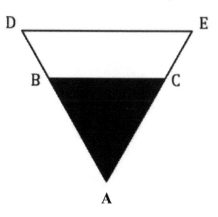

In the diagram above, $\overline{DE} \parallel \overline{BC}$ and $3\overline{DB} = \overline{BA}$.

37

What is the value of the area of the shaded triangle divided by the area of the unshaded trapezoid?

38

If the area of triangle *DEA* is $4\sqrt{3}$ square inches, what is the perimeter of trapezoid *DECB* in inches?

---- ▲ ----

CONTINUE ➡

<u>**Answer Keys**</u>

CONTINUE

CONTINUE

Unit 1: (114 Q)

Skill 1: (pg. 7)
1. D
2. B
3. C
4. A
5. C
6. D ✓
7. B
8. A

Skill 2: (pg. 10)
1. A
2. A
3. D
4. B ✓
5. C
6. C
7. D
8. B

Skill 3: (pg. 13)
1. B
2. C
3. C
4. A ✓
5. B
6. D
7. A
8. D

Skill 4: (pg. 16)
1. A
2. A
3. D
4. B
5. B
6. D
7. C
8. C

Mid 1 R: (pg. 20)
1. C
2. B
3. C
4. B
5. D
6. D
7. B
8. D

9. A
10. A
11. A
12. B
13. C
14. D
15. C
16. 6
17. 2
18. 7
19. 88
20. 3

Skill 5: (pg. 27)
1. C
2. D
3. B
4. B ✓
5. A
6. A
7. C
8. D

Skill 6: (pg. 30)
1. A
2. C
3. D
4. B
5. A
6. D
7. C
8. B

Skill 7: (pg. 34)
1. A
2. C
3. D
4. D
5. B
6. C
7. B
8. A

Unit 1 R: (pg. 40)
1. D
2. A
3. B
4. C
5. D

6. B
7. B
8. D
9. A
10. D
11. A
12. B
13. C
14. A
15. C
16. D
17. B
18. B
19. C
20. B
21. C
22. A
23. A
24. C
25. D
26. C
27. D
28. A
29. C
30. B
31. 11
32. 12
33. 1/2 or 0.5
34. 70
35. 128
36. 6
37. 160
38. 600

Unit 2: (122 Q)

Skill 8: (pg. 53)
1. C
2. B
3. B
4. C
5. A
6. D
7. D
8. A

Skill 9: (pg. 56)
1. B
2. C
3. A
4. D
5. B
6. C
7. A
8. D

Skill 10: (pg. 59)
1. D
2. A
3. B
4. D
5. C
6. A
7. C
8. B

Skill 11: (pg. 63)
1. B
2. B
3. C
4. C
5. D
6. A
7. A
8. D

Mid 2 R: (pg. 66)
1. C
2. D
3. A
4. C
5. B
6. B
7. A
8. D

9. C
10. A
11. C
12. D
13. A
14. B
15. D
16. 6
17. 4
18. 48
19. 22
20. 520

Skill 12: (pg. 74)
1. A
2. B
3. B
4. D
5. D
6. A
7. C
8. C

Skill 13: (pg. 77)
1. C
2. D
3. B
4. C
5. B
6. D
7. A
8. A

Skill 14: (pg. 80)
1. A
2. D
3. C
4. D
5. B
6. B
7. A
8. C

Skill 15: (pg. 83)
1. C
2. C
3. B
4. D
5. A

Unit 2 R: (pg. 88)
1. C
2. C
3. A
4. B
5. A
6. B
7. D
8. C
9. B
10. B
11. D
12. C
13. A
14. D
15. B
16. A
17. D
18. C
19. D
20. D
21. A
22. D
23. A
24. B
25. C
26. A
27. D
28. C
29. B
30. B
31. 9
32. 18
33. 1
34. 25
35. 1/4 or 0.25
36. 8
37. 100
38. 900

CONTINUE ▶

Unit 3: (178 Q)

Skill 16: (pg. 102)
1. A
2. B
3. C
4. A
5. D
6. B
7. D
8. C

Skill 17: (pg. 104)
1. A
2. C
3. D
4. C
5. B
6. B
7. D
8. A

Skill 18: (pg. 107)
1. A
2. C
3. D
4. B
5. B
6. D
7. C
8. A

Skill 19: (pg. 110)
1. A
2. C
3. B
4. D
5. D
6. C
7. A
8. B

Skill 20: (pg. 114)
1. C
2. B
3. B
4. A
5. D
6. A
7. C
8. D

Skill 21: (pg. 117)
1. B
2. B
3. A
4. A
5. C
6. C
7. D
8. D

Skill 22: (pg. 119)
1. A
2. B
3. D
4. C
5. A
6. C
7. D
8. B

Skill 23: (pg. 122)
1. D
2. A
3. C
4. C
5. D
6. B
7. A
8. B

Mid 3 R: (pg. 126)
1. C
2. C
3. D
4. B
5. C
6. B
7. D
8. B
9. A
10. A
11. A
12. C
13. B
14. D
15. D
16. 2
17. 143
18. 300
19. 5/2 or 2.5
20. 52

Skill 24: (pg. 133)
1. A
2. B
3. C
4. C
5. B
6. D
7. A
8. D

Skill 25: (pg. 137)
1. D
2. B
3. D
4. A
5. C
6. A
7. B
8. C

Skill 26: (pg. 140)
1. C
2. C
3. B
4. D
5. A
6. D
7. B
8. A

Skill 27: (pg. 143)
1. A
2. D
3. B
4. C
5. D
6. B
7. A
8. C

Skill 28: (pg. 146)
1. A
2. B
3. A
4. C
5. B

6. D
7. D
8. C

Skill 29: (pg. 148)
1. C
2. C
3. A
4. A
5. D
6. D
7. B
8. B

Skill 30: (pg. 151)
1. D
2. A
3. C
4. A
5. B
6. C
7. D
8. B

Unit 3 R: (pg. 160)
1. D
2. C
3. D
4. B
5. B
6. B
7. A
8. C
9. A
10. B
11. D
12. C
13. B
14. A
15. C
16. A
17. C
18. A
19. D
20. D
21. D
22. D
23. A
24. C

25. C
26. D
27. B
28. B
29. B
30. A
31. 17/4 or 4.25
32. 1
33. 63
34. 0.01
35. 60
36. 18
37. 40
38. 2/23, .086, .087

CONTINUE

Unit 4: (178 Q)

Skill 31: (pg. 173)	**Skill 36: (pg. 188)**	19. 4	6. B	25. D
1. B	1. C	20. 1	7. D	26. A
2. D	2. B		8. C	27. A
3. C	3. C	**Skill 39: (pg. 205)**		28. B
4. C	4. A	1. B	**Skill 44: (pg. 221)**	29. C
5. B	5. B	2. D	1. C	30. C
6. D	6. D	3. C	2. D	31. 10
7. A	7. A	4. A	3. C	32. 2
8. A	8. D	5. B	4. A	33. 3
		6. D	5. B	34. 0
Skill 32: (pg. 177)	**Skill 37: (pg. 191)**	7. A	6. B	35. 9 or 15
1. D	1. B	8. C	7. A	36. 7
2. C	2. A		8. D	37. 2008 or 2013
3. A	3. D	**Skill 40: (pg. 209)**		38. 5
4. C	4. B	1. D	**Skill 45: (pg. 223)**	
5. A	5. D	2. A	1. D	
6. B	6. C	3. D	2. B	
7. D	7. A	4. C	3. A	
8. B	8. C	5. B	4. C	
		6. A	5. D	
Skill 33: (pg. 179)	**Skill 38: (pg. 195)**	7. B	6. C	
1. A	1. A	8. C	7. B	
2. D	2. B		8. A	
3. D	3. C	**Skill 41: (pg. 211)**		
4. B	4. C	1. D	**Unit 4 R: (pg. 232)**	
5. C	5. B	2. A	1. D	
6. C	6. A	3. C	2. B	
7. B	7. D	4. B	3. C	
8. A	8. D	5. D	4. A	
		6. C	5. A	
Skill 34: (pg. 182)	**Mid 4 R: (pg. 198)**	7. A	6. D	
1. B	1. D	8. B	7. D	
2. A	2. D		8. C	
3. B	3. A	**Skill 42: (pg. 214)**	9. A	
4. D	4. C	1. A	10. B	
5. D	5. D	2. C	11. D	
6. C	6. A	3. B	12. C	
7. C	7. B	4. D	13. C	
8. A	8. C	5. D	14. D	
	9. D	6. C	15. D	
Skill 35: (pg. 185)	10. A	7. A	16. B	
1. B	11. B	8. B	17. B	
2. C	12. B		18. A	
3. A	13. C	**Skill 43: (pg. 218)**	19. A	
4. A	14. B	1. A	20. C	
5. D	15. C	2. B	21. B	
6. C	16. 2	3. A	22. C	
7. D	17. 1/7, .142, .143	4. D	23. B	
8. B	18. 1	5. C	24. A	

CONTINUE

Unit 5: (162 Q)

Skill 46: (pg. 246)
1. C
2. A
3. C
4. A
5. D
6. B
7. D
8. B

Skill 47: (pg. 248)
1. C
2. C
3. A
4. D
5. A
6. D
7. B
8. B

Skill 48: (pg. 251)
1. D
2. C
3. C
4. B
5. A
6. D
7. A
8. B

Skill 49: (pg. 255)
1. A
2. A
3. C
4. D
5. D
6. C
7. B
8. B

Skill 50: (pg. 257)
1. B
2. B
3. A
4. D
5. A
6. D
7. C
8. C

Skill 51: (pg. 260)
1. D
2. C
3. C
4. A
5. B
6. D
7. B
8. A

Skill 52: (pg. 263)
1. B
2. A
3. D
4. D
5. C
6. A
7. B
8. C

Mid 5 R: (pg. 268)
1. C
2. B
3. C
4. A
5. D
6. A
7. D
8. B
9. C
10. D
11. C
12. A
13. B
14. A
15. B
16. 45
17. 4/5 or 0.8
18. 5/2 or 2.5
19. 864
20. 0

Skill 53: (pg. 275)
1. A
2. B
3. D
4. C
5. B
6. D

7. A
8. C

Skill 54: (pg. 278)
1. B
2. B
3. C
4. A
5. A
6. C
7. D
8. D

Skill 55: (pg. 282)
1. C
2. C
3. D
4. B
5. A
6. A
7. D
8. B

Skill 56: (pg. 284)
1. B
2. B
3. C
4. D
5. A
6. C
7. A
8. D

Skill 57: (pg. 287)
1. A
2. A
3. B
4. D
5. B
6. D
7. C
8. C

Skill 58: (pg. 291)
1. D
2. C
3. A
4. A
5. C

6. B
7. B
8. D

Unit 5 R: (pg. 298)
1. C
2. C
3. A
4. D
5. C
6. A
7. C
8. B
9. D
10. C
11. B
12. C
13. B
14. C
15. B
16. D
17. A
18. A
19. C
20. B
21. D
22. D
23. D
24. A
25. B
26. A
27. D
28. D
29. A
30. B
31. 6
32. 240
33. 4
34. 225
35. 13.3
36. 45
37. 9/7, 1.28, 1.29
38. 9

CONTINUE